The *Girl* from Nip 'n' Tuck

PART I

The Girl from Nip 'n' Tuck

PART I

DIANNE H. LUNDY

PRIMIX
PUBLISHING
THE WRITE CHOICE

Primix Publishing
11620 Wilshire Blvd
Suite 900, West Wilshire Center, Los Angeles, CA, 90025
www.primixpublishing.com
Phone: 1-800-538-5788

Published by Primix Publishing: 08/17/2023

ISBN: 978-1-957676-78-4(sc)
ISBN: 978-1-957676-79-1(e)

Library of Congress Control Number: 2023912084

Contents

This book is dedicated to all the teachers in my life with special thanks to the following:

Mrs. Esther Smith, Grades 1–3
Mrs. Marguerite Dean, Grades 4–6
Mrs. Dolores G. Hollis, Grade 7
Rocky Branch Elementary School

Mrs. Mary Louise Johnston, English I
Mrs. Margie Benefield Antley, English II
Mrs. Marjorie Wade Terrell, English III
Mrs. Corrie Armstrong, English IV
Mrs. Lucille Stewart, Home Economics
Farmerville High School

Dr. Earl Wilcox, Honors English
Harding University

Flavil D. Hollis, my father,
Who taught me many lessons in life

Special thanks also to Hooshang Khorasani for the cover design for this book.

Chapter 1

The main street apparently ended at the river with no bridge in sight. Dianne Hollis wondered if anybody ever crossed the river, or if life in this town just ended at the river's edge.

She eyed her surroundings dubiously as she climbed the steps on her way to yet another job interview. Exactly how many interviews this made was unclear, as they were all beginning to run together in her mind.

Sometime later she almost burst through the door as she exited the session. "Let's go!" she exclaimed, pitching her voice to rise above the clatter of typewriters in the waiting room. Her remark was directed to her father, F. D. Hollis, who had driven her to the unfamiliar location.

They walked briskly to their vehicle, a beige Ranchero, which was parked nearby.

"Well, did you get the job?" he inquired.

"I don't know, Daddy. I guess they'll notify me," she replied.

F. D. started the engine and pulled away from the curb Dianne studied the landscape as they left the bleak-looking town behind. Sparsely populated with white wooden houses, it was definitely a rural community.

Waterproof, what a place, she thought. *It's probably just as well if I don't get a job here. There are certainly not many prospects of available men—not unless you count the farmers.* A vision of herself carrying a sack lunch to someone on a John Deere tractor popped into her head. She closed her eyes tightly and then opened them, willing the picture to exit her mind.

Her train of thought was interrupted as F. D. punched in the cigarette lighter. *Oh, great,* she fumed to herself. *Now I'll have to endure the smoke.* To her relief, he cracked a window.

He took a long drag on the cigarette and then drawled out a surprising question in his slow, Southern manner. "Well, if I were hiring a home ec. teacher, the first thing I would ask her would be could she fix a man's pants."

Dianne stared at him almost as if he were from another planet.

"Can you fix a man's pants?" he asked her point-blank.

"Of course, I can," she almost sputtered, "but that's not what we teach in sewing."

"Oh, really? Then what do you teach in sewing?" he countered.

"We teach people how to make clothes using a pattern," she explained.

He flicked the ashes into the ashtray as he sarcastically remarked, "Well, I don't see what good that is if you can't fix a pair of pants."

Dianne could see that arguing was a waste of time. Nobody ever won an argument with her father. She rolled her eyes and held her tongue.

Respected by all, and feared by some in their community, F. D. Hollis was not a man to be taken lightly. Of average height and with a stocky build, he prided himself on dressing in a dignified manner. A coat and tie were standard dress for work or important business meetings. Bright blue eyes accented his round face. His head, slightly balding, with gray hair, was usually topped with a hat whenever he was outdoors.

As they rode in silence, Dianne caught a glimpse of herself in the side mirror. There could be little doubt that she was F. D.'s daughter. She had the same full face, so like his, with an almost duplicate nose, short eyebrows, and a quirky mouth. Her green eyes, accented with her favorite green eye shadow, replaced his blue ones.

She had also inherited his short neck, the feature that she most despised because it forced her to wear her chestnut brown hair in a short, straight style. They were too much alike, she pondered, as they sped down the road. That was probably why they didn't get along much of the time.

The silence remained unbroken as F. D. finished his cigarette and crushed it into the ashtray.

How did I ever get into the predicament of looking for a job at the last minute? she asked herself. Her mind drifted back to her college days, which had ended just a few short weeks ago.

Chapter 2

Dianne had attended Harding College in Searcy, Arkansas for four years. The small private Christian college with a student body of twelve hundred had appealed to her in a catalog that she had received just before she graduated from Farmerville High School. Although it was more expensive than state schools, she had managed to make it with the help of two scholarships and some money that her mother, Dolores, had saved for her education.

She had changed her major from dietetics to vocational home economics at the beginning of her sophomore year. The vocational courses had just seemed more interesting. Besides, education was in her blood, as both her parents were teachers.

As graduation approached, all her friends had been busily making plans to move for new jobs or to get married. She, on the other hand, had been still undecided about the future when a bulletin board announcement caught her eye.

"EXODUS to Des Moines, Iowa. Christian workers wanted who are willing to relocate." It sounded like an adventure, just what she had been looking for.

She had discussed the idea with her friends. At least one girl, Babs Clark, was also interested in the job opportunity. Dianne had sent a letter to the contact person listed in the bulletin.

About a week later she had been surprised by a long-distance phone call to her dorm late at night regarding the letter she had written. Everyone had gathered around the phone excitedly as she and Babs had made arrangements to fly to Des Moines.

Just one problem had remained—getting permission from Virgil Lawyer, the Dean of Students, to make the trip. The college was very protective of its students and no one was permitted to go on out-of-town trips without permission from both the dean and their parents.

She could almost still hear his voice ringing in her ears as she had spoken to him about the trip.

"You want to do *what*? Leave in the middle of final exams?" he had almost shrieked in disbelief.

"I'm exempt from finals because I'm a senior with at least a 'B' average in all of my courses," she had reasoned.

"What about baccalaureate?" he had continued to quiz her.

"We'll be back on Saturday night, so we'll be here in time for baccalaureate," she had assured him.

"Very well," he had reluctantly agreed, "you have my permission to go."

It had been a whirlwind trip. Dianne and Babs had flown on student passes, which meant "stand-by status." No apparent problems had occurred on the flight until they arrived at the Des Moines airport. It was then they discovered that their luggage had been delayed. That meant no dress clothes for the interviews. They should have heeded it as a bad omen. But they didn't have much time to mull over the situation as they were chauffeured about, from one interview to another. Everyone was very pleasant and the interviews had seemed promising.

The return trip from Des Moines had proven to be more of a hassle than the original flight. After several delays due to inclement weather, they had been allowed to get in line to board the plane. Babs, who was in front of Dianne, passed through the checkpoint without incident. Dianne, however, had been pulled aside by one of the attendants and was not allowed to board. The attendant explained that she had to wait because of her stand-by status to see if any more seats were available.

Sick with worry, Dianne had watched all of the other passengers get on the plane. She had taken two Excedrin earlier that morning for a headache, and when that had failed, she had taken two more. By that time she was feeling as if she could fly without the plane.

About five minutes before departure the attendant had let her through the gate. She had rushed up the steps and hurried to find Babs. Just as she stepped into the General Class section, everyone began to cheer, and several men stood up to give her a standing ovation. "Yeah, Dianne, we didn't think you were going to make it," one of them had shouted.

"What's going on? Why are all of these people cheering, and how do they know my name?" she whispered to Babs.

"I told the stewardess what happened and that if you didn't get on, I had to get off," Babs explained. "I also think the men have had a little too much to drink."

The girls and their luggage made it back to Searcy at the same time. The next few days had raced by with baccalaureate, graduation, packing up, and saying goodbye to friends of the past four years.

Dianne had lounged around home for about a month, still waiting to hear from the Des Moines school district. Then a phone call had changed everything.

"Dianne, it's Babs. Did you hear from those people about a job yet?"

"No, I haven't, Babs."

"Well, I called them, and they said that the positions have already been filled. I just wanted to let you know so that you could start looking for another job."

Dianne had slowly hung up the phone. That had been the beginning of her new job search—sending out letters and making phone calls to area parishes—all to no avail.

She snapped back to the present as the Ranchero turned into their driveway. The Hollis house, a neat red-brick structure with white shutters, sat on top of a hill overlooking a meadow and a pond. A small herd of cows dotted the landscape as they grazed leisurely on the thick grass in the meadow. Behind the house was a barn and a bountiful summer garden. *This is definitely country living,* she thought, *and it's what I've known for twenty-one years. But it's not what I want for the rest of my life. Somehow, and some way, I'm going to change from John Deere green to bright city lights.*

Chapter 3

Dianne was past being frustrated. She was almost desperate. The window of opportunity for finding any kind of teaching job was closing fast. Life wasn't supposed to be this way. You went to college; you graduated; you got a job. That was the natural order of things, but things weren't working out for her. She was still determined to leave her home community of Rocky Branch, also known as "Nip 'n' Tuck," in Union Parish.

Salvation appeared through her mother, Dolores, who was attending Northeast Louisiana University to work on an advanced degree. Dolores came home one afternoon and announced that interviews for teaching jobs were being conducted on campus. She thought Dianne should at least try to find a job through those means. Dianne put on her best dress and headed out to Northeast the next day for the interviews. There were no home economics jobs available, but one interviewer from Calcasieu Parish did have a job opening for a science teacher. The only problem was that Dianne did not have enough hours for certification to teach science. There was still time for her to take six additional hours during the second summer session at Northeast, so she was offered a job in Lake Charles, contingent on her completion of the course work. She signed the contract with a silent sigh of relief.

The six-week session flew by, and Dianne successfully passed both courses, making "A's" in both of them. Science had always been one of her favorite subjects, so she felt she could handle the responsibility of teaching it.

About a week before school started, Dianne and Dolores made a trip to Lake Charles to locate the school, Forrest K. White, and to find a place for Dianne to live.

After a visit to the school board office to receive directions, they managed to find the school. They met the principal, Mr. Mims, who was a very large and imposing man. Several students were running in and out of the building as he took Dianne and Dolores on a tour. "They just can't stay away," he commented, shaking his head.

Mr. Mims gave Dianne an idea of where she could find a place to stay. A lady known as "Aunt Doll" often rented out rooms to single girls. "There's just one problem with renting a room from her," he noted. "All of the girls I send over there keep getting married."

Dianne stored that remark away in the back of her mind for future reference. After all, she was a single girl, and finding an eligible man was still on her mind.

"Aunt Doll" lived up to her name and proved to be a lovely person. But Dianne was never quite comfortable with renting just a room with "kitchen privileges." She was used to having her privacy. After the first month, the problem solved itself when "Aunt Doll" informed Dianne that she would have to move out to make room for someone who was coming to visit.

"Aunt Doll" felt rather guilty about asking Dianne to leave on such short notice, so she took it upon herself to find another place for her tenant. There was a vacant apartment just down the street. "They don't usually rent to single girls," she said, "but I assured them that you would be an excellent tenant."

With her housing problems behind her, Dianne was free to concentrate on her teaching duties. She had attended the first day of orientation for teachers. It had flown by like a film in fast motion, with so much to remember that her brain felt almost muddled. Her room was located on the bottom floor in a corner next to an entrance. It was a rather stark-looking facility. Windows without blinds or curtains ran across the outside wall. Two other walls were covered with green chalkboards. A lab demonstration table and a teacher's desk sat in the front of the room. There was only one storage cabinet. The rest of the space was occupied by approximately thirty student desks, most of which were in rather sad condition.

Dianne was not sure what to do about lesson plans, as she had no experience whatsoever in teaching science. The first day was filled with assigning books, making out roll sheets, and other general duties. She was assigned to teach two classes of eighth grade science and three classes of ninth grade General Science. She felt that it was too early to make any kind of prediction about the abilities of the students, but it did not take long for their differences to surface.

Chapter 4

Dianne was having a hard time remembering the names of all of the students. It was so overwhelming! Many of them had surnames of French origin, which were difficult for someone from another part of the state to pronounce. Names such as Boudreaux, Fontenot, Leger, and Tramonte were like Greek to her. However, the one name that she did get right was that of Craig Herbert because she remembered a story that her father had told many times from his days in the army.

The story went that there was any army sergeant who was calling roll for the troop that F. D. was assigned to. He came to the "H's" and called out the name "Herbert Hebert," mispronouncing the last name as "He-bert." No one answered, even though the sergeant called it several times. When roll call was over, he asked if there was anyone whose name had not been called. One man stepped forward.

"What's your name?" the sergeant inquired.

"Herbert Hebert," (A-bear) the man replied.

So, that was one French name that had stuck in her mind.

Dianne thought that it would be easy teaching three classes of one subject and two of another because that meant only two basic lesson plans per day. She quickly learned, as all teachers do, that each class had its own personality and that all classes did not progress at the same rate. Keeping them together was a definite challenge.

Two of the classes became her favorites. Second hour General Science was the quietest and most cooperative group. They were generally pleasant and easy to work with. Fourth hour General Science was a more difficult class to handle, but the students were fun to work with, although mischievous.

The fifth hour General Science class was the slowest of any of the classes. The students appeared to be academically disadvantaged, and many of them had a hard time passing any kind of test. Fortunately, it was the smallest of the five classes. The two eighth grade classes were about evenly matched, although sixth hour proved to be more of a challenge because it was the last hour of the day, and everybody, including Dianne, was ready to go home.

Dianne had hardly any materials to work with except for the Teacher's Edition of the General Science books that she had received. All of her files and bulletin board materials contained information pertaining only to home economics. She did manage to scrape together some materials suitable for the one bulletin board located at the front of her room. She found that students were helpful in getting bulletin board materials if they were given extra credit. Aside from that, she had only her wits to rely on.

Her neighboring teacher, Mr. Fuller, helped her with some ideas for simple experiments, and for that she was forever indebted. The most popular experiments seemed to be those involving the use of fire with the Bunsen burner, leading her to wonder if she were teaching some future arsonists.

Before many weeks had passed, some of the students began to emerge as her favorites. Two of the most intelligent boys, Mike Miller and Lee Lavoi, seemed to almost adopt her as their second mother. They liked to hang around and talk to her at lunch and after school. They even found her phone number and often called her at night, just to find out what she was doing.

Another boy, Bobby Morris, who was in her fourth hour class, was quite a prankster and could always be counted on for a laugh or two during class, whether Dianne wanted it or not. Much to her annoyance, he kept comparing her to their former science teacher from last year, Miss Johnson, who, he cheerfully informed her, lasted only one year at the job.

Another student, Joe Jenkins, also liked to tease Dianne whenever she was on bus duty. One day she corrected him when he stepped over the safety line before the bus arrived. "Get back over the line, Joe," she directed.

"Not until you give me a kiss," he challenged, not realizing what a ridiculous sight he made, standing all of his four and one-half feet high with his face upturned, halfway expecting Dianne to follow through with his request.

Before she could reply, Mr. Mims, who was standing nearby, sternly reprimanded Joe. "Don't let the students play around with you," he instructed a much-chagrined Dianne.

One of the boys in fifth hour, Bruce Thompson, was not a very strong student, but he seemed to think of himself as a "lady killer." Looking somewhat like a cross between Bobby Darin and Elvis, he had no trouble attracting girls. He seemed to have a bit of a crush on Dianne. One Friday he informed her that his parents were going to be out of town all weekend. "Why don't you come over and visit me?" he suggested.

"Thanks, but, no, thanks, Bruce. I've already got enough problems," Dianne replied, much to his disappointment.

Bruce's parents had come in for a parent conference due to his grades. It was one of the first parent conferences that Dianne had experienced, and she felt very uncomfortable, hardly knowing what to say. It was apparent from their appearance that they were well-off financially, and that might have been part of Bruce's problem. However, Dianne did not realize it at the time. A few weeks later, Bruce, who had his own car, was in an auto accident, which resulted in him breaking one of his legs. Dianne went to visit him while he was in the hospital. It was not until sometime later that she realized that in order for a junior high student to own a car he would have to be over-aged, and that was also a large part of Bruce's problem.

Some of the girls were just as memorable. One girl named Linda Perry asked, "Miss Hollis, can I ask you a personal question?"

Dianne was not sure what to say. Thinking that maybe the girl had some kind of problem that she needed help with, she said, "Yes, I guess so."

The question that followed would forever cure Dianne of falling into that trap again.

Linda proceeded with her question. "Are you a virgin?".

Thoroughly embarrassed, with cheeks turning red, Dianne replied, "Why in the world would you want to know that?"

Undaunted, Linda persisted, "Well, are you?"

Dianne resolved the situation be replying, "Well, that is really something that I cannot reveal at this time."

Despite giving it her best effort, Dianne was not happy teaching science all day long. She had naively believed that her love for science would carry her through almost any situation but had soon realized that was not the case. Luck was with her when one of the home economics teachers resigned at midterm because her husband was being transferred. With the assistance of Mr. Mims, Dianne inherited two eighth-grade home economics classes and gave up two of her science classes to a replacement teacher, Mr. Mullins.

There were still several weeks left in the semester when Dianne took over the home economics classes. They did not readily accept her as their new teacher, giving her insight into how to win over hostile students, a lesson which would prove valuable later in her career.

Midterm brought new students to the home economics classes, and Dianne was thankful for the help that she received from the other home economics teacher, Mrs. Walters. The classes were to cover three basic topics—sewing, cooking, and child development. The students did remarkably well with their sewing projects, some of them even completing a ruffled pinafore with a lined top.

The cooking labs were not always successful, resulting in several batches of burnt cookies, as well as burnt biscuits. Dianne had to shop for groceries after school. Then she had to take them home with her until the next day. One night she thought that she had brought in all the refrigerated items from her car, only to discover the next morning that a can of biscuits intended for crusts for fried pies had exploded in the car trunk.

During the child development unit the girls worked with the kindergarten students. At the end of the unit they planned a party for the children. They decided to make peanut butter cookies and Kool-Aid for refreshments. To Dianne's relief, the cookies turned out rather well, or so she thought. After the lab was over she discovered that the jar of peanut butter was cracked, resulting in glass being in some of the cookies. They had to start all over again the next day. The party was deemed a success, and the kindergarten students presented Dianne with pictures that they had drawn, representing their impressions of the visits with the girls. She stored the pictures in her files, wishing that all of her memories about teaching could be such happy ones.

Chapter 5

*L*ake Charles, being located next to the Gulf, was susceptible to hurricanes and inclement weather. The climate was very humid, and Dianne's apartment was not air-conditioned. She had been contacted by one of her cousins, Mary Browning, when she had first arrived in Lake Charles. Mary practically adopted Dianne as her second daughter, and Dianne spent many hours visiting Mary and her husband, E. T., enjoying the comfort of air conditioning, as well as the pleasant company and delicious food.

As luck would have it, a major hurricane struck the coast during Dianne's tenure in the city. Evacuation was recommended, but not mandatory. Dianne decided to "stick it out." Lake Charles, being rather flat, was not very accommodating to any type of rainy weather. The streets often flooded, making travel hazardous, if not impossible. During the hurricane Dianne cautiously eyed the water, which was edging halfway up onto her front yard. Eventually, the flooding in town was so great that people were actually water skiing in the streets, an event which was documented by the local newspaper. Fortunately, the storm did not do much damage, except for the rain.

Mary informed Dianne that her apartment was not in a very good section of town.

"You're living on the wrong side of the tracks," she commented.

"I kind of got that idea," said Dianne. Her apartment was

located down the street from two lounges, "The Mambo" and "The Bamboo." It would get pretty noisy on Saturday nights, especially at closing time. Dianne just stayed inside and kept all her windows and doors locked.

One day Dianne put out her garbage can as she left for work. When she returned that afternoon the can was missing. She reported the incident to her landlord. A couple of days later he stopped by and asked Dianne if she could identify her garbage. "I think so," replied Dianne.

"Well, I think I found your can. I was a couple of blocks over. I'll bring it by and you can check it," he said.

When he came by, surely enough, it was hers. She concluded that it had most likely been a prank pulled by some teenagers in the neighborhood.

In the fall Dianne flew out of town to attend the wedding of her former roommate and close friend, Becky Holt. Becky lived in Birmingham, Alabama with her parents and her brother, Paul. Dianne was designated as the maid of honor, a position which she happily accepted.

Becky, being an art major, had rather unusual taste in color. She had decided on a color scheme of aqua and purple. All of the attendants had to make their own dresses of aqua crepe—not a problem for Dianne, being a home economics major. When she arrived in Birmingham the day before the wedding, Becky was still trying to finish making her own wedding dress. Ever the procrastinator, she had put it off until the last minute, and she was having difficulty completing the task. Dianne stepped in to rescue her. They stayed up until the wee hours of the morning, and Dianne finished putting in the zipper just before the wedding. They made it to the church on time, and everything went according to plan.

Following the reception, Paul drove Dianne to the airport. He even walked her to the steps of the plane. Dianne felt a little ridiculous holding onto her purple bridesmaid's bouquet as she boarded the plane. She couldn't help wishing that Paul might be the man she was looking for, but time would prove that was not the case.

Money was tight during that time. Dianne was making only $5,600 for the entire year's work. The rent and utilities were fairly inexpensive, and her car was paid for, leaving only food to worry about. She cooked fairly simple meals, rarely indulging in anything expensive. Once, however, she decided to purchase some fresh shrimp, a mainstay of the Cajun cuisine in Lake Charles. Not knowing how much to buy, she ended up with more than enough for a meal, and she ate fried shrimp for several days in a row.

She awoke on the morning following her third meal of shrimp to discover that her top lip had swollen to almost twice its size. Mistakenly thinking it was an insect bite, she reported for work, as usual. Of course, the disfigurement was immediately noticed by the students. She had to endure teasing for most of the day, especially after she commented that she thought something had bitten her on the lip. As the swelling continued, she became concerned and contacted Mary, who promptly advised her to seek medical attention. Only after visiting a doctor did she learn that she had been the victim of an allergic reaction to shrimp.

Missing work was not something that Dianne could afford to do very often, as teachers were allotted only ten days of sick leave per year. Unfortunately, she caught the influenza virus shortly after Christmas, forcing her to miss over a week of school. The substitute hired in her place was not a science major, Dianne learned upon her return to school.

"I didn't know anything about science. I'm an art major, so I was teaching them how to decorate an apartment," the substitute commented, as she and Dianne conferred on the progress of the classes that she had kept. "All of the classes were fine, except for second hour," she continued. "They gave me a really hard time."

"I can't understand that! They are my best class!" Dianne exclaimed.

The next week Dianne returned to her familiar routine. A girl in second hour insisted that she had to talk to Dianne outside in the hall, so Dianne reluctantly stepped outside the door to see what the problem was. After several minutes of conferring about a test grade, they re-entered the classroom. To Dianne's surprise, she was greeted with a chocolate cake that was decorated with the words "Welcome Back."

"Boy, we really missed you, Miss Hollis," said Terri Morris. "I couldn't stand that other teacher!"

"Yeah, don't ever be absent again," chimed in Jimmy Lemoine, as he presented her with a card signed by the entire class.

"Well, that explains why you were so bad while I was gone, I suppose. Believe it or not, I missed all of you students, too."

Dianne reached a decision before the end of her first year of teaching. She decided to resign from her job effective at the end of the year in order to seek employment elsewhere. Although she had made some friends and was fond of many of the students, she felt that it would be better to look for a job closer to home.

"Lake Charles has too many Cajuns and too many hurricanes," she commented to some of her family members. *And not enough eligible men,* she thought to herself.

At the end of the year Dianne purchased one of the school yearbooks. She was brave enough to ask the students to autograph the book if they so desired. When she later looked at the book, she reflected on the comments which had been written.

"Miss H. Stay as sweet and nice as you are. You're a neat science teacher. Remember all our good times in 2nd hour. See you at your wedding, or will I?" *Terri, the girl who spear-headed my "Welcome Back" party. What a fun student!*

"Miss H. It has been fun in your class. Too bad you're not going to be around this school next year. Good luck in the future always." *Carol, a good student and a quiet girl.*

"To a teacher that needs to get married." Peanut, always worried about my social life.

"Miss H. I have really enjoyed being in your class. I have had more fun in your class than in any other classes put together. Lots of luck in finding another job."

Patricia, petite, blond-headed, another quiet student.

"You're out of your tree! Would you believe a bush? Evacuate Lake Charles, never." *Mike, a favorite student, with the little private joke about him being 'out of his tree.'*

"Miss H. It's been fun in your class. Like when you fuss at us a lot. Lots of luck in the future." *Susan, another quiet student. Glad to know she enjoyed being fussed at.*

"Miss H. It's been a blast in your science class. I wish all of our classes were like this. Although we've been mean sometimes, we're really nice kids. Good luck next year." *Hamp, a real motor-mouth.*

"To one of the nicest teachers I know and a cute one, too. I have enjoyed being in your class. Good luck for the rest of your life." *Karen, Susan's sister. Were they twins?*

"To the best teacher I've had all year, but I hope I don't get you next year." *Debbie, I hope I don't get you, either!*

"To a great teacher whom I've enjoyed very much. Too bad you can't teach me next year because I will probably know more than you. Good luck with all of your boyfriends. I hope you get married soon because you are tempting. Anyway, I am going to be the best man." *Jimmy, again. Always the kidder!*

"To a fun teacher. It's been great this year and you made it that way. You'll really have to stop acting tough, though. You just can't keep a straight face. I've still got your phone number, so guess what!" *Lee, the Kleenex Kid. I'll miss talking to him on the phone.*

"Miss H. You said not to write anything dirty, so I'll try my best. You are a really groovy teacher who doesn't know when to walk out of class." *Docia, good thing I said not to write anything dirty!*

"To a very 'determined' and 'sweet' teacher who has tried to make her classes enjoyable, even certain 'circumstances' came up. Keep up the good work. I really enjoyed having you this year. Better luck next year with a better class." *Lynette, what a great student! I need lots more like her in the future.*

"To a great science teacher and a teacher I will always remember. Good luck in future teaching." *Richard, a quiet boy, and one of my rally students.*

"To one of the nicest, sweetest, kind of cute, mean teacher from one of your sweetest, nicest, kindest, and most considerate, mature, and, most of all, disciplined student in the class. Good luck in the future." *Bobby, the biggest prankster, and definitely the most memorable student I taught at F. K. White.*

Dianne emptied out her desk and turned in her keys and her records. She then proceeded to pack up her belongings in her apartment in short order. It was too hot to tarry long in an apartment that wasn't air-conditioned. She headed back to Rocky Branch, the very place that she had vowed to leave, to spend the summer at her parents' home as she began yet another job search, hoping that she would find a job more to her liking.

Chapter 6

*I*t was déjà vu. Dianne hadn't learned much French during her tenure in Lake Charles, but she certainly knew the meaning of that term! *Can this really be happening to me all over again?* she wondered. *Surely my luck has to change for the better.* And change for the better it did. She applied, once again, to several of the local parishes, even applying to a state-run school for mentally retarded students. The school was located in Ruston, and it was under the direction of one of her cousins, Edward Dettenheim. Getting a job there seemed almost a certainty, but, after thinking it over, she decided against the move. She wrote Edward a letter to that effect.

Soon afterwards, she received a reply from a letter that she had sent to Rapides Parish. The Director of Personnel, Harold Parks, was asking her to call to schedule an appointment for a job interview. Her aunt, Hazel Fulton, her father's sister, had lived and taught in Rapides Parish for many years. Hazel's husband, R. V., was an uncle to Harold's wife. Dianne was hoping that the connection would help her in getting a job somewhere in the parish.

F. D. agreed to drive her to Rapides Parish for the interview. They stopped by the Fulton house, and Hazel accompanied Dianne to the School Board Office. Mr. Parks was very cordial, and he offered her a job at the Ruby-Wise Junior High School teaching home economics, General Science, and girls' P. E. The school's principal, Mr. John Slay, was also in attendance. Dianne stated that she would like to see the school, so Mr. Slay offered to take her on a tour. She then checked with her aunt, who was waiting outside.

Hazel exclaimed, "I have a pie in the oven! I need to call home and tell the men to take it out before it burns."

Mr. Parks allowed Hazel to use his phone. After hanging up, she said, "They were watching that pie and already took it out. They weren't about to let it burn!"

The two men laughed appreciatively because Hazel was well known for her excellent cooking abilities.

"There is one thing that I should tell you before you decide about taking the job," commented Mr. Parks. "There is a big integration lawsuit underway in the parish. I don't think it will have much effect on the rural schools, so you should be pretty safe."

Dianne, Hazel, and Mr. Slay made the trip to Kolin, and he showed her around the junior high part of the school. As Dianne picked up some of the textbooks to take with her for lesson preparations, her aunt noted, "Well, I guess she's taking the job. She's taking some books home."

The next problem that Dianne had to face was, once again, finding a place to live. She consulted a real estate firm and settled on an apartment located on Madeline Street in Alexandria. Just by coincidence, it happened to be the apartment where Hazel and R. V. had formerly lived before buying their house. The apartment would not be vacant for another week, so her aunt volunteered the use of a guest room at her house. Dianne readily accepted the invitation.

Conditions at Ruby-Wise were much more pleasant than those at Forrest K. White. For starters, the school was air-conditioned a welcome relief from the hot and humid conditions that Dianne had endured in Lake Charles. The junior high students had their own wing, complete with a gym and dressing rooms. The wing had three classrooms, one for each grade, seventh through ninth. There was a science lab and a home economics lab, both of which were assigned to Dianne. Students did not have lockers. They had to store their books under their desks. Junior high teachers moved from room to room as they met with their scheduled classes.

"Who is that?"

"Is she our new teacher?"

"I don't know, but whoever she is, she's cute."

Those remarks were overheard by Dianne as she wove her way through the mass of students crowding the hallway on the first day of school. She finally made it to the room assigned to her, the middle classroom of the junior high wing. It belonged to the eighth grade, her homeroom.

She had nervously anticipated this day, a new beginning at a new school. Knowing that most of the day would be consumed with mundane tasks such as assigning books and making out class rosters, she had not prepared any formal lesson plans.

Teachers were required to write the names of students in all of their textbooks. This proved to be quite a task, as each homeroom teacher had to assign books for all of the subjects taught to their grade.

Following the advice of her aunt, she used the remaining time by assigning students to write essays on their summer activities. It was a long and trying day, and Dianne was glad to hear the final bell ring. She wasted no time getting to her car and heading home, thankful to be off her aching feet.

Chapter 7

*I*t was 1969, the year of the historic landing on the moon, and Dianne had watched the event on her T. V. in her bedroom at her parents' home. There had been a gospel meeting going on at their church that summer, and F. D. had volunteered the use of his bedroom for the visiting preacher. That, too, was a historic event because F. D. ordinarily didn't give up his bed for *anybody*.

Dolores, like a dutiful country wife, had been worried about what to do regarding feeding the preacher, but they soon learned that he, along with the host family, would be invited out every night. "Now I see why everybody was always so eager to let the preacher stay at their house," F. D. commented, after his fourth straight night of dinner engagements.

They had barely made it home to see the "moon walk" after one of the sermons. On the way home Dianne teased her younger sister, Sallie.

"I wonder if they have already landed on the moon," mused Sallie, as they approached their driveway.

"Look, I can see them," exclaimed Dianne, pointing to the full moon.

"Where?!" asked Sallie excitedly, half-believing her sister.

"I'm just joking, silly. Nobody can see that far," said Dianne, chuckling as she spoke.

Dianne decided that the moon landing would be a good topic for her introductory lesson plans, and she used that for her second day's lessons. After that, she turned to the textbooks for inspiration. The seventh graders were studying General Science. The eighth graders were scheduled to study Earth Science for the first half of the year and Home Living during the second term. Ninth graders were assigned a Physical Science book, and it was one of the more poorly written texts that Dianne had encountered.

She used the teacher's edition of that book and faithfully followed the instructions for experiments to the best of her ability with the materials that she had on hand. However, when it was suggested that she "obtain a broken windshield, and wearing heavy gloves, carefully demonstrate to students how it was put together," she rebelled.

"This is one of the worst science textbooks that I have ever seen," she grumbled to her fellow teacher, Mr. Henry Megison.

"There are some older texts stored in the closet, if you want to see if there are enough of them to use," he suggested.

Dianne dragged the dusty books out of the closet and managed to scrape up enough for the rather large class of almost thirty students. "I think you will find these books to be more interesting," she explained to the class, as she assigned them to the students.

As with her first year's teaching experience, Dianne soon discovered the classes at Ruby-Wise had their own personalities. The ninth graders were one of the most perfect examples of an "average" class that she would ever encounter. Their abilities ranged from one student who was rated as a "borderline genius" to a large number of "average students," as well as a few who were rated "below average." She always looked forward to meeting with them each day.

The seventh graders, likewise, were a generally cooperative group, although there were a few "stinkers" in the bunch. Class with them was also generally an enjoyable experience. The eighth graders were the downside of her day. They were the smallest group, and there were a few good students in the class. However, many of them lagged far behind their grade level in their abilities, and they did not seem too concerned about passing any tests. When she complained about the class to some of the other teachers, their teacher from the sixth grade, Mrs. Warner, declared, "You'll never get much work out of them. If they had a brain, I never found it."

Her favorite class was the ninth-grade girls' Home Economics I class. They met in the home economics lab room. It was equipped with four large tables, sixteen sewing machines, and four kitchen units. When they were down there, it was almost as if they were in another world, and Dianne felt very close to some of the girls.

Teaching P. E. was not something that she was comfortable with, so Mr. Megison directed the class most of the time, with Dianne supervising the girls' dressing room. Mr. Slay called her in one day to tell her that she was expected to coach the girls' basketball team.

"I don't know a lay-up from a forward pass," she said. "Trust me, my coaching the team would be a complete disaster."

Mr. Slay relented, and the coaching duties for both teams were assigned to Mr. Megison. Dianne, in turn, agreed to sponsor the cheerleaders, considering that to be a more than fair trade-off.

Dianne soon settled into a routine, reporting for work each day and spending a large part of the night either typing up lesson plans and tests or grading papers. Things seemed to be going pretty well, and her life was beginning to get back on track, or so she thought. Then, at midterm, a tremendous change occurred that would affect her for the rest of her life.

Chapter 8

The winds of change were blowing through the Rapides Parish school system, and the results would have far-reaching effects. Everywhere anyone turned, the desegregation lawsuit was the talk of the town. Grumblings were heard from every segment of society, and they festered beneath the surface like a long-dormant volcano suddenly awakening and ready to erupt. Dianne had listened to the news reports and had also mentioned to her family and friends that she might possibly be transferred to another school. But she still remembered what Mr. Parks had said about the rural schools most likely being exempt from the lawsuit, so she was not particularly concerned.

The School Board stalled as long as they could, but they finally had to make a decision on which teachers to transfer to achieve a ratio of three white teachers to one black teacher in each school, or as close as possible to that number. Students were dismissed from schools for several days in order for the transition to take place.

At Ruby-Wise the teachers met in the cafeteria for lunch, after which the announcement was to be made as to who would be transferred. Dianne, accustomed to eating only a sandwich in her department at noon, was feeling a little uncomfortable after consuming the rather large meal.

"I wish I hadn't eaten so much," she whispered to her friend Eunice Spears, the librarian, who was sitting beside her.

Mr. Slay stood up to speak, and a hush fell over the crowd. "Well, it's time to make the announcement of who will be leaving," he said. "Miss Hollis, Mrs. James, and Mrs. Lee, I guess you all had better read this letter first."

The letter was passed down to the designated teachers, and Dianne was dismayed to see her name listed as being assigned to A. Wettermark High in Boyce.

"I don't even know how to get there," she commented as she passed the letter along to the next person on the list.

Dianne rose from the table and made a fast exit to the ladies' restroom, trying to hold her emotions in check. Once out of sight of the rest of the faculty, she burst into tears. Several of the other teachers who were concerned about her followed after her.

"I'll be okay," she assured them. "I'm just shocked. I didn't think that they would be able to find a black home ec. teacher who was also certified to teach science. I don't know how I am ever going to find the place, either. I don't have the foggiest notion of where to look."

"Don't worry," said Eunice. "I know where it is. My husband, Sam, and I will drive you out there after school today."

Dianne went back to her room and began to try to gather up the things that she thought she would need. Departing teachers were told to leave explicit instructions for the teachers who were assigned to replace them, so she began working on that, also.

Mr. Slay came by her room to check on her. He was not in the best of moods. "In my opinion, they made a really bad choice in the teachers they picked to transfer," he told her. "You and the first-grade teacher are the last ones that I would have chosen. You are the only teacher in the history of the school who has been certified to teach both home ec. and science."

Later that afternoon she rode out to view the school with Eunice and Sam. The school was across the street from some ram-shackled houses. All the black people came out on their porches to stare at the trio as they sat in the car, soaking in the atmosphere of the school. Then a young black man drove up in his car and parked across the lot, also gawking at them. Dianne was beginning to feel very uncomfortable.

As she took a long look, her heart sank, because the school was obviously sub-standard. *God, I don't know what I've gotten myself into, but, please, somehow and some way, help me to get through this,* she prayed silently, as they drove back to her apartment.

That night Dianne began breaking the news of her transfer to the family members who lived in town. The first person she called was Aunt Hazel. "Just thought I would let you know that I got my transfer orders," she said.

"Where are you going?" Hazel inquired.

"I'm being sent to Wettermark in Boyce," she replied.

"Well, I just don't think it's right, sending all of you young teachers off to the black schools."

Dianne could hear Uncle R. V. yelling in the background, "Is that Dianne on the phone? Where are they sending her?"

"Wettermark, in Boyce," her aunt replied.

"She ought to just quit. That would show them!" he yelled again.

"I can't quit, Aunt Hazel. I need the job," Dianne interjected.

"I know you do, honey, and I am so sorry. Keep me posted," said Hazel, as they ended the conversation.

The next person that she called was her cousin Jerrine Harrell. "I got my transfer orders today," she said, repeating the information for the second time.

"I don't see how you are going to drive all that way out there every day," her cousin commented.

"I don't, either, but I'll make it someway," Dianne declared.

Dianne decided to wait until the weekend to break the news to her parents in person.

The next day the transferred teachers were sent to their assigned schools to meet with the principals. When Dianne walked through the front door of the school the first thing she saw was a large bulletin board with Martin Luther King, Jr.'s picture in the center announcing the fact that it was "National Negro History Week." *How appropriate, and how ironic, she thought. Just my luck to get transferred to an all-black school during National Negro History Week.* She walked into the main office and introduced herself to the principal. He instructed her to go to the school library.

Dianne found her way to the library and looked around. There was a section of books dedicated to black history and also a good number of books on white history. There were also a lot of filmstrip projectors and filmstrips just sitting out in the open with no protection from student vandalism. *Maybe they don't have anywhere to lock them up,* she reasoned, as she tried to decide on what she thought would be a good seat. She chose a seat close to the head of the table next to a large dictionary, halfway hoping that it would help to hide her. That turned out to be a mistake because the principal stood at that end of the table and smoked the whole time he was conducting the meeting. The drifting smoke headed right for Dianne's face.

The principal opened the meeting with a ten-minute lecture on his credentials. *I guess he thinks that he has to prove that he is as good as we are,* she thought, as she sat mesmerized by the large diamond rings on his hands. She had never seen a man wear so much jewelry.

The meeting lasted for almost an hour, and everyone was beginning to get restless before it finally ended. There were only six black teachers left at the school, along with the black principal and the black assistant principal. Dianne was surprised at how courteous and helpful they were to the unhappy newcomers.

Following the meeting, Dianne managed to find the home economics department. The door was in rather bad shape and the lock had been beaten, causing her difficulty in even getting into the room. The department consisted of one large room that contained both the cooking and sewing labs. The cutting tables also served as student desks.

As she began to look over the sewing machines her heart almost stopped because they were treadle models. She remembered her younger days of learning how to sew on her grandmother Rose's old faithful treadle machine, and the memories were not always happy ones. To her relief, closer examination showed that they had been converted to electric models. *Thank you, Lord, for small favors,* she thought.

She walked around the department, pulling out drawers and opening cabinets in the kitchen unit. Equipment was jumbled in the spaces with no apparent order. *How will I ever get this stuff straight?* she wondered. *Thank goodness, at least there's a washer and a dryer,* she observed, as she continued her exploration of the department.

There were no books in sight, and no one seemed to know anything about them.

"There should be some books in the bookroom," the principal commented when Dianne inquired about them.

The janitors could not locate any of the books that she needed, so Dianne was left, once again, with only her wits to rely on for her lesson plans.

Thoroughly exhausted, both physically and emotionally, she headed home after a trying day and settled down to watch the news as she ate a light supper. Her attention was captured with a special announcement from the Rapides Parish School Board.

"All teachers will report back to their original schools tomorrow. Repeat, all teachers will report back to their original schools tomorrow." That was the only part of the announcement that really sank in. Dianne couldn't believe it at first. It seemed too good to be true.

The school board, it seemed, was uncertain about their orders from the court. Rumors were circulating that there was also to be an integration of the students. Rather than having to move teachers twice, they wanted to make sure that the orders were clarified before proceeding with the desegregation plan for teachers in the system.

Chapter 9

The students at Ruby-Wise were excited and relieved to have their teachers back. Dianne cautioned them that it was probably only temporary. Students in all of her classes wrote up petitions requesting that she not be transferred. Mr. Slay told them that it wouldn't help the situation, so they gave the petitions to Dianne as souvenirs.

"Don't get your hopes up," she said. "Sooner or later the teachers will probably have to go back to the schools that they were assigned to."

Surely enough, that was the case. Announcements were made both at school and on the T. V. newscasts that the courts had ruled that the desegregation plans must be followed. All reassigned teachers were ordered to report to their new schools beginning the following week.

Dianne decided to make a trip to Rocky Branch to break the news to her family about the job transfer. Her grandmother, Rose Gunter, had already heard that Dianne might be transferred when Dianne had visited her earlier during the Christmas holidays.

Rose had cried, feeling certain that Dianne would be raped by one of the boys at the black school. "One of those boys is going to get you," she sobbed, "I just know it!"

"No they won't, Ma. I'll be okay," Dianne had reassured her.

Dolores, also, was worried about her daughter going into an unknown situation. "I don't see how you are going to tell them apart," she said. "They all look alike, you know. And what about the germs?" she continued. "You'll get sick being exposed to all of the germs in that place."

Sallie had been unusually quiet during the whole discussion. Then she chimed in with a question. "Aren't you scared, Sister?" she asked, addressing Dianne by her family nickname.

"No, I'm not scared. I'll be okay," Dianne replied.

There weren't too many things that she was scared of, thanks to Dolores. During the time they were growing up, Dianne and Sallie had sometimes been left alone when Dolores had to go to run errands or go to meetings. "Don't be afraid," she had always told them. "The dogs will protect you if anybody comes around."

In reality, the dogs probably wouldn't have been much protection. Dianne's dog, Ruby, was a black-and-white rat terrier, while Sallie had a black cocker spaniel named Jettie. More than likely, they wouldn't have been much help against an intruder. But Dolores never lied, a principle which she had instilled into her children at an early age. So, if she said that they should not be afraid, they believed her. As a result, they grew up being unafraid of almost anything.

F. D. exhibited a different viewpoint on the matter. "Well, Sister," he said, "You've been baptized by water. Now you are about to be baptized by fire."

"Daddy, as far as I'm concerned, all teaching is a baptism by fire," she retorted.

On the following Monday, Dianne drove out to Wettermark, highly aware of the butterflies that refused to stop fluttering in her stomach. She had consumed almost half a bottle of Pepto-Bismol on the way to school, but it brought little relief. She wanted desperately to turn her blue '65 Chevy BelAire around and head back to her apartment, but sheer determination kept her going until she reached the school's parking lot.

She was the first teacher to arrive, and she was reluctant to get out of her car. Then another white teacher drove up and got out, so Dianne worked up the nerve to make her way towards the building. *I can do this, I can do this,* she kept repeating to herself silently as she headed for the teachers' lounge to sign in. She felt "slightly akin to a fool," as her mother used to say, whenever she was uncertain about a situation. She could feel the many pairs of eyes watching her as she walked through the parking lot and down the hall. It felt like one of the longest walks she had ever made.

An assembly in the gym had been scheduled for the first event of the morning. The new teachers were seated in chairs on the gym floor, awaiting the time they would be introduced to the student body. The principal's voice seemed to drone on forever, and most of what he said was lost on Dianne as she stared out at the crowd of students sitting in the bleachers. All that she could see was a sea of black faces staring back at her. *Dear God,* she thought, *they do all look alike. Mother was right! How am I ever going to learn their names or tell them apart?*

Chapter 10

Dianne began meeting with the classes later that morning. She had difficulty pronouncing some of their names, much to the amusement of some of the students. The day went by in a blur, and she didn't know much more about the students or their classes than when she started.

Unable to locate any books, and uncertain about exactly what the classes had covered, she devised a plan. The smallest class, which was composed of senior girls, would study a wedding unit. All the other classes would study a foods unit based on the *State Curriculum Guide for Home Economics I.*

As the days passed by, she grew more familiar with the students and managed to master the pronunciation of most of the names. She was surprised to learn the black students, just as the other students she had taught, each had their own individual looks and personalities.

Guess I was wrong about not being able to tell them apart, she thought to herself. I'll have to tell Mother she was wrong, also.

Dianne, as always, soon settled into a routine. The students were attentive to the lessons and contributed to class discussions as best they could. Generally cooperative and respectful, they seemed to be somewhat in awe of the white teachers who had invaded their school. She was surprised to find she actually encountered fewer discipline problems than she had faced with the all-white classes.

A few of the students, though, did manage to get into trouble between classes or at lunch time. Some of them were caught fighting, but the problems did not spill over into class time. One day, just as Dianne was reaching outside the room to close her door after the tardy bell, she came face to face with the principal.

"Miss Hollis," he said, "I just wanted to come by and let you know that Derrick Baptiste will not be in your class today. I have him down in the office. He managed to set fire to a trash can at lunch time." Derrick was one of the most mischievous students in her classes. He was a real "wiggle worm" and could hardly sit still for the lessons.

"Why am I not surprised?" she asked. "Thanks for letting me know."

At the end of the second week she decided to give written exams in order to determine just how much progress she was making with the classes. After handing out the test papers to each class, she watched the students carefully as they worked on the tests. She was expecting some of them to try to cheat on the exam, but that was not the case. They were very quiet, and all of them appeared to be working really hard.

She did not have time to grade the tests at school, so after she got home she made out the answer keys. She was eager to see exactly what they had learned. As she began marking the incorrect answers, she became greatly enlightened as to the real abilities of the students. She had already known many of them could not function at their grade level when it came to reading and writing skills. What she learned from the test papers showed her they were a lot worse off than she had even imagined.

There were a few good scores and a sprinkling of average grades. However, many of them had "faked" their way through the test, making it appear that they were working when they actually knew nothing about the topics. Some of them had merely copied the questions over again into the spaces provided for the answers. Those who were worse off in reading abilities had simply traced over all of the typed letters on the test so everyone, including Dianne, would think they were actually working. She was somewhat discouraged by the number of "zeros" on the test.

This must be why they never used textbooks, she thought. That might also explain why there are no test grades in the gradebook, only grades for the end of each six weeks.

She decided to have the foods classes make posters about the Basic Four Food Groups at the end of the nutrition unit. She managed to gather up enough magazines for them to cut pictures from. Many of them could not afford to buy poster paper, so she furnished it for them. They were very excited as they worked on their projects, and Dianne was pleased when so many of them turned out well. She fastened them onto the walls, displaying them all around the room.

She invited the principal down to view their work. He was amazed at their accomplishments. "That is the most work I have ever seen out of some of those students," he commented.

The Rapides Parish Superintendent of Schools, Mr. Allen Nichols, was making it a point to visit every teacher who had been transferred during the lawsuit. He, too, was impressed by the work that the students had done.

"Miss Hollis," he said, "Everywhere I've been, the teachers are mad and complaining. Here I find you smiling and working."

"I got the best end of the deal," she informed him, almost cheerfully. "I got all home ec. classes, while the other teacher has to teach three science classes and only one class of home ec."

As the weeks passed by, Dianne and the students began to get more used to each other. She finally succeeded in pronouncing their names correctly and was able to match each name to the correct face. Occasionally, though, her Southern accent gave them their laugh for the day. They found it especially amusing whenever she said the words "rice" or "ice."

They were generally friendly and helpful. They met her each morning and carried her books to the room. The same task was repeated every afternoon as they carried her books out to the car when school was dismissed. They also loved to run errands and do chores. Some of their favorite tasks included dusting the erasers, sharpening pencils, and cleaning the chalkboard.

Dianne was taken off-guard one day when one of them asked her if they could wash the chalkboard. "I don't know," Dianne commented. "It doesn't look that dirty to me."

"Oh, please, let me go to the cafeteria and get some pickle juice," the girl begged.

"Pickle juice, whatever for?" Dianne inquired.

"We always wash the board with pickle juice," the girl insisted.

"Well, I suppose it will be okay," said Dianne, chuckling to herself, as it was her turn to laugh.

To her amazement, the girl quickly returned with a jar of pickle juice. Afterwards, the board had never looked so clean. *Well, I guess she really knew what she was doing, after all,* Dianne mused to herself, as she inhaled the odor of pickle juice for the rest of the day.

As Dianne and the students grew more comfortable with each other, the students began to pry her for personal information about herself. In most cases, she managed to evade their questions without giving out too much information.

She was astounded at one question that was posed by one of the male students.

"Miss Hollis, are you going to cook for the principal like the other teacher did? he inquired.

"Cook for him? What are you talking about?" she asked.

"She be cookin' all kinds of good food for him. Pork chops with rice and gravy, turnip greens and cornbread," he replied.

"Fried chicken, too," chimed in another student.

"And chocolate pie," added another.

"Yeah, she be carryin' him big ol' plates of food at lunch time," said yet another student.

"No, I don't think I'll be doing that," said Dianne slowly, as she pondered the information.

Dianne tried to add interest and humor to her lessons by telling little anecdotes and jokes. But aside from laughing at her pronunciations and her Southern accent, the students rarely saw the humor in what she was telling them. One exception occurred during the wedding unit in the senior girls' class. Dianne had just finished teaching a lesson on flower arranging and had shown the girls a filmstrip on that topic.

"The flowers will stay fresh longer if you put an aspirin in the water when you arrange them," she commented.

The entire class ended up laughing at that remark with one student declaring, "Miss Hollis, now I've heard everything. Put an aspirin in flower water. That is too funny!"

When the six-week grading period was almost over, Dianne was surprised to find a note in her mailbox early on a Friday morning. "Please report to the principal's office during your planning period today."

She was totally perplexed as to why she was being summoned. *Maybe he wants me to cook lunch for him,* she thought.

"Miss Hollis, come in and have a seat," he said when she reported as requested. "I have had a call from the school board office," he continued. "You are to report back to Ruby-Wise school on Monday morning."

"Why? What happened?" she managed to stammer, as she sat in total shock.

"The teacher you traded places with is not certified to teach science," he replied.

Dianne walked slowly back to her room, lost in thought, and almost unable to believe it.

She decided that it would be best to break the news to the students herself.

"Don't you like us anymore?" one of them asked.

"Do you really have to go?" another one inquired.

"I don't have anything to do with it," Dianne explained. "I have to go wherever the school board sends me. It is part of my job."

As the day progressed, a steady stream of students came by the room to say goodbye to Dianne. Many of them were sad to see her go.

Almost every girl from the senior class came by. "I just wanted to say that I enjoyed your class," one of them said.

At the end of the day Dianne packed up her belongings in short order and prepared to leave Wettermark behind. She had taken to keeping her things in a cardboard box so that she could be prepared to leave at a moment's notice, since the school board could not make up its mind where to send her. She turned in her keys and left for home, elated at her good fortune. Little did she know that her short stay at Wettermark would prove to be an albatross around her neck in future years.

Chapter 11

On the following Monday Dianne headed back to Ruby-Wise. She was greeted with "Welcome Back" banners and cheers from her former students. She spent most of the class time that day exchanging tales with the students about the past six weeks adventures. One boy in the seventh grade told her, "You know what, Miss Hollis? When I asked her if I could go to the office to get an aspirin for my headache she told me that if I didn't shut up she was 'going to give me an ass burn!'" Dianne decided to pass up that remark without comment. *You probably gave her a headache!* she responded silently.

Students in the eighth grade reported their bad luck, also. "When she got mad at us she gave us an "'F' to the fifth power," one student remarked. *And this class probably drove her nuts, too,* Dianne thought to herself.

In the ninth-grade girls' sewing class, even more stories followed. "When I showed her my garment she said that it was all wrong. Then she took it and just ripped it apart with her hands," said Kathy.

"And when I got ready to put in my zipper she told me to sew backwards around the whole zipper," added Sally, "I told her that I didn't think Miss Hollis would want me to do it that way. She said that she was teaching the class now, not Miss Hollis."

"Well, I never heard of putting in a zipper that way," observed Dianne. "Maybe they didn't have any zipper feet at their school."

"You know what else?" whispered Billie. "She made Jenny's whole dress for her. Jenny just kept coming up and asking for help and she said that she would show her how to do it. Then she would sew it for her."

"Well, it's too late to do anything about that now," replied Dianne. "I guess Jenny just lucked out."

Dianne had made a quick inspection of her departments and discovered that several important items were missing. "I can't find my gradebook, my keys, or the Green Register," she commented to Mr. Megison, her fellow teacher.

"You need to let Mr. Slay know about that right away," he replied.

Dianne reported the problem to Mr. Slay. "Grades are almost due," she noted, "and there is no way that I can calculate them without the grade book."

"Phone the teacher and tell her that you need the items back as soon as possible," he instructed.

Dianne followed his orders and called the teacher at the other school. After several long delays, she finally got her on the other line. "I can't stop now and bring that stuff to you," she said. "I'm busy teaching."

Dianne reported the results of the phone call to Mr. Slay, and he was furious. "Make out a list of everything that is missing and let me have it as soon as you get through. Don't worry. I'll get the stuff back for you," he said.

Dianne had to keep his geography class while he went to town to get the missing items. At the end of the day he stopped by to give them to her. "There is one other thing that I want to tell you," he said. "She has been giving the students a lot of "F's" as punishment for misconduct. I want you to ignore all of that type of "F" when averaging their grades."

"Yes, I have already heard about those, and I was planning to omit them from the averages," she replied.

Things soon settled down to normal as Dianne and the students reverted to their regular routine. The ninth-grade girls completed their sewing projects. They decided to model their garments in a style show for their mothers and the girls in the sixth, seventh, and eighth grades. The mothers were invited to the home economics lab for refreshments afterwards. "It was really nice. You all did a great job," was the comment heard over and over, as Dianne and the girls basked in the praises.

There were some refreshments left over, so the ninth-grade boys were invited down after all of the guests had left. They made short work of the leftover treats, reluctantly admitting that they were "pretty good eats."

The style show was such a hit that Dianne and the girls decided to put on a play for the younger girls. It was titled "The Evolution of Sitting," and it was an original play that had been written by Dianne's classmates during her college days. Dianne cleverly matched each girl to a character in the play that resembled her own personality.

Donna, the prettiest girl in the class, was selected to be "Eve," the first woman and the symbol of all womanhood to come. Sally, a sweet and shy girl, was selected to be "Southern Belle Sally."

"I hope you can find a hoop skirt," said Dianne, as she assigned the part. Rhonda, a quiet girl with strawberry blond hair was "Wild West Winnie."

"I think you might have a secret yearning for adventure," Dianne told her.

She felt that her best assignment was that of "'Millie,' 'Maxie,' and 'Minnie Mod,'" three girls who would wear mini-skirts and demonstrate the incorrect way to sit in such attire. She assigned the parts to the girls in class who were known to be a bit on the wild side. She wasn't sure if it would work, but on the day of the play they showed up with green, pink, and purple girdles hanging out of their short skirts. They went through their antics of bending and sitting incorrectly, much to the amusement of the audience. The class had gone all out with the stage decorations, music, and costumes. Carol Swain, one of the best readers in the class, served as the narrator.

The play was quite a success, and Dianne felt that producing it had been worth all of the extra time and effort. It had even been fun!

The eighth-graders switched from science to Home Living at midterm. Dianne dreaded having labs with that group, but they performed surprisingly well. They tackled their sewing projects with enthusiasm. The boys made chef's aprons and hats, while the girls made laundry bags and skirts. They even managed to bake a batch of cookies without burning them, much to Dianne's amazement. Home Living was listed as their "best subject" in *The Panther*, their school newspaper. *I guess they are better at hands-on projects rather than academics,* she reflected.

Chuck, one of the eighth-grade boys, told Dianne that his mother was seriously ill with cancer. Dianne and Eunice decided to visit her and take her a potted hydrangea as a gift. As Chuck rode out to the house with them he tried to prepare them for the visit. "She has a lot of tubes hooked up to her," he said.

When they arrived and entered the bedroom, his mother apologized for her appearance. "Chuck tried to prepare us," said Eunice gently. They made it through the visit and drove home in a somber mood.

His mom passed away a short time later. The week after the funeral, Dianne observed Chuck's younger sister, Beth, as she was on after-school bus duty. Beth's dad had tried, but it was obvious from her mismatched clothes and hair badly in need of a barrette that a mother's touch was no longer present in the household. Beth looked so small, sad, and alone. Dianne blinked back a few tears, thinking that it was one of the saddest sights she had ever seen.

She decided to straighten and inventory the science lab, enlisting the aid of two of the best ninth-grade science students, David and

Paul. They were "in their element" in the science lab and were excited to see all of the chemicals and demonstrations materials on hand. "Okay, you two. You're going to have to stop gawking and get to work," she instructed. She had ordered some fish to stock the aquarium, so she told Paul to fill it up with water. He picked up a beaker and began emptying it over the rocks. A few minutes later Dianne noticed that the rocks were starting to fizz.

"Where did you get that beaker?" she asked Paul.

"I just picked up the one that was over by the sink that already had some water in it," he replied.

"Oh, no!" she exclaimed. "That wasn't water. It was hydrochloric acid for an experiment tomorrow. I think the rocks are melting."

The three of them rushed over to the aquarium, which by then resembled a glass of Alka seltzer as it rapidly filled with bubbles from the bottom of the tank.

"I can't believe you did that!" said David, almost doubling over with laughter.

Paul was totally embarrassed by the whole incident. "I know that you two will never let me forget this," he said, shaking his head in disbelief.

His turn for revenge came a few days later. "Paul locked David in the book closet," Mr. Megison informed Dianne as she entered his room for class after recess.

"How in the world did that happen? Couldn't he just open it from the inside with the doorknob?" she asked.

"No, the knob is behind a shelf, so he couldn't reach it," replied Mr. Megison.

"I can't believe that somebody as smart as David would let himself be locked in a closet. How did he look when you opened the door?" she inquired.

"He looked pretty sheepish."

Well, I guess Paul got the last laugh, after all, she thought, chuckling to herself as she pictured David trapped in the closet.

She broadened her relationship with the students as they became better acquainted. One of her favorite ninth-grade students, Lee Mercier, kept falling asleep during science class. "If you keep sleeping in class I'm going to pour a glass of water on your head one of these days," she teased. After several more incidents of napping, she carried out her threat as his classmates gleefully watched the event unfold. Lee never napped in class again.

Another of her favorite students, Leo Williams, was also a ninth grader. Leo loved to joke around with Dianne, although he never caused any trouble in class. His mother, Janet, was an aide at the school. She and Dianne became well acquainted as they ran off copies of tests for Dianne's classes. One day Dianne mentioned to Janet that Leo's grade for the six weeks was hanging in the balance. "He is just wedged in there between a 'C' and a 'D,'" she reported.

"Well, if he deserves a 'D' you just go right ahead and give it to him," said Janet.

When the time to average grades came around, Dianne decided on the "D." A few days later when report cards were passed out, Leo was in shock. "You really woke him up with that 'D,'" his mom reported. "I think that you will see a great improvement in his study habits from now on. You are his favorite teacher and you can get more work out of him than anybody else."

Some of the girls reported to her that one of the ninth-grade girls was planning to run away from home. "She brought extra clothes to school with her, and she says that she is really going to do it," one of them insisted. Dianne relayed the information to Mr. Slay, who promptly began an investigation. He found out that the girl and her father had argued the night before, resulting in her being whipped, and that was why she was planning to run away. Thanks to Dianne's intervention, a potential crisis was averted.

Back at home Dianne's social life had not improved much over what it was in Lake Charles. At her apartment she was visited by

Brenda, a girl who was looking for the former tenant. Not knowing anyone her age in town, she became acquainted with Brenda and began to see her on a regular basis. She agreed to accompany her new friend to the Pentecostal church during a revival.

Visiting other churches was something familiar to her because Dolores had always made it a point to attend other community churches during their revivals. Dolores felt that supporting neighboring revivals would boost attendance during revivals at the church she belonged to. Dianne found the Pentecostal church to be very similar to an Assembly of God church that she had visited in her younger days.

When she was referred to as "one of the understudies" she realized that Brenda was trying to convert her to the Pentecostal religion. She broke off the relationship, explaining that she could never convert to another religion. "I was brought up in the Church of Christ and I attended a college of the same religion," she explained. "Besides that, at one time my daddy was a deacon in the church. Converting is just not an option for me."

Her apartment, once again, was not in the best section of town. The walls were not well insulated for sound. The couple who lived on the adjoining side of the duplex had some rather strange habits. They argued frequently late at night, forcing Dianne to run a fan in her bedroom in order to drown out the noise so that she could sleep. Every Thursday night they would go out and get drunk. Then, without fail, they would come home at 2:00 a.m. and throw up loudly. One night after they came home late the woman locked the man out of the house, and he ran around banging on all of the doors and windows, waking Dianne in the process.

Dianne's newspaper disappeared several times after it was thrown onto the front porch. Although she suspected that the neighbors were taking it, she didn't have any proof. She went into her detective mode, determined to find out once and for all why the paper kept disappearing. One afternoon when it was almost time for the paper delivery she listened for it to hit the porch floor. Like clockwork, she heard footsteps coming out of the neighbors' door as the porch boards creaked softly. When she checked, as she suspected, the paper was gone. Rather than confront the hostile couple, she solved the problem by picking it up as soon as it was delivered.

Also, somebody kept putting fish heads into her garbage can. She never could figure out if it was a prank or if someone was really cleaning and eating the fish. Either way, it was a disgusting and smelly mess to clean up. *Boy, if I ever catch who did this, they are definitely going to get a piece of my mind,* she fumed, as she cleaned out the garbage can for the third time.

Dianne was a creature of habit, and she kept waking up early on Saturdays, thinking that she had overslept and was late for work. After several false starts of jumping out of bed, only to remember that it wasn't a school day, she solved the problem by putting a note that read "IT'S SATURDAY!" in front of her alarm clock. One Saturday morning she was finally enjoying sleeping in when she was awakened by water dripping onto her head. *Now what?* she wondered, as she looked upward for the source. She discovered that the roof had sprung a leak and water was leaking all onto the bed. She had to get up and call the realtor to get the roof repaired, once again losing some much-needed sleep.

Her social life did an about face one night when she received an unexpected phone call.

"Is this Dianne Hollis?" an unfamiliar, sexy male voice inquired.

"Yes, it is. Who is this?" she replied.

"A secret admirer."

"Really? What's your name?"

"I can't tell you that."

"No, really, who is this?"

"Why don't you try to guess?"

"I'm not much good at guessing games."

"Well, give it a try. You might be surprised."

"Okay, is it George?" she inquired, referring to a running joke that she had shared with her last two roommates. She and Becky had nicknamed one of their suitemates "George," based on the old television show *Topper,* because "George" was always coming and going like a ghost.

"Wow, I can't believe you guessed it right. Yes, my name is George."

Dianne was pretty sure that he wasn't being truthful, but she continued to play along. "George" kept calling her for several weeks, holding lengthy conversations. Finally, he asked her to go out on a date. She reluctantly agreed, mostly out of curiosity.

"What do you think I look like?" he inquired the night before they were supposed to go out.

"I really have no idea," she replied.

"Guess, anyhow."

"I really can't even begin to guess."

"Okay, then, what do you see me wearing?"

"Gosh, I don't know."

"Well, think. You can think of something."

"Okay, I guess, a pullover sweater."

"What color?"

"Blue."

The next night when George came by to pick her up he had on a blue sweater, just as she had described. They went for a drive and dropped by the Alexandria Senior High basketball game. They didn't stay too long because it was too noisy for Dianne's taste. He dropped her off at her front door and she scooted inside, quickly saying her goodbyes. *Boy, that was really weird. I'm not sure if I want to keep seeing him or not,* she pondered.

George continued to call her almost every night. He was a tall, slender man with light brown hair and brown eyes. Over all, he wasn't bad-looking. Still, Dianne wasn't comfortable with the situation. One day he called shortly after she had gotten home from work. The apartment was still hot, as she had just put the air conditioner on. She took off her dress as she was talking, letting out a sigh of relief, glad to be out of her working clothes.

"What did you just do?" he inquired.

"Took off my dress," she replied.

"What are you wearing now?"

"My slip."

"What color?"

"None of your business!"

This is just getting weirder and weirder, she thought. I don't think he is the guy I'm looking for.

George came by her apartment a few more times when she said that she was too busy to go out. One night he even helped her grade some papers. Then she made up her mind.

The next time he called she broke the news to him.

"I don't think I can see you anymore."

"What?! Why not?"

"It's just not working out."

"Well, I think that you at least owe me an explanation."

"I just don't think you're my type. I think it's best if we break off the relationship."

Dianne felt relieved, like a burden had been lifted. The guy was probably harmless, but there was something about him that just didn't seem straight-forward. For starters, she never really believed that his name was George. In fact, he had been rather elusive about any data regarding his background. *It's all for the best,* she reasoned. *I'll still find the right man. It will just take time.*

George didn't give up that easily. He came by the apartment again several times and knocked loudly on both doors. Dianne knew it was him because nobody else ever came to visit. She just stood her ground and refused to open the door. Finally, he quit coming by, and he was out of her life, or so she thought.

As the end of the school year approached Dianne decided to take some of the girls with her on a weekend excursion to her parents' home in Rocky Branch. Debbie Foster, Billie Nalley, and Rhonda Ryland were the girls who were chosen for the trip. When they arrived in Rocky Branch Dolores and F. D. were cordial hosts, doing their best to make sure that everyone was comfortable and well fed. At the dinner table F. D. was his most charming self, entertaining them with some of his most humorous stories. All in all, they had a jovial time and Dianne felt it was a good experience for the girls.

When graduation time arrived Dianne was sad to see so many of her favorite students leave. She knew she would never forget that group, no matter how many more years she continued to teach. She attended the graduation ceremony and was introduced to the tradition of the "Book of Memories" that was passed on from the ninth-graders to the eighth-graders, who were becoming the "senior group" at the school.

After the ceremony Mr. Slay carried out another school tradition by taking the ninth-graders out to eat. Dianne was invited to attend but had no way to get home, as she rode to the event with Eunice and Sam. Lee Mercier offered to take her home in his car, but she had serious doubts about riding with him.

"Lee Mercier has offered me a ride in his car if I go with the group to eat. What do you think?" she asked Mr. Megison.

"Have you seen that 'rattletrap' he calls a car?" replied Mr. Megison.

"No."

"Well, I don't know, do what you want to."

She made up her mind quickly. "Sorry," she told a much-disappointed Lee, "but I guess I had better just go on home."

She finished up the remaining two weeks of school in short order, looking forward to having a few weeks off from dealing with students. She cleaned out her apartment and decided not to renew the lease, hoping she could find more suitable living arrangements for next year. Headed back to Rocky Branch again, she stopped to say goodbye to Aunt Hazel and Uncle R. V. on her way out of town.

"I managed to get everything into my car except for my garbage cans," she informed them.

"I'm gonna go get those cans. There's no use in lettin' 'em go to waste," said R. V.

"Be careful on your trip home, and tell the folks I said 'Hello,'" added Hazel.

"Okay, I will. I love you both. Goodbye for now," said Dianne.

Dianne had made another decision before the school year had ended. She had decided to take some additional courses at LSU in order to become a certified dietician. "It's just not worth all of the trouble and turmoil that I had to go through this past year," she wrote to her cousin Mary Browning. "I'm going to see if I can get into another line of work, but I'm holding onto my job at Ruby-Wise just in case things don't work out."

After depositing most of her belongings at her parents' home in Rocky Branch, Dianne headed for the LSU campus in Baton Rouge. She had pre-registered and elected to stay in the graduate women's dorm. After consulting with an advisor, she signed up for two classes, Advanced Nutrition and Organic Chemistry. Both classes proved to be pretty time-consuming and required lots of study time. Although she had maintained a "B" average in the chemistry class, she decided to drop it and concentrate on nutrition, figuring that she could take it at a later date. The nutrition class had proven to be harder than she had thought it would be.

She went back to Rocky Branch for the Fourth of July break, looking forward to seeing all of her relatives. F. D. always had a big fish fry for his brothers and sisters on the Fourth. It was a family tradition.

"Never trust a woman professor whose first name is 'Harvey,'" she said, referring to her nutrition teacher, as she complained to Dolores about the difficulty of the class.

She had learned that in order to be a certified dietician she would have to take a year's worth of undergraduate classes and then intern for a year before getting a full-paying job. I think this is going to be too much trouble, she pondered, as she pored over the nutrition formulas night after night. I believe that my best bet would be to work on my master's degree and keep on teaching. I guess it just wasn't in the cards for me to be a dietician, after all. Good thing I held onto my job at Ruby-Wise. I guess it will be good to see all of the students again, too.

Chapter 12

On a hot day in August 1970, Dianne returned to Pineville with her old faithful '65 Chevy BelAire loaded to the point of almost overflowing. She pulled into Hazel and R. V.'s driveway, glad to be back in familiar territory. She had phoned Hazel of her plans to return, and Hazel had found an apartment for her at the other end of Payne Street, the same street where she and R. V. lived.

"Hi, Uncle V. I'm back. Could I get my garbage cans back from you?" she inquired.

"Sure, you can. They're sittin' right out there by mine. You can come back and get 'em after you unload your car," he replied.

After receiving directions to the landlord's house, Dianne retrieved the key and proceeded to the front door to give the place a "walk through."

It was a small duplex apartment, just three rooms and a bath, but it suited Dianne's needs just fine. It had a window air conditioner, and, even better, a washing machine. Dianne wasted no time unloading the car and setting about to make the apartment her own. A few days later she decided to add a second window air conditioner and a dryer. *It will be really nice to be cool and also not to have to go out to do laundry,* she reasoned to herself, as she splurged on the new appliances.

Returning to Ruby-Wise a few days later was a new experience for her. It was the first time in her teaching career she was returning to the same school with many of the same students. The school had a very low turnover rate with both students and faculty, although a few new faces always appeared at the beginning of a new school year. She found it was a definite advantage to already know most of the students in the eighth and ninth grades. The seventh graders were new to her, but she had taught some of their brothers and sisters.

"The Megison," as Eunice had jokingly dubbed him, imparted some of his wisdom to Dianne on her first day back. "You know the old saying about teaching, don't you?" he inquired. "They say you don't really get to be a good teacher until your third year. The first year you know nothing. The second year you think you know it all. Then by the third year you are ready to really start teaching."

"Well, I hope that holds true for me," Dianne replied.

Dianne had the highest esteem for her two fellow junior high teachers, Henry Megison and Ruth Hyde. Mrs. Hyde, a small and petite person, was always the perfect lady. Impeccably groomed and speaking in the softest of voices, she maintained complete control of her classes without ever losing her cool. Dianne often envied Mrs. Hyde's discipline methods, but she couldn't follow them. They didn't suit her personality.

Mr. Megison, who also served as the assistant principal, was more jovial and was well liked by the students. Dianne appreciated his sage advice that was often laced with humor.

"Watch out if somebody sends you an eraser," he warned. "That means there is a supervisor somewhere in the building."

A new face had been added to the faculty. Don Sexton had joined the school to serve as guidance counselor and also as a coach for the boys' basketball teams. Girls' basketball had been discontinued due to lack of interest.

Dianne was already sponsoring the cheerleaders, and she remembered all the fun she had when she was in the boosters during her high school years. So, she came up with the idea of forming a booster club for the junior high girls. It was met with great enthusiasm. The girls joined in droves and decided to call themselves "The Pantherettes." They set about selecting patterns for the uniforms.

The patterns and material were ordered from Wellan's Department Store, and they arrived shortly afterwards. Dianne volunteered to make the letters for the uniforms, her first of many experiences at providing her sewing skills for a school's benefit.

The cheerleaders traditionally selected a young girl to be their mascot at the ball games. Don Sexton's daughter, Suzie, was a perfect candidate. Although Suzie was very shy, her mother, Geri, taught her a simple cheer to show to the girls. Everyone was enthralled with having such a cute mascot. With her blonde hair and blue eyes, little Suzie added a special touch to the games' atmosphere as she waved her blue and white pompoms along with the cheerleaders.

Dianne soon learned that sponsoring the boosters was a lot more time-consuming and a greater responsibility than sponsoring just the cheerleaders. For starters, she was responsible for a lot more people and for their behavior at the ballgames. In addition, she had to attend all of the games, including the away games. That meant riding the bus along with the boisterous students. Sometimes there were two games a week, so that activity began to consume a lot of her spare time.

Most of the trips went without incident, but several of them proved to be memorable. On one trip Dianne caught two of the girls smoking in the restroom of a school they were visiting. She reported the incident to Mr. Slay and left the punishment up to him. On another trip she noticed on the way home that the students were noisier than usual. There seemed to be a lot of giggling and laughter coming from a certain section of the bus. After warning them several times to "quiet down," she decided to investigate the source of the noise. Making her way to the back of the bus, she found that an extra passenger had been smuggled between the seats. It was a girl who was fittingly nicknamed "Squirrel." Dianne elected to suspend the student responsible for the prank from attending the next ballgame.

The ball teams had their ups and downs, winning some games by a surprising margin and losing others by only a few points. One day Don was complaining to some of his fellow teachers about the sluggishness of some of the team members. "Some of those boys run like they have on lead-soled shoes," he lamented. "I thought they ran a lot faster than that during practice."

"Well," commented Dianne, "I think I know what part of the problem could be. Jeffery Mitchell told me he ate two packages of hot dogs and a whole loaf of bread before the game the other day."

"What? You don't mean that! I'm going to have to have a talk with that boy!" exclaimed Don. "No wonder he can't run."

Dianne continued to sponsor the boosters and cheerleaders throughout her remaining tenure at Ruby-Wise. Although a few more unpleasant incidents occurred, the majority of the activities were filled with pleasant memories.

Dianne really missed the brilliant, funny, and lovable ninth graders from the previous year. Her eighth-grade homeroom of the previous year had become the ninth-grade "seniors" at the school. Moving up a grade had not improved their abilities or personalities. In fact, many of the boys didn't actually pass to the ninth grade. They had been socially promoted because of spending two years in the eighth grade.

She had reported their lack of progress to Mr. Slay as the previous year had progressed. He had taken it upon himself to come over and talk to them. "Some of you boys are going to look awfully funny sitting in here in a couple of years with this year's fifth-graders," he warned. At the end of the year he told Dianne to write "Furniture Move" on the records of those students who did not actually earn enough credits to pass to the ninth grade. "They don't deserve having 'promoted' listed on their records," he declared.

Most of the discipline problems in that class occurred with the over-aged boys. One boy who considered himself to be quite macho wrote "Born to Raise Hell!" on the outside of his notebook. When this was reported to Mr. Slay, he called the boy in and confiscated the notebook. The next day the boy's father came charging into the office, demanding to know "Who took my son's notebook?"

Mr. Slay, who was a rather tall and large-framed man, was sitting behind his desk when the man entered his office. He stood up, unfolding himself from his chair and said, "I'm the man who took the notebook."

The father backed up a couple of steps, somewhat surprised by the size of the man he was ready to take on. "Ah, that's okay. I just wanted to know who it was. You keep it!" he stammered as he backed out of the office.

Her salvation came through the seventh and eighth grade classes both of which contained some really good students. It was really nice to have an eighth-grade homeroom where the students actually cared about their grades. A problem did arise in the seventh grade with a record number of forty-three students that year. Unfortunately, there weren't enough students in the overall school enrollment to justify hiring another teacher, so that class remained large for the rest of the year. Luckily, most of them were good students who caused few discipline problems, despite the overcrowded conditions. "I don't think they can move around enough to get into trouble," she commented to her friend Eunice.

Dianne tried to add interest to the science classes with demonstrations, experiments, films, and field trips. The school had a roll-a-lab which she used to transport the materials from one classroom to another. One of the favorite experiments in the ninth-grade class included the formation of carbon from sugar by pouring hydrochloric acid over it. Students would watch excitedly as the carbon began to form and give off an obnoxious odor. "Mr. Megison says that you are always coming in and stinking up his room with your experiments," one student reported to her.

"Well, that's his tough luck," Dianne retorted jokingly as she cracked a window.

In the eighth-graders' study of earth science, she obtained some molds of volcanoes and glaciers. She made enough plaster of Paris models for each student in class and had them paint and label the parts. *I think I may have found their talent,* she thought, as they pored over the delicate work.

She also arranged to take that class on a field trip to the Don Theater to see the Walt Disney film, "The Living Desert." One of the boys in the class, Steve Jenkins, was extra small for his size. In fact, the other boys often entertained themselves at recess by stuffing him into one of the trashcans, feet first. "I'm going to get in with a child's ticket," he announced.

"Oh, you can't do that! You'll never get by with it," cautioned Dianne.

"Yes, I will. I do it all the time," he confided.

She watched carefully as he made his way towards the ticket window. Surely enough, he passed for a child under twelve and got in for half price. "Told you I could do it," he boasted.

In seventh-grade science she decided to have them make leaf prints using a technique that she had learned from F. D. when he had worked for the Louisiana Wildlife and Fisheries Department. The problem was finding some leaves for them to gather and identify.

"The school owns a plot of timberland adjacent to our campus," Mr. Slay informed her. "You can take the students on a field trip through there to get the leaves they need."

"Okay, but I think I had better go over the trail first to see what's in store," she replied.

I always knew that winning that trip to forestry camp in 4-H would come in handy some day, she thought to herself, remembering the time that she had beaten out all of the boys in Union Parish, winning first place in the forestry project.

She asked for a couple of volunteers to go with her on a scouting expedition to lay out the trip. Two boys, Dennis and Kent, volunteered to accompany her. The next day after school they headed out to the forest plot. "You can get there from the back of the campus," Mr. Slay had told her. What he didn't mention was that the entrance was a set of steps that went up and over the fence rather than a gate.

The two boys scurried over and waited for Dianne to follow. "Okay, I'm coming over, but don't you two dare try to look up my dress," she threatened.

After a hot and dusty traipse through the woods they headed

back, walking by the side of the road. "Can you buy us a coke at Tauber's store?" they begged.

"Okay, I guess you deserve it," said Dianne. The boys drank the cokes as she drove them home.

The next day the students were all excited about the upcoming field trip. Upon checking roll and collecting permission slips, Dianne learned that Dennis was absent. "I can't believe he didn't come today after helping me out yesterday," she commented to the class.

"There's a good reason why he's not here," said the Megison, when she reported the absence to him later. "It seems that Kent rubbed Dennis's face with some poison ivy leaves yesterday when you were in the woods. He had to go to get a shot today."

"Oh, brother, what will they think of next?" Dianne exclaimed.

The ninth-grade girls' Home Ec. I class continued with the usual traditions of cooking, sewing, and child development. Some of the cooking labs went off without a hitch, while others proved to be more of a challenge. One group of girls wanted to make some oatmeal cookies, so Dianne suggested that they use the recipe in their textbook. They mixed up the cookies and baked them according to recipe directions. Some really delicious smells were coming from their oven. When they took the cookie sheets out of the oven and tried to remove the cookies, every single cookie fell apart. "Miss Hollis, what happened to our cookies?" They almost cried as they posed the question. "We did everything right."

Dianne took out the textbook and began to read through the recipe. "Well, girls," she replied, "I think I know what caused the problem. This recipe has no flour. Somehow the printer left it out of the ingredient list. I'm really sorry. We should have checked it more closely."

When the Christmas holidays approached, the girls wanted to sponsor a Christmas tea for the faculty. They excitedly planned the menu and decorations, making the invitations to give to each faculty member. The school had been closed for the Thanksgiving holidays, and the cooking lab had not been used for several weeks. After mixing up their cookies and cakes they proceeded to put them into the ovens. This time, instead of a delicious odor, a rank and putrid odor began to fill the lab room. "Miss Hollis, what's wrong? Why does this stuff smell so bad?" they asked.

"I don't know, but I'm about to find out," Dianne replied.

Upon opening the drawer beneath one of the ovens which seemed to be the culprit of the almost unbearable odor, Dianne discovered a nest of baby mice which had succumbed to the heat. "Well, I guess that lets those cookies off of the refreshment list," she observed, as she removed the cookie sheet from the oven, dumping the cookies into a trash can. Somehow, everyone had suddenly lost their appetites. Two boys volunteered to clean out the stove and get rid of the mice, much to the relief of the girls in the class.

During the second semester the class worked on their sewing projects. Dianne always cautioned the students against buying either black or white material. "Black is too hard to see if you need to take some stitches out," she said, "and white gets dirty too easily."

One girl, Lisa, ignored the advice and bought white material anyhow. She also did not follow the directions for backstitching at the end of every seam. By the time the garment was finished it was looking a little worse for wear.

The girls decided to put on the usual spring style show modeling their garments for their mothers and the girls in the sixth, seventh, and eighth grades. Dianne was narrating this time. The cue for each girl to come on stage was when her name called out as Dianne began to describe each garment. When she got to Lisa's name she glanced over to the entrance and saw that the girl was missing, so she skipped down to the next model. Afterwards she found Lisa and asked her what happened.

"I took my dress home to wash it last night," said Lisa, "and it fell apart in the washing machine."

"Well, remember all of those times I kept telling you to backstitch," said Dianne. "Now you know why."

During the child development unit the girls went over to work with the kindergarten students. They had great fun telling stories, singing, and playing games with the children. At the end of the unit they sponsored a party for the children and had them to dance around a Maypole. "Wow, that was so much fun," said one of the girls. "Do we have to start having class again after this?"

Students were required to study health for part of the year during their P. E. classes. Dianne was responsible for supervising the students who were in the Megison's room watching films and filmstrips and answering questions while the rest of the classes rotated out to the gym. The filmstrips included a series on the human body systems. One of the filmstrips on the endocrine system showed some drawings illustrating the changes that both males and females went through during puberty. After the seventh-grade girls had viewed the filmstrips one of them came up to Dianne the next day with tears in her eyes. She was holding a note in her hand.

"I didn't want to give you this, but my mamma said that I have to," she blubbered.

What in the world? Dianne wondered, as she began to open the note.

The mother, it seemed, was most upset because of the viewing of the diagrams of the unclothed human bodies in the endocrine system filmstrip. "You should be ashamed of showing materials like that to the students," the note read. "My daughter was most embarrassed, and I am sure that the other students in the class were, too."

Dianne carried the note over to Mr. Slay. "Why don't I take a look at the filmstrip, and then I'll make a decision on what to do," he said.

After viewing the filmstrip he called Dianne back into his office. "I wouldn't worry too much about the note," he said. "They can see a lot worse stuff than that in *National Geographic*."

Dianne reported the incident and the results to the Megison. "I wondered why that filmstrip was so popular," he remarked, chuckling as he walked down the hall.

Dianne wasn't very athletic. She never had been. She couldn't run, and she couldn't jump. But the one thing that she could do was play volleyball, and she played it very well. In college she had joined a sorority, Theta Psi, because a lot of her friends were in it. What she hadn't realized until later was that most of the members were also athletes. They won almost every kind of intramural competition that the college had to offer. Dianne had played on the championship volleyball team, and she had not forgotten the skills that she had learned.

On a warm spring day the Megison announced that he was going to take the boys outside to play baseball. "You and the girls can stay here and play volleyball," he told Dianne. "The nets are already set up for you."

As the girls began to play, the temptation was too much for her, and Dianne couldn't resist hitting a few serves. The girls were impressed and begged her to play some more. "I can't play in a dress unless I have on some shorts underneath," she protested.

"Okay, but you have to bring them tomorrow," they insisted.

That afternoon before leaving school she found an illustrated note on her desk. "Dear Miss Hollis, Please, please, don't forget to bring your shorts and sneakers tomorrow so that you can play volleyball with us. Gloria Cole."

Word soon got around the school and a report about Dianne's athletic endeavors was noted in the school paper. *Oh, boy, will I ever live this down?* she wondered.

One of the least pleasant parts of the job at Ruby-Wise was the afternoon bus duty. Students who didn't board the bus immediately after school had to wait for their bus connection to arrive. In addition, some of the high school students were dropped off, also, to make another bus connection. Watching students from kindergarten through the high school age group was no easy task. It was hot in the fall and cold in the winter. The duty teacher was required to roam around the waiting area, checking on all of the students.

One day the Megison came over to talk to Dianne. "Come over here for a minute. There's something I need to tell you," he said. "We have been having a problem with some of the candy and the candy money disappearing from the office. We are pretty sure that we have it narrowed down to two students. We think that it is Johnny Johnson and Kitty James. One of the ladies in the office, but I'm not saying who, took one of the chocolate bars and laced it with some Ex-lax a few days ago. We left it out in the office after school, and it disappeared. The next day we called Pineville High to see if Johnny and Kitty were there. Johnny was absent. We've got it figured out. One of the two is acting as the lookout while the other one sneaks in the office and steals the candy and the money. Your job tomorrow will be to ignore them and let them have their chance to get in there again."

"Okay, I'm game," replied Dianne.

The next day the trap was set. The tempting box of candy and money was left on top of a filing cabinet in the unlocked office. A mirror had been hung over the filing cabinet in just the right place so Mr. Slay could see the box when sitting at his desk in the adjacent office.

"They're busted!" the Megison reported to Dianne the next day. "Mr. Slay saw a hand reaching into the box, and when he opened his door, it was Johnny. His hand came up from the box so fast that the suction pulled the box up off the filing cabinet."

Eunice had been carpooling with Dianne for quite some time. Her husband, Sam, would drop her off at Dianne's apartment and pick her up there after he got off work. One afternoon after all of the students had left, Dianne noticed a small gray striped kitten playing in the flowers by the bus stop. "Oh, look, it's a kitten," she said to Eunice, as they were heading out to Dianne's car. "I wonder where it came from."

"Mrs. Tauber across the street has some cats. Maybe it's one of hers," suggested Eunice.

"Well, let's take it over there and see. We can't leave it here," Dianne stated firmly.

"Hi, Mrs. Tauber," said Dianne, as she entered the store holding the kitten. "We found this kitten over in the school yard, and we wondered if it belongs to you."

"No, no, it isn't mine," exclaimed Mrs. Tauber. "You can't leave it here. My mama cat won't let it stay here."

There were several men sitting around in the store, just to pass the time of day. "I can take it off and kill it for you," one of them offered.

"No, I don't think so," replied a horrified Dianne, as she clutched the kitten closer to her chest. "I think I will just take it home with me."

"Well, it looks like we're stuck with the kitten," she reported to Eunice as she climbed back into the car, kitten in tow. "I don't even know if it's a boy or a girl."

"It's a boy," announced Eunice, upon closer examination of the kitten. "You'll have to take him. I have loose birds inside my house. You can stop at the store and get some cat food and you'll need a litter box and some cat litter, too."

Oh, great, what am I getting myself into now? wondered Dianne, as she set about finding the needed items at the Pineville A and P grocery store.

Dianne and the kitten made it through the night. He sat in her lap the next morning as she ate breakfast. Then he wasted no time in chowing down on his own breakfast.

"Wow, look at you," Eunice exclaimed as she came through the door and saw the kitten, who by then had expanded his stomach several sizes. "You're a little butterball now!"

"Have you named him yet?" she asked.

"No, I'm just waiting to see if a suitable name comes to me," said Dianne.

That afternoon upon returning to her apartment after school, Dianne poked her head through the door and saw the kitten lying on the couch. "Boo," she said. "Hey, little kitty. How was your day?"

Dianne and the kitten continued to bond over the next few days. Then one morning instead of eating his food, the little kitten began vomiting. He didn't eat anything all day. Dianne rushed him to the Fitzgerald Animal Hospital as soon as she got home from school.

"What we have is a really sick kitten," Dr. Fitzgerald told her. "He's been out in the wild, and he probably hasn't had any of his shots. He has a bad case of distemper."

"Can you save him?" begged Dianne.

"Well, we are going to try our best, but you will have to leave him here for a few days."

The kitten rallied, and Dianne was allowed to take him home after a few days of treatment. About a week later, he started exhibiting the same symptoms, so she rushed him back to the vet's office.

"He's had a relapse," reported Dr. Fitzgerald after he examined the kitten. "We'll try to pull him through, but a lot of times they don't recover from a second case of distemper."

Dianne drove home totally depressed. God, I know that somehow you must have sent me the kitten, so please, please, let him get well and come back home with me, she prayed silently as she returned to her apartment.

A few days later she had a call from the vet's office. "You can come and pick up the kitten. He's well now," the receptionist told her.

A few weeks later the kitten was well enough to travel, so Dianne decided to take him home with her on a trip to Rocky Branch. She didn't have a cat carrier, so he just rode on the seat beside her.

"Have you named him yet?" inquired Dolores, as Dianne arrived home and deposited the kitten onto the kitchen floor.

"No, I can't think of the right name. I've just been calling him 'Boo,'" Dianne replied.

Upon hearing "Boo" the kitten perked up his ears and let out a meow. "See, he already thinks that's his name, so you might as well call him 'Boo,'" advised Dolores, who was a great lover of all animals.

So, "Boo" it was, and "Boo" it would remain for the next sixteen years.

Eunice decided to leave Ruby-Wise at the end of Dianne's second year at the school. She transferred to Boyce High School, which was closer to where she lived. Dianne was sad to see her go, but she could understand the reasons for the transfer.

Eunice's successor was a wonderful lady named Margaret Paul. She had a warm and nurturing personality that endeared her to everyone with whom she came in contact. She and Dianne became friends, and Dianne spent many hours at her house visiting with her and her husband, Leslie, and their three children, Mary Margaret, Richard, and Cindy. Dianne even went along with Mary Margaret to pick out her wedding dress.

Eventually, Mrs. Paul left to teach at a school in Alexandria. The new librarian was Marion Sullivan, who also became one of Dianne's friends. Dianne did not socialize too much with other people on the faculty, but it was handy to stop in the library to chat on the way back from the lunchroom. Marion had a different personality than Mrs. Paul, but she and Dianne seemed to share a sense of humor regarding their outlook on teaching.

Mrs. Hyde retired and was replaced by a very young teacher named Barbara Kurtz. Barbara was engaged, and her last name soon became Hare when she married Bill Hare shortly after the school year started. Dianne and Barbara became friends as they spent many hours discussing their efforts in the classroom. One week when Bill was out of town Barbara decided to accompany Dianne to a ballgame, riding the bus with the boosters, cheerleaders, and basketball players. "You're in for a noisy time," warned Dianne.

"Oh, that's all right, I can take it," replied Barbara.

They went to Dianne's apartment first for a simple meal of hamburgers and fries. "I'm sorry that I don't have a deep fat fryer for the fries," apologized Dianne. "I keep thinking that I will buy one, but I never have."

Dianne's life seemed to be on the right track, except for her social life. She had completed several years of teaching in Rapides Parish. She had bought a new car, a '71 Ford Torino, to replace the old Chevy. She was working on her master's degree. The only thing she didn't have was a man in her life.

George still hadn't given up. He called the school every year to see if she was still working there. Dianne figured out that George had gotten her name off her mail that was in her front porch mailbox and then had gotten her phone number from the phone book. She had gotten an unlisted phone number when she moved to Pineville, and the school did not give out personal information about its teachers. So, he couldn't track her down.

Well, I guess I found the bright city lights I was looking for, she reflected, but I still haven't found the right man. I will just have to trust in God to send him to me when the time is right. Until then I will just concentrate on doing the best job that I can with my teaching career.

Chapter 13

Dianne was always glad to see summertime roll around. Getting a break from the students was a welcome relief. Despite the fact that she wasn't too fond of traveling, she did manage to make several trips to visit some of her former friends from college. Becky and her husband, Don, graduated together from Harding College a year after they got married. Dianne was on hand to congratulate them and to snap their pictures as they walked down the aisle together for a second time. She flew to Birmingham the following summer to visit them for a week at the home of Becky's parents. By that time Becky was pregnant with what would be the first of their three children. "Wow, I'm going to be an aunt," joked Dianne.

One of her very close friends from Harding, Lola Murray, asked her to serve as a candle lighter at her wedding to David Crouch in Hattiesburg, Mississippi. Dolores and Sallie accompanied Dianne as she drove Dolores's car on the trip. They had a close call with disaster on the way back home following the wedding. Just as they approached a truck that was hauling a racecar on a trailer, the wheel came off the trailer and headed straight for their car.

"Oh, my God, we're going to be killed," screamed Dolores. "It's going to come right through the windshield."

Dianne managed to swerve just before the tire hit their car, and it bounced off the right front fender, just missing the windshield.

They hobbled home with a crippled car, after being stopped once by the Mississippi State Police for having a broken headlight.

"I figured something like that would happen," declared F. D. as he surveyed the damage later that night.

"I think that's going to be the end of my travels for a while," Dianne informed her family, thankful that the damage was no worse than it was. "I think that I will just stick closer to home after this and work on my master's degree at Northeast University in Monroe."

Dianne was somewhat familiar with the Northeast campus, as she had attended one summer school session while still enrolled at Harding. However, the registration process proved to be somewhat confusing. When attempting to register, she was informed that she must first have an adviser to sign her schedule. Following the directions given to her by a kind soul in the registration line, she managed to find her way to the education department.

Once there, she viewed the closed doors, each of which had the name of its occupant listed in bold letters. One door caught her eye. That particular professor, it appeared, was fond of "Peanuts" cartoons, as he had several of them taped to the outside of the door. She and Becky had been huge "Peanuts" fans during the year they had roomed together.

Well, I guess he's my best choice, she reflected, smiling as she read the cartoons. *Anybody who likes "Peanuts" can't be all bad.*

The professor, Dr. John Brady, turned out to be a robust, silver-haired man with gray eyes and silver-framed glasses. He possessed both a friendly personality and a ready smile. *Good choice, Dianne,* she silently congratulated herself, as they conferred on her schedule.

Dianne spent two summers at her parents' house in Rocky Branch, arising at 5:00 a.m. in order to make the commute to Monroe for a 7:30 a.m. class. She usually ate breakfast in her room in order to avoid inhaling F. D.'s cigarette smoke. *I wish he would sleep a little longer so that I could stay at the dining table and eat in peace,* she often fumed as she carried her coffee and toast back to her room.

She quickly learned that most of the education classes required for a master's degree in education were real sleepers. A few, however, did stand out in her mind. One was a class on Principles of Secondary Education. It was supposed to be a "cripp course," but, with her usual luck, the regular professor was on leave, and she drew a substitute, Dr. Earl B. Snodgrass. There was standing room only in the class during the first class meeting, with about fifty students in attendance. Upon hearing the course requirements of twenty-five outside reading cards, an oral presentation, and a term paper, the number thinned out considerably on the second and third days until only about twenty students were left.

As if he weren't torturing them enough, Dr. Snodgrass also added the requirement of two tests per day on the reading material from the textbook—a pretest, and a post test. Dianne was about ready to throw in the towel, but she couldn't because she needed the class in order to graduate. *Why do I have such luck?* she pondered, as she pored over the required reading assignments.

He also informed the class that most of them probably shouldn't even be in graduate school. "You may be surprised to learn that you are not even graduate material, he taunted. He set about making his point by giving them two standardized tests, one in English, and one in math. "You will see what I mean when you get your scores back, he insisted.

Dianne knew that she was good in English. In fact, she had considered majoring in it before deciding on home economics as her field. However, she had taken only one math class in college since that was all required for her degree. She did her best on the tests and, along with the other students, waited for her scores to come back, good or bad as they might be.

She was quite surprised to learn that she had made the best score in the class on the English exam, beating out two English teachers and a librarian. Her math score wasn't too shabby, either, being in the top five of the class. That was an even bigger surprise.

"I didn't know I remembered that much about math," she confided to one of her fellow students.

She set about completing the research for her term paper, deciding on the topic of the state of the family in American society. Being a teacher of Family Living, she was concerned that families seemed to be on the decline. She was glad to learn through her research this was not the case, and that family life in her country was still strong.

The paper was due the week after the Fourth of July break, so she planned to write and type it during that time. F. D. had scheduled his usual family reunion for that holiday. She was in the middle of typing the paper when the noisy clan descended on the Hollis household. She didn't even bother to go out to greet them, not that it mattered.

"Where's Dianne?" they demanded to know. "We saw her car outside, so we know that she has to be here somewhere."

Well, I guess there's no escape, she thought, I'll have to go out and say something to them. Then I will explain that I have to get back to work on my paper.

She continued typing throughout the day, stopping only for a quick lunch with the relatives. She finished much later, in the wee hours of the morning. *Boy, was that stressful,* she reflected, as she crawled into bed for some much-needed rest.

She did not feel that the paper was one of her best works, but she had no choice but to hand it in at the next class meeting.

"I'm going to start grading your papers right away," Dr. Snodgrass informed them. "I should be able to give you an assessment by our next class meeting."

Dianne was on needles and pins. She was usually pretty confident about her work, but with this particular professor, one could never tell.

When the class met the next day, the professor began to discuss the results of his grading session on the papers. "Some of these papers reflect really poor work," he announced. "In fact, some of them don't even rate a score of fifty percent satisfactory. I am not through grading all of them yet, so you will have to come by my office to check your scores which will be posted on my door within the next two days."

Dianne drove home with a heavy heart, certain that her paper was one of those which had met with disapproval. *Why didn't I spend more time on it,* she fretted. *I know I could have written a better paper than that!*

When she went to check on her score she was doubly surprised to see that she had earned a ninety-nine percent on her term paper. Relief washed over her like a wave surging upon the shore. *Thank you, God,* she thought, as she sent a silent prayer upstairs. *I just might make it through this class, after all.*

When the final day of class came, Dianne was relieved to take the final exam and get it all over with. "Miss Hollis, I need to talk to you for a minute after class," the professor informed her.

Oh, brother, now what? she wondered.

"You have done really well in this class. I was wondering if you would be interested in becoming a graduate assistant under me and working on your Ph. D.?" he asked.

Dianne almost reeled over with shock, but she managed to keep a calm face.

"Well, I thank you for the offer," she replied, "but I really can't afford it. I have to keep my job in order to have an income."

"I understand, but you really should give it some thought. You would be a good candidate for a Ph. D.," he said, as the conversation ended.

Another memorable class was Media in Education. A popular class with a large enrollment, it was definitely more interesting than those that dealt strictly with educational topics. Everyone in the class was quite friendly, and Dianne became friends with two people in particular. One of them was a lady named Ethel Parks, who was getting recertified so that she could teach home economics in Ouachita Parish. She and Dianne also had several graduate home economics classes together.

The other was a beautiful redheaded woman with gray eyes and a striking figure. Her name was Martha Bass, and she and Dianne would remain friends for a number of years to come. Martha lived in Monroe and worked as a librarian in the school system there. She was quite opinionated and outspoken, but Dianne found most of her remarks to be rather humorous.

The main project for that class was to be some sort of visual and auditory presentation. Dianne decided on a set of slides with auditory accompaniment. She went to the Union Parish Library and found a book titled *If Not for You*, a story about a big sister who had problems with her little sister following her around all the time. Since it reminded her of her younger days with Sallie, it was the perfect choice.

Using the available classroom equipment, Dianne made her slides and auditory tape.

Her presentation on storytelling for young children was a great success, and it received a round of applause from the classroom audience. After class that day the professor, Dr. Wallace Williams, asked her if he could borrow her materials.

"You did such a fantastic job that I would like to use your materials as an example for my future classes," he explained.

"Well, yes, I suppose that will be okay, as long as I can get them back," Dianne replied.

The classes that Dianne enjoyed the most were those in her field of home economics. She took a total of four graduate home economics classes under the direction of Dr. Ann Kapp and Dr. Daisy Daniels, both caring women with warm personalities which endeared them to their students. The hardest class, by far, was the one on Pattern Design under Dr. Kapp. Dianne spent many hours working on the tedious assignments, trying to master the techniques necessary for the required projects of designing, making, and modeling two garments. *I don't know if I will ever use this information again, but it is a lot of fun learning how to do all of this stuff,* she reflected.

She was on a tight schedule, and during the last semester she didn't even have time to eat lunch. Before that, she had rushed home the previous semester at 2:00 p.m., often driving at 100 miles per hour because she was so hungry, not having eaten since 5:00 a.m. *Boy, will I ever be in trouble if Mother and Daddy ever learn that I am driving this fast,* she worried, as she sped over the two-mile stretch which lay just across the D'Arbonne River and was often used late at night for illegal drag racing. Fortunately, the road was not patrolled very often, so she never got a speeding ticket, and Dolores and F. D. never knew about such reckless behavior.

One of the most dreaded courses by all the graduate students was Research. It could be good or bad, depending on which professor one ended up with. Dianne learned from her friend Martha that taking it in summer school wasn't quite as bad as taking it during the regular semester. "You have to do just one paper," Martha informed her, "but in the regular semester you have to do a lot more work."

Being a librarian, Martha was an expert on research techniques and sources, so she showed Dianne around the library at Northeast, pointing out to her what resources she needed to make use of. "If you make an 'A' on your paper I'm going to be really mad," she threatened. "I did the research on mine and wrote the paper in three days. The professor gave me a 'B' on it because he said that nobody could do a research paper that fast."

"But, Martha, you're a librarian, and you know all of the sources," observed Dianne.

"I tried to tell him that, but it didn't make any difference," Martha replied.

Dianne settled on the topic of using the overhead projector in teaching. Thanks to Martha, she was able to complete the necessary research in short order. Martha also helped her find a lady who was an expert in typing research papers.

"How much do you charge?" Dianne inquired, as she handed the materials over to the typist.

"I get two dollars a page. I should probably charge more, but I'm trying to help you students out. The professor says I help you too much, but I know what he wants and how he likes the papers typed," the lady replied.

"Wow, Martha, I don't know how you ever found her, but thanks so much," said Dianne, as they climbed back into the car to leave.

"Well, just let me know how you come out with it," said Martha.

Dianne picked up the perfectly typed paper a few days later and handed it in to the professor, glad to have one more obstacle to graduation out of her way. She waited anxiously for the results on her grade.

Several days later the professor posted the grades on his door. Dianne was, once again, happy to learn that she had made an "A" on yet another paper. *Boy, I guess Martha will be really mad about this when I tell her what I made,* she reflected.

"I hate you," exclaimed Martha, when she learned about the "A." "But, I hate that professor even more! Don't worry, we're still friends. It's not your fault!"

One class that Dianne was really looking forward to taking was Adolescent Psychology. Maybe this class will help me with all of those weirdo problems that I keep encountering with rebellious teenagers, she reasoned.

"Well, I hope you like that class better than I did," commented her friend Martha when she told Martha of her plans. "I couldn't stand that professor. He's just a little dried-up runt, and all he did was brag about himself. Make sure you sit on the front row. He likes people to sit up close to the front."

Dianne walked into the class, wary of both the professor and the surroundings, thanks to Martha's advice. She found a seat near the front and waited in anticipation as the professor, Dr. Markus Seigenthal, walked into the room. *Well, Martha was right about his appearance,* she observed. *Let's hope his teaching is better than she predicted.*

"Good afternoon, students," he began the class. "How are you all doing today?"

Dianne listened attentively as he launched into a description of the course and its requirements. This doesn't sound too bad. Maybe Martha was exaggerating. She does tend to get a bit carried away at times.

As the class continued to meet, the professor entertained them with stories about his experiences counseling adolescents. Then he came up with the idea of letting them have debates on different topics that often caused conflicts between teenagers and their parents.

"We'll let half of the class take the part of the parents, while the other half of you can be the teenagers," he instructed. "However, I have to check it out with the administration first."

"Well, it looks like the debates are off," he reported to the class the next day. "I called the administrator and talked to him. He wanted to know what the debate topics were going to be, so I started calling the list out to him. He was agreeable to all of them until I got to the topic of premarital sex. Then his response was, 'Noooo, I think we had better leave that one out.'"

There was a unified moan from the class, as most of the students were over thirty years old, and many of them were married with children.

Boy, this is really ridiculous, fumed Dianne silently. How Victorian can you get?

"In light of these developments, I have made a decision," he announced. "We are not going to have any exams, and as long as you continue to attend class you will get an 'A' for your grade."

"What about the final exam?" one student inquired. "Will we have to take a final?"

"No, there will be no final exam, either. I will give you an essay topic, and you can hand in your essay on the day of the final."

"What are we supposed to do about our comprehensive exam for our degree?" another student asked.

"Don't worry about that, either. I am going to give you the question that will be on that exam, too," he replied.

When Dianne reported the turn of events to Martha, she almost cringed as Martha vented her wrath. "Oh, you don't know how mad that makes me. You have all the luck!" Martha exclaimed.

Dianne and Martha decided to take time out from their studies for some recreational activities. Their friend Ethel, from the media class, had a camp on the Ouachita River.

"Ethel has asked me to go with her family to their camp for supper and water skiing," Martha informed Dianne. "Why don't you come, too?"

"I didn't know you could ski," Dianne replied. "Besides, Ethel didn't ask me to go."

"Oh, don't worry about it. I'll ask her if you can come."

"But I don't have any suitable clothes with me," fretted Dianne.

"Doll, just call your mother and get her to bring you some. You can spend the night with me. No problem," promised Martha.

"Well, okay, I guess I can do that."

Dolores was shocked to receive a call from her daughter requesting the clothes. "I can't believe you are actually spending the night with somebody," she observed several hours later as she delivered the clothes to Dianne in one of the school's parking lots.

"Just be careful."

"Oh, Mother, you know I'm always careful," responded Dianne.

Soon afterwards Dianne and Martha found themselves aboard a ski boat, watching as Ethel's children and their friends continued skiing until dusk. Martha gave it several tries and ended up falling into the water. Dianne wasn't that brave and decided to stay dry.

Almost all of the food was gone by the time they made it back to the camp. "I saved both of you a plate," Ethel informed them. "That's the only way there was going to be any food left for you."

"Thanks, these hamburgers are really good," Dianne said as she bit into a juicy burger with all of the trimmings.

As darkness fell, Martha and Dianne headed back to town in Martha's car. Martha began to entertain Dianne with stories about her dating experiences and her techniques for fighting off men who tried to get too intimate.

"When they try to go too far I just start reciting the Lord's Prayer," she told Dianne.

"That really works?" inquired an astounded Dianne.

"Well, most of the time, but there's one time that it didn't," admitted Martha, as they prepared for bed at Martha's apartment.

"What did you do then?" asked Dianne.

"I told him that I was a lesbian," said Martha solemnly.

Dianne paused as she was about to crawl under the covers of the double bed. *Oh, God, what have I gotten myself into?* she worried, until she realized that her friend was only joking.

Dianne continued to visit Martha occasionally as they worked their way through the courses required for their master's degrees. One night Martha asked Dianne to stay and go to a show with her.

"But, Martha, I have nothing to wear again," she protested.

"You can wear one of my pantsuits, doll."

"It will be too long for me, and besides, it probably won't fit."

"Well, just give it a try. Roll it up at the waist."

Dianne exited the bathroom a short time later wearing an apricot-colored pantsuit with a white shell top. "Wow, this really fits, Martha," she exclaimed. "You have great taste in clothes."

"It looks better on you than it does on me," teased Martha. "Now, let's go to get something to eat, and then we'll go to the show."

After exiting the restaurant and heading for their car, Dianne and Martha were greeted with wolf whistles and whoops from a passing car that did a U-turn and headed back their way.

"Martha, hurry up and get the doors unlocked! Those men are

trying to pick us up," shouted Dianne, as the car began to pull back into the parking lot.

She and Martha jumped into the car, laughing, as they locked the doors.

"Boy, this pantsuit of yours is really magic," joked Dianne.

"It's not the suit, it's the girl," retorted Martha.

"No, it's the suit," insisted Dianne.

Arriving at the show, they purchased their tickets and picked out their seats.

About halfway through the show, Dianne changed positions and noticed that the man on her left was staring at her.

"Martha," she whispered from the side of her mouth, "the man beside me is staring at me. What am I supposed to do?"

"Just ignore him."

"Okay, but it won't be easy," she replied, as the man shifted his posture, resting his elbow on the armrest and propping his face upon his hand as he boldly continued to leer at her.

"That does it! I'm going out to the lobby to get some popcorn. If he follows me out there, I'm going to duck into the ladies' restroom," she confided, in a soft whisper.

Walking swiftly, she made her way out to the lobby and then into the ladies' restroom, just to be on the safe side. When she exited there was no sign of the lecher, so she proceeded to make her purchases and headed back to her seat.

Great, he's still there, she observed, as she crawled over several sets of legs to get back to her seat. I think he's actually enjoying having me climb over his legs. When this is over I'm getting out of here, but fast!

When the movie ended, the lecher stood at the end of the aisle, smiling and waiting for them to exit.

"Martha, scram as fast as you can," she directed as they beat a quick retreat to the car.

"This is positively the last time I wear any of your clothes. This whole night has been too much for me!"

"I'm telling you, it's the girl, not the pantsuit," Martha repeated, as they drove back to her apartment.

Dianne continued working on her class assignments, thankful that the end was almost in sight as graduation drew near. One day she opened the mailbox to find a letter from Northeast addressed to her.

What is going on now? she wondered, as she tore open the envelope.

"Dear Miss Dianne Hollis," the letter stated. "This letter is to inform you that you are being assigned to another advisor. Your new advisor will be Dr. Wallace Williams."

Dianne couldn't wait to report the news to Martha.

"That doesn't surprise me one bit," stated Martha. "That's how he operates. Whenever he finds a student that he likes in one of his classes, he gets himself appointed as their advisor. He especially likes young, attractive women."

"Great," said Dianne. "I didn't want a new advisor. I picked out the other one because he likes 'Peanuts' cartoons. Besides, he's nice."

"That's too bad," replied Martha. "But take my advice. Don't fight it. You're stuck with him now, so make the best of it."

"Guess I've got no choice," sighed Dianne.

A few days later Dianne received a notice to report to Dr. Williams' office.

"Martha, I've been summoned to his office. Now what am I supposed to do?" she inquired worriedly.

"I can tell you what it's probably about," said Martha. "He has been calling his students to his office and telling them what the questions are on their comprehensive exams."

"How can he do that?" Dianne asked disbelievingly.

"All of the questions are sent to the advisors. They are the ones that make out the tests for the graduate students."

"But, Martha, I've never cheated on a test in my life, and I don't want to start now."

"Just go, doll. Make the best of it."

Dianne reported to his office at the designated time, leery of what fate might be awaiting her. She knocked on the door cautiously and reluctantly.

"Come in," the professor's voice rang out through the frosted glass paneling which lined the top half of the door.

Dianne entered the room, feeling like a lamb being led to the slaughter, and wishing she hadn't sprayed on so much cologne before she left home.

"Miss Hollis, good to see you," he began. "I called you here today to discuss your comprehensive exam. I have found that it is helpful to students if they have somewhat of an idea of what their questions are going to be."

Oh, boy, here it comes, she thought, as the professor edged his chair closer so their knees were almost touching. *Please, God, give me the strength to get through this ordeal!*

"You have a question on pattern design," he informed her, looking straight into her eyes.

Dianne bit her bottom lip to keep from laughing. The name of the class was Pattern Design. *Big help.* "Okay," she said.

The session continued until all of the subjects had been covered.

That was "much ado about nothing," she pondered as she drove home afterwards. At least I can say that I still haven't cheated on a test, since I didn't really learn anything I didn't already know.

Most of the professors had been pretty nice about the comprehensives. Some of them even went so far as to tell the students exactly what questions to expect. Dianne began to study in earnest for the exam, making herself out a schedule to follow about a month in advance of the examination date. She spent hours each night reviewing the information

Then she made a decision. Since I know the topics for each course, I am going to write out an essay for each question. I don't care what the question may be, somehow, I am going to make my essay fit it.

A few days later she dropped by Martha's apartment, surprised to find the usually neat premises in disarray with papers scattered everywhere.

"I don't know what I'm going to do about these comprehensives," Martha complained. "I have no idea where to start studying. I'm just going in circles."

"Calm down," instructed Dianne. "I'm going to make you out a schedule. You stick to it and you'll have covered all of the courses by exam time. Now, give me a list of what courses you have taken."

Dianne handed Martha the completed schedule shortly afterwards. "Dianne, you're a real lifesaver. I don't know what I would have done without your help," admitted Martha.

"Just follow the schedule, and you'll be okay," Dianne reassured her as she exited the apartment.

For the next few days Dianne threw herself totally into her studies, reviewing all the information she could and memorizing the essays she had written on each topic. She even elected to skip the bridal shower for her cousin, Donna Carol Hollis, who lived in Columbia.

"Tell her I'll be there for the wedding," she yelled to Dolores and Sallie as they prepared to leave for the shower.

The comprehensive exams were set for Tuesday during the week before graduation. Dianne decided to stay home on Monday and study rather than attend her classes. Most of the important information in the classes had already been covered.

Dianne reported to the assigned room at 1:00 p.m. as instructed in a letter she had received. She carried with her a picture I.D., several pens, and a small stapler. The test monitors passed out the materials quickly and Dianne began to study the questions pondering over her answers carefully.

Her train of thought was interrupted several times as Martha, who was sitting in the desk beside her, laughed out loud, unable to contain herself. *I don't know what her problem is, but I am definitely going to find out when this is over,* Dianne thought as she dragged her mind off Martha's apparent amusement regarding the exam.

Several hours later Dianne looked up to realize that she was one of only three students still taking the test. The time was almost up so she hurried with the final answer and began to staple her topics together, one by one. *Here's hoping I passed,* she thought, as she handed in the essays.

She drove home and fell into bed, too exhausted to even eat supper.

The next morning she arose bright and early to head for her Pattern Design class. It was the last day of class, and they were going to have a style show and refreshments at the home of their instructor, Dr. Kapp.

Dianne found the house, or at least she thought it was the right one. There were no other cars in the driveway. *I wonder where everybody else is,* she thought, as she walked up to ring the doorbell. After a long wait, someone finally fumbled with the doorknob and the door swung open.

Dr. Kapp stood in the doorway wearing her robe with curlers in her hair. "Oh, you didn't come to class on Monday, did you?" she exclaimed. "We changed the time for today. We aren't meeting until eleven o'clock this morning."

"I'm so sorry," replied a mortified Dianne. "I had no idea. I'll go visit a friend and return at that time."

She headed straight for Martha's apartment where she was greeted by a very surprised hostess. "What in the world are you doing here at this time of morning?" Martha demanded to know.

Dianne explained the situation.

"Well, you might as well come in. I have to leave for class, but you can stay."

"Thanks so much, Martha. I really appreciate this. I do have one question for you, though. Why were you laughing so much during the comprehensives yesterday?"

"Oh, that's easy to explain. I had no idea of the answers to those dumb questions. I don't know if I even passed the blessed thing!"

"Oh, I'm sure you passed. We should find out sometime this week."

"I hope so. Well, ta ta, doll. I'm off for class. Make yourself at home and be sure to lock the door when you leave."

Dianne settled in and began watching an old Cary Grant movie on TV. She reached for a piece of butterscotch candy from the dish on the coffee table. *I don't know why I eat this stuff. Martha just keeps it out for decoration. I think it's been here for several years,* she reflected as she carefully chewed on the gooey glob, unable to understand how anyone could leave a bowl of candy sitting around untouched.

As eleven o'clock approached, Dianne left the apartment, carefully locking the door behind her. This time, cars were lined up in Dr. Kapp's driveway.

"Welcome back," said Dr. Kapp, as Dianne entered amid the bustle of excited students.

Everyone was changing in one of the bedrooms, and Dianne followed their example. As she pulled her first original design dress on she discovered that it no longer fit. It was much too big. "Oh, no. I forgot that I lost fifteen pounds since I started summer school because I didn't have time to eat lunch," she explained.

"That's okay," replied Dr. Kapp. "As long as you completed the project and we can see what it looks like, you have nothing to worry about."

Several days later, the comprehensive exam scores were back. Dianne went by Dr. Williams' office to see if she passed. She held her breath as she looked for her name on the posted list of passing students. *There it is. I passed! I passed!* she silently cheered.

"Your answers were very, very good," commented her other home economics professor, Dr. Daisy Daniels, later that day. "In fact, they are the best that I have ever read on a comprehensive."

"Really? Thanks," replied Dianne, grateful that her technique of writing the essays for each question had paid off.

Martha, too, had passed, they soon learned. "I don't know how I passed, but I passed and that's all I care about," exclaimed a very ecstatic Martha. "We are marching down that aisle together, girl!"

Later that week Dianne picked up her cap and gown from the bookstore and headed for graduation practice. "Let's be sure to meet here tomorrow night," she told Martha as the practice session ended. "I want to get some pictures of us in our caps and gowns."

Graduation proved to be a long and drawn-out ceremony, but Dianne didn't care. She had made it through a tempestuous journey to reach her goal, attending one summer session at LSU, one night class at LSUA, and four summer sessions at Northeast. She had burned a lot of gasoline in the process and also a lot of midnight oil.

Exactly how useful the information would prove to be remained to be seen. Useful or not, she would be getting a substantial raise, something that she desperately needed. At one point she had been existing on soup and crackers, and all that her cat, Boo, had to eat was dry cat food. Fortunately, that situation had lasted only about a month after she bought her new Torino, as she had gotten a small raise when she returned for another year of teaching.

She would be returning to her teaching position armed with new knowledge and new self-confidence, having obtained her Master's of Education degree from Northeast Louisiana University. She was proud of her accomplishment, and F.D., Dolores, and Sallie were equally proud for her.

Underneath her gown Dianne had worn one of the dresses she had designed and made in her Pattern Design class. It was the ultimate symbol of her accomplishments, something that she alone had created and made.

She and Martha posed together for pictures after the ceremony, triumphantly holding their hard-earned diplomas in front of them. Their smiles said it all. It was their night, and nobody could take that away from them.

Chapter 14

When Dianne returned to Ruby-Wise for another year the student body had changed. The desegregation lawsuit had continued with the integration of students. Ruby-Wise had received all of the students from an all-black school located close by in the community when that school was shut down.

The students arrived with mostly "A's" and "B's" on their school records. Unfortunately, the grades did not reflect their true abilities. Many of them could not read or even complete math problems at their grade level.

"We've got students in the fourth and fifth grades who can't even add two plus two," the Megison informed her. "It's a pretty bad situation."

Dianne was experiencing some of the problems herself with students in the junior high who could not read, either. "What am I supposed to do with them?" she wondered as she and Barbara Hare were comparing notes on student progress.

"At this point there's not a lot we can do," Barbara observed.

A few weeks later report cards were distributed. The office was soon overwhelmed with phone calls and visits from upset parents when their children, who had been making "A's" and "B's," were suddenly bringing home "D's" and "F's."

"Things got pretty hot in the office today," the Megison informed

Dianne. "Parents have never seen grades like that on their children's report cards."

"Well, it's sad, but if they can't do the work, they can't get passing grades," Dianne responded.

One exception to the rule was an eighth-grade black transfer student named Michelle Coleman. Michelle was like a shining star peeking through a dismal and clouded sky. A neat and attractive girl with a cheerful attitude, she easily kept up with her white classmates, often outscoring them on exams.

"My aunt is a teacher," she confided to Dianne. "She helped me a lot with my homework when I was in the lower grades."

Dianne was relieved to have attained tenure in the parish as she began her fourth year of teaching at Ruby-Wise. Although students were usually on their best behavior whenever a supervisor came to observe, one could never tell when a problem might arise that could be a blight on a teacher's record. Arriving without prior notice, the supervisors would often slip into a seat in the back of the room, write vigorously on their notepads, and then leave just before bell time without ever telling the teacher what they were doing right or wrong. They also had an uncanny knack of showing up at Ruby-Wise on the day before school was to be dismissed for the Christmas holidays.

"Honestly, why do they have to pick the worst day of the school year to observe us?" Dianne complained to her fellow teachers.

"They say that they are going in alphabetical order and that just happens to be where our school falls," said the Megison.

"Well, it's bad enough to be observed, but students are definitely not on their best behavior on the day before the holidays," Dianne retorted.

Her prediction came true when a supervisor showed up to observe her seventh-grade science class. Dianne was relieved that particular class had been chosen because they were usually among the best-behaved students she taught. The lesson was on biology and Dianne had selected some of the lab specimens which had been preserved in formaldehyde for examples.

Feeling rather proud of herself for having lucked out with such a good lesson plan, she began passing the examples around the class as they discussed the topic. The rather squeamish girls viewed the samples and quickly passed them on to the eagerly awaiting boys. Several of the impish boys delighted in taunting the girls with the specimens while commenting on their "gory" appearance.

Dianne was mortified, observing the disapproving frown on the supervisor's face. "I think that we had better just put all of the specimens back up here in the front of the room," she announced as she quickly collected them back from the students.

Great, there goes my chance for a good report, my usual luck she thought. I suppose it's to be expected on the day before the holidays. Even a good class can go bad.

Three supervisors stood out as being the most helpful. One was Mr. Tommy Stepp. He showed up one day when Dianne was conducting a ninth-grade lesson on light and color with a demonstration on the stage in the school's gymnasium. The lesson went very well and the students were enthralled with the vivid lights and color changes they observed. Dianne breathed a sigh of relief as the lesson ended without incident.

"Mr. Stepp was pretty impressed with your lesson," the Megison reported to her later. "I think he liked what he saw."

Dianne had told Mr. Stepp about some materials that she needed and a few days later they arrived. "That's one of the first times I actually got any help from a supervisor," she commented.

Another helpful supervisor was Dr. Jessie Hutchinson. He observed Dianne teaching a ninth-grade science class that happened to be on their best behavior that day. Dianne told him that she needed some more copies of the older book that she was using. He promised to try to find some more for her. A few days later the requested books arrived, much to Dianne's delight. *That's one supervisor I'm never going to forget,* she vowed.

The most memorable and most beloved supervisor was the vocational supervisor, Mr. Byron Stafford. A cordial man with a down-to-earth personality, Dianne felt that she could talk to him about any problems she had regarding teaching. He would make every effort to get anything that a teacher needed.

"You know how he operates, don't you?" inquired the Megison. "If you want something, he will get it from another school if they aren't using it. He swaps things around all the time. Don't let him know if you have anything you aren't using or you might not have it for very long."

"Thanks for the warning. I'll keep that in mind," said Dianne.

As the year progressed Dianne continued her usual work with her classes, along with sponsoring the boosters and cheerleaders. They decided to have a fund-raiser for the two groups by selling cookbooks. Prizes for the top sellers were to be awarded.

Two sisters, Regenia and Marlene Quattlebaum, won the prizes, hands down. They were two of the most outstanding and creative students that Dianne would ever teach. She could always count on them to go the extra mile on any project they undertook. They got their creative abilities from their mother, Mary, who made her own Christmas cards. She was well-known for sending out several hundred cards each year to friends and relatives.

Regenia and Marlene were also active 4-H members, and Mary was one of their Adult Leaders. They invited Dianne to their home to view their collection of pet rabbits, one of their 4-H projects. Dianne was impressed by the animals and the apparent care that they had received.

"May I hold one of them?" she asked.

"Sure, let me pick out a good one for you," said Regenia.

"It won't bite me, will it?" Dianne inquired as she stroked the rabbit's soft fur and long ears.

"No, they're perfectly tame," replied Marlene.

"Well, you girls have certainly done an outstanding job, as always. It's too bad all of my students don't have your talents."

As midterm approached the desegregation lawsuit, once again, took first priority in the news. The school board, it seemed, had lapsed in meeting their requirements of the black-to-white teacher ratios. Another mass transfer of teachers was going to be necessary.

"Well, I did my time already," Dianne commented to her fellow teachers. "Surely, they won't send me off again."

Once again, students were dismissed from school for a day while teachers were informed of who was to be transferred. Dianne almost held her breath during lunch, awaiting the announcement. To her surprise, no mention of the transfer was made.

"What gives?" she asked the Megison as they headed back to their rooms afterwards.

"Mr. Slay is going to use a different approach this time," he told her. "He is coming around the rooms to tell teachers individually about the transfers."

Dianne went back to the home ec. lab to catch up on some much-needed work. A short time later Mr. Slay appeared in the doorway.

"Well, I'm afraid I've got some bad news for you again," he announced.

"What?" Dianne exclaimed.

"You are being transferred to Carter C. Raymond High School in Lecompte."

"You've got to be kidding. Why am I being sent off again? I can't believe this! I don't even know where the place is," she moaned.

"Well, it's true," he said, handing her the paper to examine. "I'm really sorry. There's nothing that I can do about it."

"What about certification? The last time they sent a teacher here who wasn't even certified to teach science."

'They have assured me that this one is. They said that they weren't going to make that mistake again."

"Great, just great! I'm not giving up yet. I'm calling Mr. Stafford about this!"

The next morning she got Mr. Stafford on the phone. "They are sending me off to another black school when I already went the first time. This just isn't fair! Can you do something to help me?" she pleaded.

"I have already tried, but it didn't do any good. There are about five or six of you teachers who are in the same situation," he replied. "They said that you didn't stay for a whole semester and that is why you are subject to being sent back."

"But I didn't ask to come back. They sent me back because the other teacher wasn't certified."

"I know that, but they said that it didn't matter. They aren't making any exceptions this time."

"I swear, I have the worst luck!" she exclaimed.

"There is one piece of good news that I can give you," he added. "You are now considered a 'displaced teacher.' That means that if an opening comes up in a school that you want to transfer to and you are qualified, by law, you must be given the first chance to transfer."

It was a small consolation, but one worth remembering, she decided.

Dianne began breaking the news of her second transfer to her family and friends. Most of them were incredulous. Her friend Margaret Paul reassured her. "Leslie knows where the school is located. We can drive you out there to see it, if you would like to go."

"Thanks, I would really appreciate that," responded Dianne.

The next afternoon they drove out to the school, which, by that time, was deserted. Dianne eyed the facilities dubiously.

"Well, at least this school appears to be in better shape than Wettermark," she noted.

Unlike the previous transfer, teachers were given several weeks advance warning.

The transfers were to take place during the week after midterm in order to avoid as much disruption as possible.

"I want to meet with the other teacher at her school before I actually have to transfer there," she told Mr. Slay.

"I'll call the other school and see if it can be arranged. When would you like to go?" he asked.

"As soon as possible. Sometime this week during the afternoon would be best," she replied.

Later that afternoon Mr. Slay appeared in her doorway. "It's all set," he informed her. "You can go tomorrow afternoon. I'll cover your classes for you. Just report to the front office and someone will show you to the home ec. department."

"Thanks, this will be so much better than having to start out blindly like I did the last time."

The next day she headed out for the school, glad that she had made a scouting trip in advance. *Here I go again. I really can't believe my luck.*

Entering the front door she walked into the office and introduced herself. The assistant principal escorted her to the home economics department. *This guy looks really familiar,* she thought. *Where have I seen him before? Whoever he is, he's definitely good-looking!*

The teacher, Mrs. Dorothea Collins, an older and gracious lady, was very cordial. She and Dianne spent nearly an hour discussing what had been covered and what the classes were studying. A class was meeting in the sewing lab at the time and the students eyed Dianne curiously. She tried not to stare at them. *I don't want to do anything to alienate them at this point,* she decided.

"Let me ask you one other question," she stated. "Are you certified to teach General Science?"

"Yes, unfortunately, I am," Mrs. Collins replied. "However, I told them that 'certified' is certainly not 'qualified.' Now I have a favor to ask of you," she continued. "I would like to visit your department in advance, also."

"Of course," replied Dianne. "Just let me know when you want to come."

Dianne left just before the final bell for dismissal. As she walked down the hall she heard a long, loud wolf whistle aimed in her direction. *Well, I guess I made an impression on somebody,* she thought as she headed for her car.

Several days later Mrs. Collins arrived to view Dianne's department. They spent almost an hour going over the materials that Dianne had prepared in advance.

"You certainly have a nice department," Mrs. Collins commented. "It will be nice to work in an air-conditioned building, but I really hate to leave my students. I have been teaching some of those families for years."

"I know what you mean, but I guess we have to do what we have to do," Dianne replied. "Let's just hope it all works out for the best."

Basketball season was underway and a pep rally had been scheduled for Dianne's last day at Ruby-Wise. She had been packing to leave for several days, carting things back to her apartment in her car each day. It was a sad task.

"Well, I guess I'm headed for my last pep rally," she commented to Barbara as they headed down the hall and into the gym. "I hope I can make it without crying in front of the students."

"Oh, you're tough. You can do it," Barbara assured her.

As the pep rally drew to a close a student named Wendel Birkicht walked to the front microphone. "At this time I would like to ask Miss Hollis to come up here," he announced.

Dianne approached, wondering what he could possibly be up to.

"Miss Hollis, on behalf of the student body I would like to present you with this going-away present," he said, as a large beautifully wrapped package was carried in from the side of the stands.

"Thank you. I don't know what to say," Dianne almost stammered.

"Open it! Open it!" came the cry from the students in the stands.

Dianne tore off the wrapping and was surprised to find a deep fat fryer inside.

"I know Mrs. Hare had something to do with this," she exclaimed, blinking back the tears as she spoke. "My thanks to all of you. I will never forget you."

As she walked off, the students gave her a standing ovation.

———

"Boy, that was a surprise," she admitted to Barbara later. "I can't believe that you picked Wendel for the job. He's usually so bashful."

"He volunteered," said Barbara. "He was pretty nervous about it, but he was determined to go through with it."

A short time later Dianne carried the last load of her belongings out to her car and, once again, turned in her keys and her gradebook. She drove off without looking back, knowing that this time she was gone for good.

There's no turning back now, she thought sadly. I know I can't go back. There's no way to go except to go forward. I don't know what the future holds, but, once again, I will just have to trust in God that He knows best. I won't give up! I will make it. I just know I will.

Chapter 15

*D*ianne headed for Carter C. Raymond High the following Monday. *She wasn't as nervous as she had been the first time she was transferred to an all-black school. Well, at least this time I know that they don't all look alike. They are people, just like everyone else,* she reflected as she drove the unfamiliar route, a much longer commute than the one to Ruby-Wise. *I guess I will just have to get used to all of this traffic. I'm definitely not looking forward to the extra expense of more gasoline or driving so far in bad weather.*

She picked up her keys and gradebook from the office. The assistant principal was, once again, on hand to greet the new teachers. "I'm trying to figure out where I know you from," Dianne commented as she picked up her materials. "What is your name again?"

"Clifton Cowan," he replied.

"Were you by any chance the assistant principal at Wettermark a few years ago?" she asked.

"Yes, I was there until I got transferred over here."

"Well, I think you were there when I was sent there for about six weeks."

"Sure was. Sure was. I knew you looked familiar."

"Well, that makes me feel better. At least I know one person at this school."

Dianne headed down the hall to the home ec. department,

bracing herself for what was bound to be a difficult day. She looked straight ahead, fully aware that she was being sized up by the rows of students lined up against the walls of the hall. She was relieved to finally reach the door and let herself inside, locking out the noise from the hall and trying to compose herself before the bell rang for school to begin.

The day began with homeroom, which lasted for ten minutes. The main purpose of it was to check roll for the attendance report. The school had no intercom, so teachers were expected to read the daily announcement from a ditto sheet which had been run off for that purpose. Dianne followed the instructions to the best of her ability, having trouble with the pronunciation of some names, once again.

"We all here," announced one girl. "I'll tell you who's absent. Demarkus Traylor and Jeanette Simmons. They never come, but everybody else be here."

"Okay, thanks for the help," said Dianne, counting the number of students in the room to see if it matched the number in the roll book. Eighteen present and twenty on roll, so I guess she knows what she is talking about. At least I have a tenth-grade homeroom, not eighth graders like I had at Ruby-Wise.

She was thankful when the bell rang to signal the end to homeroom. That was definitely a new way to start the day, and probably not something to look forward to. First period was her planning period, and she was anticipating having some time alone.

A girl walked through the door and sat down at one of the sewing machines. She pulled some material and a pattern guide out of a large bag, threaded the machine, and began to sew. Dianne was flabbergasted. *Why is this student coming in here now?* she wondered. The girl said nothing but continued working steadily. *Well, I guess I will just leave her alone and see what happens. Maybe she had some sort of arrangement with the other teacher.*

As the period ended the girl packed up her belongings and left as soon as the bell rang.

Boy, was that strange, Dianne thought, but I won't worry about it now. I have much bigger problems to tackle for the rest of the day.

She began meeting with the classes as soon as the bell for second period sounded. The first class, Home Economics II, was a group of sixteen students. They sat quietly, listening to Dianne's explanations of class procedures. Dianne tried to find out exactly what they had been studying and how far along they were, but nobody could tell her with any certainty.

The day continued with a General Science class that met in a vacant room at the end of the hall in the elementary building. It was a long walk, and Dianne wasn't too happy about having to go back outside once she had settled in her room for the day. A stark and cold facility, the room was not very conducive to a good class atmosphere, especially with the elementary students having their recess right outside the windows.

Most of the students came to class without a textbook.

"Where is your textbook?" Dianne inquired of student after student.

She was met with some strange responses.

"I lost it in the ditch," explained one student.

"My little brother tore it up," said another.

"Mine got wet," commented another.

"Our house burned down," added yet another.

"The dog ate it," responded a jokester.

"Now, I know that is one of the oldest excuses in the world," declared Dianne. "I want all of you to make an effort to find your books by tomorrow. You will be needing them every day."

The students were restless, and they, as well as Dianne, were glad when the period finally ended, as they headed out for lunch.

Well, I can see that is probably going to be my worst class. At least I have a few minutes to rest up while I eat my lunch. I can see that I am going to need all of my strength to make it through the rest of the day.

The class after lunch was a combined class of Home Economics III and Home Economics IV. To Dianne's relief, it consisted of girls only. *No boys to worry about, for once,* she thought, thankfully.

The fifth-hour class was an exploratory Home Living class for eighth graders. Dianne was surprised to see a few white faces in the bunch. She learned later that the white students were those who could not afford to go to the nearby private school that was established when the court ordered the integration of seventh and eighth graders in the Lecompte school district.

The final class of the day, Home Economics I, was made up of mostly ninth graders. They were a wiggly bunch, ready for school to be over with. Dianne had no better luck in finding out what they had covered or what they knew.

Well, I'm not sure how much good it did for me to come out here ahead of time, she reflected as she gathered up her belongings and prepared to leave for the day. They don't seem to know very much about anything. I think I am going to use the same technique with them that I used at Wettermark. Tomorrow I am going to start everyone on the basic level of a foods unit, and I will just work from there. If they know more than I think they do, I can always skip on to more difficult material. But, for now, it's foods for everybody and chapter one for the General Science students.

She headed home to dig out the materials she needed for the next day's lessons, thankful to have made it through the first day at another black high school.

The next day Dianne found a note in her mailbox summoning her to the principal's office during her free period. *Just what I needed,* she fretted. *I need all of my time to get ready for my classes.*

She reluctantly reported to the office at the designated time.

"Come in, Miss Hollis," said the principal, rising as she entered the room. "Please be seated. I am meeting with all of the transferred teachers to go over a few basic regulations with them."

"Okay," replied Dianne cautiously, awaiting what he had to say.

He went over several points that he felt all new teachers should be aware of. As he drew to the end of the discussion he sat up straighter in his chair, folded his hands on the desk, and said, "There is one thing that I want you to fully understand. There is one word that we do not use around here, and that word is 'nigger.'"

"Well, I wasn't planning on using that word, anyhow," replied Dianne as she tried to maintain her composure.

Dianne barely made it back to her room before the bell rang for first period to end. The strange and silent girl had shown up again, still sewing the entire period. Dianne had not had time to deal with her due to the appointment with the principal. *That is one problem that I am going to have to tackle tomorrow,* she decided.

She began each period with an explanation that they would be studying a foods unit. She did not tell the upperclassmen that they would be studying Home Ec. I material. *What they don't know won't hurt them,* she reasoned.

The announcement that they would be expected to take notes and would be tested on the material went over like a lead balloon.

"Take notes in home ec. I never heard of such a thing," declared an outspoken girl named Vanessa.

"Well, that's what we are going to do, so you might as well get used to it," responded Dianne. "I expect all of you to have some paper and something to write by tomorrow. For today, I will loan paper and pencils to anyone who does not have them.

Things didn't go much better in the General Science class. Only about half of the students had managed to locate their textbooks.

"Okay, we will share textbooks today, but tomorrow I expect the rest of you to come up with your books," said Dianne. "Those of you who don't bring a book will be given a written assignment to do."

That does it, she vowed, as the students headed out for lunch. This afternoon I am going back to Ruby-Wise to pick up some old copies of the "Current Science" newspapers that the students out there have already used. Boy, will these students be in for a surprise when they come without a textbook tomorrow!

During her lunch hour she phoned her former principal, Mr. Slay, with her request.

"If I can get some of those 'Current Science' papers I left down in the home ec. cabinets, it would be a big help to me," she explained.

To her relief, Mr. Slay approved the request.

She had written a brief outline of the home ec. lessons on the chalkboard to help the students learn how to take notes. As she met with the classes throughout the day she could see that quite a few students were struggling to keep up, even though she was going at what seemed like a snail's pace to her.

Well, there's another job for tomorrow, she decided. I am going to get an overhead projector from the library. I will just have to write the notes out in more detail in order for the students to be able to follow along. Reading skills are definitely a problem at this school. I guess I won't know who the best readers are until I give them a written exam.

Surprisingly enough, there were actually very few discipline problems in the classes, aside from the General Science class. As with her experience at Wettermark, most of the students were polite and respectful. They tried to participate in the lessons, even if they didn't know a lot of the answers to the questions she posed.

If I can just keep them on track, things just might work out, she reflected at the end of her second day. I will just have to wait and see what other problems may develop after they get more used to me and my teaching techniques. Only time will tell if I am taking the right approach.

Dianne had not had time to socialize much with the other teachers. She was too busy trying to keep one step ahead of the students. However, she had met the other teachers who had been transferred, as well as those who were already teaching at the school when she arrived. Each one had their own story and their own set of problems to deal with.

The chemistry teacher, Mrs. Ava Vercher, had been the first white teacher in the high school. She had come voluntarily. "I came out here for a job interview and a tour of the department," she told Dianne. "The students looked me over real good that day. I made up my mind. There was a need and I was ready to fulfill it. I took the job and I've been here ever since. There is a lot of good that can come from us being here, if other teachers will just have the right attitude about it."

Likewise, the junior high white social studies teacher, Roy McDaniel, had also been there for several years. A short and stocky man with wavy red hair and thick glasses, he reminded Dianne of Henry Kissinger. He had plenty of stories to tell about his experiences in the school, and Dianne often got her laugh for the day from talking to him.

The other social studies teacher, Don Paulk, who was also white, had also put in his time there. He, too, was quite a storyteller, and he didn't mind sharing his experiences with anybody who would listen.

"I don't have any discipline problems in my classes," he confided to Dianne. "I'll tell you my secret. There's a big hole in the back wall of my classroom. I tried to get it fixed, but it has been there for several years. Now whenever the new classes come in I tell them 'You see that hole in the back wall. That's what happened to the last student who gave me any trouble.' It works like a charm. They eye that hole, and I don't hear anything out of them for the rest of the year."

The white math teacher, Mr. Bob Hale, had also been there for several years. He was a hard worker and was well-liked by the students. Upon talking to him Dianne found out that he knew her sister, Sallie, through their church work. "Wow, I can't believe that I actually found somebody that I have a connection to at this school," she told him.

The business teacher had been replaced by another white teacher, Mrs. Kate Spaulding, who let it be well known that she was most unhappy with the transfer. "I'm going to get out of this place next year. Just you wait and see," she told Dianne. "In the meantime, I am going to do just what I have to. I'm not going to put myself out one extra bit for the people in this place."

The English teacher had been replaced with a white teacher named Mrs. Jan Kessler. She had short blonde hair which became even shorter when she bleached it one too many times. "I had to cut it all off because it broke off," she admitted to Dianne. "Now it is only about one inch long all over my head, and I can't do anything with it until it grows out."

Another white teacher at the junior high level was Mrs. Tammy Risinger. She was a tough cookie who didn't put up with any nonsense from the students. She was the bane of their existence, according to Roy.

"The students can't stand Risinger," he informed Dianne. "They plot out what they're going to do in her class. I've overheard them talking about it. They try their best to make her life miserable."

"Oh, well, better her than me," replied Dianne.

The guidance counselor had been replaced by a white teacher, Mr. Bradley Mercier, who also taught a chemistry class. "Somebody with my qualifications is pretty hard to find," he told Dianne. "There aren't too many guidance counselors who are also certified to teach chemistry."

The rest of the high school faculty remained black. The P. E. department, music department, and industrial arts departments were unchanged. There was also one black math teacher who was not transferred. Other than that, the entire high school faculty had become a majority white organization. It was something that required adjustments from the students as well as the rest of the faculty members.

Never one to leave school early, Dianne also became acquainted with the head custodian, who came around to sweep up her department. Mr. Jonas Williams was known to every teacher and every student in the school. He never knew a stranger, and if anybody ever needed help he was always the first one to volunteer.

"That Mr. Jonas Williams is a really nice man," she commented to Roy.

"You know that he's married to one of the elementary teachers, don't you?" Roy asked.

"No, I didn't know that," exclaimed Dianne. "Which one is it?"

"It's Mrs. Eunice Williams. They met here at school when she first started teaching. They fell in love and got married."

"How romantic! She seems to be really nice, too."

"Yes, she is. They're a really nice couple."

Well, I'm not having any luck with finding a man, myself, thought Dianne. Every guy I meet is either weird or married. There's got to be a decent guy out there somewhere. The question is "When and how will I meet him?"

The strange girl had shown up during her planning period for the third day in a row. Dianne decided that it was time to tackle the problem of finding out just who she was and why she was showing up during the planning period.

"Why are you coming in here every day to sew?" she asked as the girl began to pull out her materials and set up the machine.

"This is my class. I'm supposed to be in here," the girl replied.

"This is my planning period. I'm not supposed to have any students coming in during this time," Dianne noted.

"I needed a home ec. class and this is the only period I could take it. Mrs. Collins said that I could come in during first hour and just sew every day and she would give me credit."

"Oh, I see. Well, if the arrangements have already been made, I guess we will just have to stick with the plan. However, I don't see any students listed in the gradebook for this hour."

"She has me down under another class. I think it would be in your fourth hour roll. My name is Leona White."

"Okay, got it," said Dianne, flipping through the gradebook. "Well, just be sure to let me check the garment whenever you finish so that I can give you a grade. Also, make sure that you stay in here the whole hour. If I am responsible for you I can't have you roaming the halls."

Dianne had made it out to Ruby-Wise in time to fetch the "Current Science" newspapers, as she had planned. True to her word, she was ready for the students who showed up without textbooks for the third day in a row.

"Okay, I have given all of you a chance to find your books," she announced. "As I told you, beginning today those of you who do not bring your book to class will be assigned a written report."

"How are we gonna do a report if we don't have no books?" asked one student named Glenn.

"That's easy. I have some copies of the 'Current Science' newspapers up here. I am going to go around and check textbooks now. If you didn't bring your book to class, you are going to spend the rest of the period writing a five-hundred-word report from the 'Current Science' paper."

"Five hundred words! Can't nobody write that much in an hour," protested another student named Latisha.

"Well, you will just have to do the best you can. Now I see that five of you still don't have your books, so I am going to pass out the 'Current Science' papers and you can get started."

"We don't know how to do no five-hundred-page report," complained Latisha.

"That's five hundred words, not five hundred pages."

"Why can't you just give us some lines to write?" asked another student named Troy.

"It's against school board policy for teachers to assign lines now. We have to give you a report."

"What happens if I don't do it?" Troy persisted.

"Well, in that case, I will have to send you to the office. So, it's either get busy on the reports or get out of class."

"Okay, okay, I guess I'll do it. But I'm telling my mamma about this!"

"Go ahead and tell her. I'm sure she will be interested to know that you haven't been bringing your textbook to class," retorted Dianne as the rest of the class roared with laughter.

"Chalk up one for Miss Hollis," exclaimed a girl named Patrice as she gleefully made an imaginary chalk mark in the air.

"Okay, that's about enough of that. The rest of us need to get started on the lesson. Remember, bring your textbooks to class every day from now on," said Dianne.

She had also managed to scrape together enough transparencies to write out the day's lesson plans. Things seemed to be moving along smoother as she used the overhead projector, which she had checked out from the school library early that morning. It would become her mainstay in keeping order during the lessons. The students were slow in copying the notes, but at least they were all trying, and that was all that she could ask of them at this point.

Well, I can see that this is going to be a lot of extra work for me, she pondered as she watched them carefully. But, if it helps with the discipline and helps them to learn, it will be worth the extra effort. Looks like I will have to go and buy some more transparencies.

"I'd like to congratulate you on the job you're doing with the ninth-grade science class," Roy told her the next day.

"Oh, really?" asked Dianne.

"Yes, I've been hearing all day how mean and tough you are. That's just what they need. Keep up the good work," he said.

"Well, I guess I've got my bluff in on them, then," she replied. "I just hope I can keep it up."

Chapter 16

*A*lways early to arrive at school, Dianne was soon assigned the duty of making coffee in the teachers' lounge every morning. "The other home ec. teacher always made coffee for us," Roy had informed her.

Roy, likewise, usually arrived early. He and Dianne often conversed before the other teachers began to report to the teachers' lounge to sign in. Roy's amusing stories were a great way to laugh away tension, and she looked forward to chatting with him. As their friendship grew, he became her main confidant and somebody that she could always depend on to lend a willing ear whenever she was totally frustrated with the way her day was going.

"Are you going to make us a cake for the faculty meetings?" Roy inquired hopefully one morning as Dianne was filling the coffeepot. "The other home ec. teacher always did."

"I think not," Dianne retorted, giving him a long and hard look. "What else did she do around here—mow the grass?"

"Oh, well, it was worth a try. Those cakes were really good!"

"There is one thing I wanted to ask you about, though," said Dianne. "I have been looking over the home ec. gradebook and I noticed that there are very few grades for the students. Mostly they have just grades at the end of each six weeks. There are no tests and no homework grades. The really strange thing is that most of the girls seem to have 'A's' and most of the boys have 'F's.' Can you explain that?"

"Well, there's a simple answer for that one," Ray replied solemnly. "Mrs. Collins did not like boys."

"Wait a minute. You're telling me that she gave the boys 'F's' just because she didn't like them?"

"Pretty much."

"That practice is about to come to an end," Dianne declared. "From now on, everybody will be graded on their work, not on what I think of them or how much I like them."

One boy, Joseph Sampson, Dianne soon learned, was an exception to Mrs. Collins's rule. Unlike the other boys, he had received "A's" and "B's" in home economics. She also learned from the girls in her classes that Joseph was an expert sewer.

"Boy, Joseph can really sew," Debbie Newman, a senior girl, informed her. "The girls even hire him to make clothes for them."

"Really?" responded an astounded Dianne. "I have never known a male to be that interested in sewing."

Joseph was an agreeable and cheerful boy who got along with everybody. Dianne liked him immediately, and he soon became one of her favorite students.

Joseph's twin sister, Mary, was just the opposite in personality. Rough and ready, she seldom smiled or had a kind word for anybody. Dianne had little doubt that anybody who picked a fight with her would get the worst end of it.

How did their genes get so crossed? she wondered. Joseph would have made a better girl and Mary would have been a great boy.

"Geesh, I would surely hate to meet that Mary Sampson in a dark alley," Dianne commented to Roy a few days later during their early morning chat. "She is one rough character."

"That she is," replied Roy.

"Why in the world did their mother name them 'Mary' and 'Joseph'? Most of the twins I know have names that rhyme."

"I think their birthdays are in December. You know—Mary and Joseph in the Bible."

"Oh, now I get it. How dense of me. It makes perfect sense now."

The home economics department at Carter C. Raymond was larger than the ones at the schools where Dianne had previously taught. It consisted of a large sewing room that also served as the lecture room with the cutting tables doubling as desks. The cooking lab was a separate large room with six kitchen units, each containing a table and chairs. Although the appliances were in fairly good condition, the Venetian blinds that covered the kitchen windows were dusty, and some of them were falling apart. Dianne decided to postpone doing anything about their sad state until later.

There were two other rooms in the department, both vacant. One room had become a junk room with all sorts of odds and ends deposited into it. The other room was totally bare except for a chalkboard. Evidently, it was intended to be used as a lecture room, but there were no desks.

Storage cabinets for students' sewing supplies were located in one of the hallways. The other hallway, which connected the kitchen and the sewing lab, had a barren flowerbed with empty clay flowerpots. *How in the world did anybody expect plants or flowers to grow here with no sunlight?* Dianne wondered. *This has definitely got to go, and the sooner the better!*

She made short work of getting rid of the flowerpots, giving them to anybody who would take them. Then she had the janitors pull out the edging around the bed. Clean-up of the space showed that tiles did exist underneath all the dirt. *Thank goodness, that's gone,* she reflected. *Now I don't have to worry about anybody tripping over the flowerpots or the edging on their way to the cooking lab.*

The next job to tackle was the cooking lab. There were two large storage cabinets that were crammed full of cooking utensils along with aprons strewn haphazardly in the mix. It was one of the biggest messes Dianne had ever seen.

How anybody ever found anything they needed in this junk heap is beyond me, she thought. *All of these utensils have to be organized and placed into the individual kitchens before we can even think about having a cooking lab. Otherwise, the students would spend half of the lab period just trying to find the utensils they need.*

She decided to use the foods classes to straighten and organize the cooking lab. The students were excited about getting to go into the kitchen until they learned that they were actually expected to wash and dry dishes and clean cabinets.

"We're not maids," one girl named LaKeitha informed her haughtily. "I don't wash no dishes for nobody."

"You're getting a grade on this, so if you don't do any work, you will get a zero," Dianne informed her.

"Well, if you put it that way, I guess I'll do it, but I don't like it. I don't want no zero," the girl replied. "Hey, y'all. Did you know that we be gettin' a grade for this?" she yelled to her classmates.

"Yeah, we know," responded a boy named Andrew. "If you had been paying attention in class yesterday, you'd know, too."

"Forget you, Mr. Smarty Pants. Who asked you, anyhow?"

"Okay, enough with the yelling," Dianne interceded. "More work and less talking."

Dianne had pulled the aprons out of the jumble as she handed out the utensils to be cleaned and stored. She washed them in the washing machine while the students were working in their assigned groups. It took several loads to complete the washing and drying process with Dianne having to untangle the apron strings as she removed them from the washer. There appeared to be enough aprons for each student to have one, so she decided to let them pick their own aprons, labeling them with masking tape. A few students wanted to bring their own aprons, which was just fine by Dianne. "Just be sure to put your names on them," she instructed.

At the end of the day Dianne looked over the newly-straightened kitchens with their sparkling clean cabinets. The whole lab smelled of detergent, and the atmosphere of cleanliness was a welcome relief from the dusty room Dianne had first encountered. *By cracky, I think we're ready to tackle a cooking lab now. This may actually work!* she congratulated herself.

The next day she conferred with the principal about procedures to follow when purchasing food for the cooking labs. He told her to use one of the small locally owned grocery stores in downtown Lecompte. "We want to keep the tax money in the community," he said. "We always buy as many of the school supplies as we can locally."

In the foods classes that day she had the students choose their lab groups, and she explained her lab rules and procedures. They broke into groups to plan their labs. The menu was to consist of chocolate chip cookies and Kool-Aid.

"Almost everybody likes chocolate chip cookies," she told them. "They're easy to make. But just watch and see—even though everybody has the same recipe, not everybody's cookies will turn out the same. I'll just bet somebody will burn them."

"Ain't nobody gonna burn their cookies," declared LaKeitha. "We gonna eat them cookies all up."

"Ha, you'll be the first ones to burn 'em," taunted Andrew. "Our cookies will be the best. Just you wait and see!"

"Okay, you're on. We gonna see whose cookies be the best," challenged LaKeitha.

Dianne just smiled. We'll see, all right. Yes, indeed, we will see.

Later that afternoon she made out the grocery list after school was dismissed. Since there were no supplies in the lab, she had to start from scratch with the restocking. She managed to find the little store, and the proprietors were very friendly and helpful, even carrying the groceries out to her car. She headed back to school with one eye on the time. She was definitely going to be later getting home than she had been when she taught at Ruby-Wise.

Several students were still standing in front of the school when she drove up. Two of the boys offered to help her carry the sacks down to the home economics department.

"What are y'all gonna be cookin' tomorrow?" one of them inquired.

"Chocolate chip cookies," said Dianne.

"Oh, that sounds good. Can I come to the lab, too?" he asked.

"I'm afraid not. Labs are just for home ec. students," replied Dianne. "Thanks for helping me, just the same."

"You're welcome. I still think we should get some cookies, though."

She stored the supplies and headed home. It had been a very long day, and she knew that she definitely needed her rest in order to cope with the cooking labs the following day.

Dianne was on needles and pins the next day as she rushed around trying to get the supplies ready to hand out to each class while keeping the additional supplies safely stored away for the remaining labs. The students bustled about excitedly, each group sure that their cookies were going to be the best ones in their class.

As the smell of cookies permeated the lab and seeped into the hallways, students from other classes began to appear at the two lab doors, almost as if by magic. Word that cooking was taking place in the home economics department had evidently spread throughout the school. Dianne was kept busy answering the door as student after student knocked, hoping to get a free sample of the cookies.

That does it! I'm going to have to do something about this situation, she vowed after answering the door for what seemed like the twentieth time. She hastily made two signs for the doors, hoping to alleviate the problem. "Lab closed to outside students. No foods given out during cooking labs." It seemed to work because the requests for samples dwindled rapidly as soon as the signs were posted.

As the labs progressed, some mistakes were made. One group's cookies were much too dry, and they didn't even stick together.

"Did you sift the flour before you measured it?" Dianne asked.

"No, I forgot," admitted one boy named Vincent.

"Boy, you gonna mess up our cookies," exclaimed Jimmy, one of his lab mates.

"We'll just have to try adding a little water to the mix. Add a teaspoon at a time until it is soft enough to mix," instructed Dianne.

"Okay, that worked," said Jimmy, watching anxiously as Vincent slowly added the water. "Boy, Vincent, you lucky. If you had ruined our cookies, I was gonna be really mad."

Several other groups almost burned their cookies. "Remember, if you are baking more than one sheet of cookies, you have to switch the cookie sheets halfway through baking," Dianne reminded them. "If you don't, the cookies won't bake correctly."

"Now you tell us," lamented Vanessa, her most outspoken student. Dianne had not forgotten Vanessa's protests about having to take notes in home ec., and she was constantly on guard, trying to think of ways to win the girl over. *Maybe cooking labs will do the trick,* she hoped.

In all the classes the groups with boys tried to outdo the all-girl groups. They jokingly traded jabs back and forth throughout the lab periods. Finally, the class with Andrew and LaKeitha arrived. It was time for the great showdown for the chocolate chip cookie bake-off!

Dianne could barely keep from laughing as she watched both groups working diligently, each determined to beat the other in getting their cookies mixed and into the oven. The boys' groups were always the most amusing to watch because they had a tendency to be the messiest as they were working. Flour usually ended up all over the countertop and floor, and dirty utensils were stacked in the sink, awaiting a much-needed washing. The rest of the flour always ended up on them, with the fronts of their aprons being a dusty white by the time lab was over.

"Just look at the mess those boys are makin', Miss Hollis," said LaKeitha. "You gonna let them get away with that?"

"No, they'll have to clean it all up," replied Dianne. "They'll learn not to be so messy. This is their first time to cook."

"Yeah, we got it under control," Andrew assured her. "Mind your own business, girl. Anyhow, our cookies are still the best."

"Oh, no. Our cookies are comin' out of the oven right now. Miss Hollis, you taste one of these and tell us what you think."

"Ha, our cookies are done, too. Here, Miss Hollis, taste this cookie, and tell LaKeitha that it's better than those old raggedy ones she made."

"Raggedy! Boy, if you want to see something raggedy, just look in the mirror."

"Girl, yo' mamma."

"No, yo' mamma."

"Okay, enough," interjected Dianne. "Both batches of cookies look pretty good to me. It's hard to say which ones are the best."

The rest of the students had been watching the drama unfold. "Wait, Miss Hollis," one of them yelled before Dianne could bite into either cookie. "You can't taste their cookies unless you try one of ours, too."

"Yeah, Miss Hollis. You gotta try everybody's cookies," insisted another student.

Dianne took a deep breath as she surveyed the six cookies that had suddenly been placed in front of her on one of the lab tables. "Okay, I'll taste them just this once. But I can't accept samples from every group whenever we have lab. If I did, I would be eating something like sixteen cookies in one day, and you know what that means. If I kept that up, pretty soon I wouldn't be able to get through the lab door."

All eyes were upon her as she bit into a cookie and chewed slowly, hoping she wouldn't choke in front of the students.

"Well, I can see that I'm going to need something to drink with all these cookies," she commented, as she walked over to the refrigerator and pulled out a cola bottle containing the remainder of her Diet Dr. Pepper that was left over from her lunch.

"How come you get to drink a cola and we have to drink Kool-Aid?" one student protested.

"This is left over from my lunch," she explained.

"You bring your own lunch to school?" another inquired.

"Yes, I don't like eating in the cafeteria. That food is too heavy for me," she replied.

"Well, I still don't think it's fair. You get to drink cokes and we don't," the first protester persisted.

"That's what happens when I'm the teacher and you're the student. Teachers have privileges."

"Never mind all that. Just hurry up and tell us whose cookies are the best," LaKeitha insisted.

"It's hard to say. They're all pretty good," she observed after trying all six cookies. "However, if I have to pick just one, I think the prize would go to kitchen number three, LaWanda's group."

"Hold on," protested another student. "How come we get named 'LaWanda's group'? She don't own us."

"Because LaWanda's the cook. We'll have to think up some other way of naming the lab groups," said Dianne.

"Man, I think that contest was rigged," complained Andrew. "I still think our cookies are the best!"

It soon became evident that several more problems existed with the lab layout in the department. During homeroom one day, Dianne suddenly noticed that a boy named Alfred was missing after roll check.

"What happened to Alfred?" she asked the class. "I know he was in here just a couple of minutes ago."

She was greeted with silence and a few snickers from some of the students.

"Okay, what gives? I know something is up. Who wants to tell me where Alfred is?"

More silence, along with a few guilty looks as students stared down at the tables.

"He went out the back door when you weren't looking," one girl finally confessed.

"Oh, really? Well, I just can't wait for him to get in here tomorrow," Dianne said.

Well, I will just have to do something about that situation, but what? she pondered. *What I have to do is prevent him from going out the back door, and I think I know just how to do it!*

When homeroom rolled around the next day, Dianne went about business as usual, pretending not to even notice Alfred. The other students appeared to have forgotten all about the previous day's incident because no one mentioned it.

After roll check, Dianne deliberately turned her back as she pretended to look through one of her desk drawers. When she quickly looked up again, Alfred was standing by the back door attempting to open it.

"What's the problem, Alfred?" she inquired innocently. "Can't get the door open?"

Alfred gave her a sheepish look as he slinked back to his assigned seat, amid laughter from his fellow classmates.

"I wouldn't try that trick anymore if I were you, Alfred. You will find that door locked from now on during class. That way nobody can get into or out of the room without my seeing them. You see, Alfred, I am responsible for you during the homeroom period. If you go wandering off and something happens to you, I will get into trouble, too. That goes for the rest of you students, too. Stay in this room and stay in your assigned seats during homeroom."

Well, I guess I solved that problem, she thought *I can't wait to see what kind of problems I have next.*

Shortly afterwards, a problem occurred with the dressing room located in the sewing lab. Since it had a three-sided full-length mirror, the girls liked to go in at the end of class to check their hair and makeup. The boys delighted in holding the door shut so the girls could not get out.

One day an especially loud confrontation occurred. Alicia Green, a senior girl, had gone into the dressing room to comb her hair. Suddenly, she found herself locked in by a mischievous boy named Roosevelt Spears. She began banging on the door as hard as she could. "Let me out! Let me out of here right now! Whoever this is will be really sorry whenever I get out of here," she yelled.

"Roosevelt, get away from that door this instant," demanded Dianne. "Don't let me catch you doing that ever again."

The boy retreated to his seat, laughing the whole time. The rest of the class joined in with loud guffaws.

Alicia burst through the doorway. "Who locked me in? If I find out, it will be the last time they do it!"

"Calm down, Alicia. It's been taken care of," said Dianne.

After rescuing the girl, Dianne decided that something had to be done about the situation. She had a key that locked the door from the outside of the knob, so she decided that it was time to lock it and keep it locked.

"The dressing room will now be off-limits during class," she announced the next day. "The door has been locked, and it will remain locked unless somebody has made a garment during sewing class and needs to try it on."

"That sucks!" complained one girl. "Why do you boys have to go and mess everything up?"

"Don't put the blame on just the boys," said Dianne. "You girls don't really need to be spending class time primping, anyhow. If you are doing your assigned work, you don't have time to primp."

That takes of the problem temporarily, but something else has to be done. I think the dressing room will have to go, she decided. I just have to decide when and how to get rid of it.

Word that the home economics department was having cooking labs eventually filtered down to Dianne's General Science class.

"How come we can't cook like your other classes do?" inquired Patrice, the girl who had been on Dianne's side the first day of class.

"This is a science class, not a home economics class," replied Dianne.

"Well, it's just not fair," declared Troy, one of the students who had protested getting a five-hundred-word report. "We get hungry, too. Besides, it's almost lunch time when we come in here."

"All right, I'll think about it, and I'll see if I can come up with some way to work food into one of our lessons," Dianne promised.

After racking her brain, she devised a plan. It would be more trouble than the usual lesson but adding a little interest to the class never hurt anything.

"Okay, students," she announced a few days later. "Today you are going to get to eat, provided you are good and pay attention to the lesson."

She began to remove things from a rolling cart to set up her materials for a demonstration.

"What is it? What are we going to get to eat?" asked Latisha excitedly. Dianne had not forgotten Latisha's stormy protests over getting a five-hundred-word report during the early weeks of class.

"You'll just have to wait and see," Dianne replied. "Let's see if you can figure out what I am about to make. First, we need to review the two basic types of changes in matter. Who can tell me what they are?"

"I know, I know," said a girl named Shandrika. "Physical and chemical."

"Right," said Dianne. "Now we are going to start by crushing up these graham crackers. What kind of change is that?"

"Physical," chanted the class, almost in unison.

"Yes, right. Now we are going to melt some margarine in this electric popcorn popper. What kind of change is that?"

"Physical again," said Patrice.

"Right again. Does anybody have any idea of what we are going to make with these crackers and margarine?" she asked teasingly as she held up a pie pan.

"You be makin' some kind of pie crust. That's a pie pan," announced Troy.

"Very good, Troy," said Dianne as she proceeded to mold the crackers to the pan. "That takes care of the crust. Now we have to make the filling. I have here some condensed milk, eggs, and lemon juice. What kind of pie do you think we are making?"

"Got to be lemon," said Latisha.

"Right again. Now watch closely. We mix the milk and egg yolks, and then we add the lemon juice. What is happening to the eggs?"

"They're changing," said Shandrika. "They're funny-looking now."

"Yes," said Dianne. "The lemon juice has coagulated the egg yolks, so we have another type of change. That would be..."

"Chemical," chanted the class in unison again.

Dianne proceeded to spread the pie filling into the crust.

"Now, we have one more thing to do, and that is make the meringue. For that, we beat the egg whites and then add sugar. What kind of change is that?"

"Chemical," yelled Troy.

"Are you sure it's chemical?" asked Dianne. "Did we change the chemical make-up of the eggs when we trapped air in them?"

"No," said Patrice. "Boy, you dumb. That's a physical change."

"Hey, don't be callin' me 'dumb,'" protested Troy.

"Well, Patrice is right. It's a physical change only. All we have done is put some air into the eggs. The sugar just makes them stiffer." She spread the meringue over the pie filling as she spoke. "Now, if we had an oven in here, we would bake the meringue, causing one more kind of change. Who can tell me what that would be?"

"Got to be chemical this time," said Troy.

"Right you are, Troy. We are actually burning the meringue when we brown it, so it is a chemical change."

"How are we gonna eat that if the meringue's not cooked?" asked Shandrika

"It just so happens that I brought two more pies that I cooked last night," said Dianne as she uncovered the second shelf on her rolling cart. "I have paper plates and plastic forks, too, so everybody gets a piece of lemon icebox pie. I need two people to help me pass the food out. Who wants to help?"

"Pick me, pick me," insisted Troy.

"I do," said Shandrika.

"Okay, Troy and Shandrika may help."

A short time later, the students dug into their pie samples enthusiastically.

"Boy, that was fun," said Troy. "Can we do it again?"

"Not for a while," said Dianne. "We can't eat in here every day. Just remember that at least one time you got to eat in science class."

"What are you going to do with that extra pie?" inquired Latisha.

"I'm going to take it home and feed it to my boyfriend," replied Dianne.

"You got a boyfriend?" asked Patrice. "What's his name?"

"Sorry, I can't tell you that," said Dianne, smiling to herself. What they don't know won't hurt them. Keep 'em guessing. That's my motto! Now all I need is a man.

What I need is a change in my wardrobe, she thought. *Perhaps that might help in attracting the interest of some new man.* Having sewn since her early days in the 4-H club, making new clothes just came naturally to her. One of her first two purchases during her first year of teaching had been a Singer Golden Touch-and-Sew Machine. She proceeded to purchase the patterns and material for several new outfits and made short work of completing them during her spare time.

Several dresses in the Spiegel's catalog also appealed to her, so she decided to order them. One dress in particular had caught her eye. It wasn't her usual style, but she couldn't pass it by. It was made of navy-blue print material, and it had a white collar and long sleeves with white cuffs. The print had small trees with little red apples on them. Scattered among the trees were lines of white writing with the slogan "The apple doesn't fall far from the tree."

Short skirts were in style, and Dianne had become accustomed to wearing hers the length that style dictated. She hemmed the skirt of that dress so that it was several inches above her knees. It was a little shorter than her usual outfits, so she decided to wear navy blue hose with it the first time she wore it to school.

Arriving that morning feeling rather spiffy, she hummed to herself as she swished down the hall in her new outfit. Too bad there's not an eligible man here to appreciate the way I look, she thought. Oh, well, at least the students always notice what I wear and have something to say about it when I have a new outfit on!

Her mood changed rapidly as she rounded the corner by the office and saw Mrs. Carter, a supervisor, coming through the front door.

"Great, just great," she exclaimed to Roy as she hastily beat a retreat to the teachers' lounge.

"What's the problem?" inquired Roy.

"There's a supervisor here, and just look at how I'm dressed."

"What's wrong with the way you're dressed? You look just fine to me."

"My skirt is too short. Now I'm going to get in trouble! I just know it."

"You know, you remind me of another teacher we used to have here," said Roy. "Her name was Miss Hanson. She was young with long blonde hair, and she wore strange outfits and very short skirts. She had a red T-Bird, and she didn't care how she got out of that thing with those short skirts on! One day she came to school with hip-hugger jeans and a tight knit top. She came into the lounge worrying about how she was dressed because a supervisor had shown up. Paulk and I were sitting in here, and we couldn't see a thing wrong with her outfit."

"Maybe I can remain inconspicuous," said Dianne. "Or maybe she won't pick my class to observe."

"Well, back to Miss Hanson," continued Roy. "She and Paulk decided to carpool to save on gas, but it just lasted one day."

"What happened?" inquired Dianne curiously.

"She picked Paulk up in her T-Bird. Paulk's wife got a good look at her that first day, and that was the end of that," replied Roy.

Dianne taught her classes that morning with a wary eye on the door, expecting to see the supervisor walk in at any time. She felt quite relieved when lunchtime rolled around and Mrs. Carter had not visited any of her classes. *I'm safe now,* she thought as she walked towards the teachers' lounge. *She won't be coming to my afternoon classes because she's not a vocational supervisor.*

Her elation was short-lived because, as she entered the lounge, there sat Mrs. Carter.

"Hello," said Dianne.

"Hello, Miss Hollis. How are you today?" replied Mrs. Carter.

"Just fine," responded Dianne nervously, hoping that Mrs. Carter wouldn't notice the dress.

"The apple doesn't fall far from the tree," observed Mrs. Carter. "What an interesting dress."

"Thank you," said Dianne, smiling weakly.

She eased back out the door as some other teachers entered the lounge. *Boy, that was a close one. Think I will just make myself inconspicuous for the rest of the day,* she thought, as she made her way back to her room to eat her lunch.

As the weeks rolled by, the home economics classes completed their foods unit and were ready for a unit in sewing. Dianne had discovered that the sewing machines in the department were older models, but they were all in working order. She had to figure out how to thread them, as they were different from any of the other models she had worked with. Also, there were not enough machines to go around in the larger classes, so students had to share.

After covering the basics, students were given the assignment of completing a practice stitch booklet. They tackled the project enthusiastically, with the boys trying to outdo the girls. Dianne also insisted that each student must pass a practical test on filling the bobbin, threading the machine, and sewing a seam before they were allowed to begin their sewing projects. That, she soon discovered, was the easy part.

What she was unprepared for was the large number of students who failed to bring the materials for their assigned sewing projects. On the first day they were to begin their project work, only a handful of students in each class brought their materials. She was faced with the difficult task of finding an alternate assignment for those who had nothing to do.

The only choice was to assign written work to those students until they brought their materials to class. The announcement that they would be required to do written work proved to be quite unpopular.

"Do a written assignment! Boy, you just enjoy giving us written work, don't you?" declared Vanessa, the girl who had protested taking notes during Dianne's early days at the school. "It's just not fair that we have to do written work just because we don't have our materials."

"I'm sorry, but you have to have something to do. Students who have nothing to do usually get into trouble. Besides, you will be getting a grade for the work," explained Dianne.

"What if we don't do it?" asked a boy named John.

"I have already spoken to Mr. Cowan, the assistant principal. Those of you who don't do the written assignment will be sent to the office."

"You think of everything, don't you?" commented Vanessa. "Well, I guess we'll have to do it, but I'm gonna tell my mamma to get me my material. I don't want to be doing written work every day."

After a few days, the majority of the students managed to get the sewing supplies they needed. However, Dianne discovered that a few of the students were simply financially unable to purchase any materials. Having a lot of scrap material left over from her own sewing projects, she managed to scrape together enough materials for those students to use. To her relief, they all managed to finish the projects before reviews for the final exams began.

The principal called a faculty meeting a few days before graduation. "There is something that I feel that all of you should be aware of," he informed the teachers. "We always have our faculty attend graduation. They march in just before the graduates, and they are seated on the front rows of seats located on the gym floor."

"Is there any particular way we are supposed to dress?" asked one teacher.

"Yes, I'm glad you asked that question. The female teachers should wear white dresses and white shoes. The men should wear a suit or slacks with a coat and tie," he replied. "Now, we don't require you to come to baccalaureate, since we are several miles out of Alexandria. Those of you who wish to come are certainly welcome to do so. If there are no other questions, we will look forward to seeing all of you at graduation next Monday night," he said as the meeting concluded.

"Some of us are going to carpool to graduation, and I was wondering if you would be interested," said Roy as they sat in the teachers' lounge the next morning.

"I might be. Who else is in the group?" inquired Dianne.

"Well, there's me and Paulk and Miss Holt from the elementary wing. I'm driving my Volkswagen station wagon."

"Are you sure your wives trust you riding with two single women?" she teased.

"No, but we're willing to do it, anyhow," said Roy laughingly.

"Okay, I guess you can count me in. I don't like to drive at night."

"Great. Give me the directions to your house, and I'll pick you up," said Roy.

Well, that takes care of the ride. Now all I have to worry about is making sure I have a white dress and white shoes, reflected Dianne as she drove home that day.

Inspection of her closet revealed that she owned exactly one white dress, and what a dress it was! Made of double-knit white polyester, it had a low-cut sweetheart neckline and short puffed sleeves. True to her current style, Dianne had hemmed the dress to fall several inches above her knees.

If I have to go to this shindig, I'm going to look my best. This dress will have to do, she reasoned. *I'm certainly not buying a new outfit for just one night.*

A few days later when graduation night arrived, Dianne dressed carefully for the occasion, taking extra pains with her hair and makeup. She took one last look at herself in her full-length mirror just as Roy pulled up outside her apartment.

Not too shabby, if I do say so myself, she thought as she blew herself a kiss.

She made a quick exit from the apartment as she heard Roy's horn sound outside.

"Nice outfit," observed Roy.

"Thanks. It's the only white dress in my wardrobe," she replied.

"You might want to fasten your seatbelt," he instructed. "I drive kind of fast sometimes."

"Thanks for the warning," she commented as he rapidly swung the car into the street.

After two brief stops to pick up Don Paulk and Melissa Holt, they were well on their way to Lecompte. Dianne soon learned that Roy was not exaggerating about his driving. He wove in and out of traffic so rapidly that she almost lost her breath several times.

"It takes a while to get used to Roy's driving," warned Don, as Roy crept closer to the car in front of them. Before long he was right on the other car's bumper.

"Hey, Roy," yelled Don from the backseat. "Do you think you can get any closer to that car? I can't quite see the screws in the license plate!"

Dianne and Melissa laughed appreciatively.

Several minutes later, the other car pulled over to the right shoulder of the road, and the driver stuck his arm out the window and waved for Roy to pass him.

"Way to go, Roy! You ran him off the road," exclaimed Don. "And look, that's a Texas license plate. It's bad enough to run anybody off the road, but even worse to run off a Texas driver!"

"If we survive this, it may be the last time I ride with you," threatened Dianne.

"That goes double for me," added Melissa.

A short time later, they pulled into the Carter C. Raymond parking lot. It was bustling with people of all ages hurriedly making their way to the gymnasium.

"We have corsages for the ladies and boutonnieres for the men," one teacher informed them as they entered the gym. "Mr. Sanders is passing them out. Just go down the hall to your right."

They headed for the hallway that had been indicated to them. Dianne took note of the dressy attire of everyone who was in attendance.

"Miss Hollis, I think I'll let you pin this corsage on yourself," said Mr. Sanders, the industrial arts teacher, looking slightly taken back as Dianne rounded the corner.

"Thanks," said Dianne as she reached for the corsage of red carnations.

"We'd better hurry. The other teachers are lining up," observed Roy.

"You teachers will march in first and sit in the first two rows of seats," instructed Mrs. Alice Clark, one of the senior sponsors. "Just wait for the music to start."

"Here goes nothing," said Roy as they started down the aisle.

Dianne marched in holding herself ramrod straight and taking small, deliberate steps. *I wonder what they think of us white teachers,"* she thought as she took in the totally black audience. *Guess they are really looking us over.*

Graduation proceeded without a hitch, much to Dianne's relief. The sooner I get out of here, the better, she fretted. It's pretty warm in this gym without air-conditioning.

As the end of the ceremony approached, the principal stepped up to the mike to make a few closing remarks. By that time, Dianne had tuned out most of the remarks. His voice droned on until she heard the word "integration." Then she perked up her ears to see what else was being said.

"Now you see seated before you this evening our faculty," he commented. "I ask you, ladies and gentlemen, is this or is this not..." Dianne had already mentally finished the sentence for him with the words "a fine-looking faculty." She was jolted back to earth when he completed the sentence with ". . . an integrated faculty." The audience burst into applause.

Dianne was completely horrified to be put on display like some kind of animal at the zoo. She took a deep breath and then exhaled slowly. *This, too, shall pass,* she reminded herself.

After the ceremony, the foursome made their way back to Roy's Volkswagen. Dianne was a little more prepared for Roy's unorthodox driving techniques this time.

The trip home proved to be a lot calmer, and Dianne was glad to soon be back at her own doorstep.

"Thanks for the ride, Roy," she said as she exited the vehicle. "It was an event to remember."

"Oh, come on. My driving isn't that bad," protested Roy. "It just takes a little getting used to."

"Maybe so," she observed, "but I think you took a few years off my life. See you tomorrow."

The end of school rolled around almost uneventfully. However, several problems had occurred with the home ec. kitchen because she had to leave the back door unlocked so that students could get to their sewing trays. Some of the students had sneaked into the kitchen, hoping to find some food, but Dianne caught them before any damage was done.

A few days later, she went into the kitchen to get the rest of her Diet Dr. Pepper, which she always left in the refrigerator after lunch. It was gone. Dianne searched through the refrigerator, thinking that perhaps she had placed it on another shelf, but it was nowhere to be found. *I just know one of those students drank it, but which one?* she wondered. *I'm going to find out tomorrow. It had to be one of the students in the afternoon classes because I drank part of it at lunch, like I always do.*

The next day she brought up the subject during her two afternoon classes. "You know, students, I think that we must have some little elves in our department. Somehow, my cola that was in the refrigerator disappeared yesterday. Since I know that none of you would take it, that means that it had to be elves."

Students in her sixth hour class began to laugh, and then the truth came out. "It was Twanda. She drank the rest of your cola," said one of the girls.

"Twanda! I can't believe you would do such a thing."

"Well, okay, I drank it, and it was good, too."

"Guess what, Twanda. I had already drunk out of that bottle, so you know what that means, don't you?" inquired Dianne dramatically as she widened her eyes for effect. "You've been poisoned!"

"Oh, I don't care nothing about that," retorted Twanda. "What I want to do is ride in your car. Why don't you take me for a ride? But I ain't sittin' in no back seat!"

"Sorry, Twanda, but I can't do that," replied Dianne. "Besides, you don't deserve a ride, anyhow, since you stole my Diet Dr. Pepper."

That does it, she vowed. Now I know just what to do with the dressing room. That kitchen has to be blocked off from the rest of the department.

The next day she made it a point to talk to the principal. "I have one request for some work to be done in the home economics department over the summer," she told him. "I want to have the dressing room in the sewing lab torn down. Then I want the wood and the door to be used to block off the kitchen from the rest of the department."

"I think we can do that," he replied. "Just fill out a work order form, and I will get the janitors to do it over the summer."

"Thanks so much. That will be a big help to me," she said.

Dianne soon busied herself with final exams and getting the last set of grades on the report cards. She closed down the department, locking away anything that she considered valuable. Another summer had arrived, and she was looking forward to some relaxation and having another break from students and lesson plans and supervisors. *Summertime is great,* she thought, *but it's too bad I can't do something to improve my social life while I'm away from school. The right man hasn't appeared yet, but I know he's out there somewhere.*

Chapter 17

Dianne had never been much of a party-goer. She preferred spending her nights in front of the TV set, occasionally taking in a movie or two. Her aunt Hazel sometimes accompanied her to features such as *Cabaret, Heaven Can Wait,* and *Jonathan Livingston Seagull*, but mostly Dianne went by herself.

On weekends she alternated visiting her friends Margaret Paul, Barbara Hare, and her aunt Hazel and uncle R.V., who lived just down the street. Visits to her home community of Rocky Branch were usually reserved for the holidays or the summer months.

That summer Hazel decided to travel to California to visit her daughter Jan Duvall and Jan's husband, Ken. R. V. refused to go because he didn't want to fly. Dianne promised Hazel she would look in on him from time to time. One day she decided to carry him a plate of food after cooking some barbequed chicken, green beans, and potatoes. *I hope he likes this food,* she thought as she entered the driveway with the foil-covered plate sitting on the car floorboard.

"Uncle V., are you home?" she yelled, as she knocked on the back door, plate in hand.

"Dianne, come on in here, girl. You're a sight for sore eyes. I'm about to go crazy with Mamma gone off to California. I tell you, I'll be glad when she gets back. I'm about to starve to death. You know I don't cook."

"Yes, I know, and that's why I brought you this food," she replied.

"What you got there?" he asked. "If you cooked it, I know it's got to be good."

"I hope you like it. I have some barbequed chicken, beans, and potatoes."

"Just put it down over there on the counter. Now I know what I'll be havin' for supper. Eatin' canned food and sandwiches is about to get to me," he exclaimed.

"By the way," she said. "I'm going home this weekend. I wondered if you might want to go with me, since you are here all by yourself."

"Go with you! You bet I will. I'd like to see what 'Strawberry' is up to," he said, referring to F. D. by his childhood nickname.

"Okay, I plan to leave Friday at about 2:00 p.m. I'll swing by here and pick you up," she told him.

Well, this ought to add a little interest to the trip, she reflected as she returned to her apartment.

The next afternoon she picked R. V. up, just as they had planned. He was chewing his usual piece of gum as he got into the car. He had given up smoking some years ago, so he chewed Juicy Fruit gum all day long, adding a piece at a time from the pack until the wad contained all five pieces.

"Okay, I'm not gonna tell you how to drive now. I'm just along for the ride," he said as he slid into the front right seat. "I know you're a good driver. I don't ride with just anybody, you know."

During the trip R. V. talked nonstop, entertaining Dianne with his many stories and quaint observations. His father had been a Methodist preacher, and that had provided him with an uncommon insight into human nature.

Soon afterwards, they arrived in Rocky Branch. Dianne was relieved to see that R. V. and F. D. were thoroughly enjoying each other's company, and the visit seemed to be going smoothly. Both men were stubborn creatures, and whenever they were together one never knew what might happen.

On Saturday afternoon shortly after their noonday meal, both men were tired and decided to take a nap. "I'll just make myself comfortable here on this couch by the dining table," said R. V.

"That's my spot," protested F. D. "Why don't you use the couch in the living room? I'm sure you'll like it better in there with less noise."

"No, this one will be just fine," replied R. V.

"No, really, you take the one in the living room," F. D. insisted, his voice growing louder.

"Nope, I'm gonna make myself at home right here," R. V. persisted.

"Dianne, Sallie, get in here right now," roared F. D. "I've got something I want you to do."

Dianne and Sallie shot out of their respective bedrooms, prepared for the worst. Whenever F. D. yelled, everybody jumped. It was the family's mission to keep him appeased and happy at all times, if possible. He had quite a temper, and nobody wanted to catch the worst end of it.

"Pick up this couch and move it into the living room, he instructed, pointing to his favorite couch that sat by the dining table. "Then I want you to move the living room couch in here."

"But why, Daddy?" asked Dianne. "These couches are heavy."

"I don't care if they're heavy or not. Just move them. I want them moved, and I want them moved now!" he instructed.

"Okay, okay. Sallie, grab the other end, and let's get these things moved," she said.

In the end, both men got their naps, with F. D. reclining on his favorite couch and R. V. relegated to the other one.

The rest of the weekend went smoothly, and Dianne was relieved when it was finally time to head back home again.

R. V., once again, kept a constant conversation going as they drove back to Pineville.

"You know I really didn't care nothin' about that couch, don't you?" he inquired, chewing his gum vigorously. "I just wanted to rile 'Strawberry' up a little bit."

Back home once more, Dianne reflected on her social life. "The only man in my life is my cat, Boo," she often joked to her friends. Aside from visiting her friends and relatives and attending movies solo, she had only one other social outlet, and that was church.

One Sunday morning she was surprised when a lady named Charlie Howell came up to her and said, "Dianne, there's somebody who wants to meet you. Come on over here with me, and I'll introduce you."

Wondering what was in store, Dianne followed her as instructed. Charlie stopped in front of a young man whom Dianne had often seen at the services. "Dianne, this is Cedric Johnson. Cedric, this is Dianne Hollis. Now you two have been introduced, so I am going to leave you to get acquainted."

Dianne was flattered, but thoroughly flustered, to think that somebody had been observing her during the services without her knowledge. Cedric was a quiet, well-mannered young man who had excellent taste in clothes. Dianne learned that he worked as an accountant for one of the clothing stores in town, so that explained his stylish wardrobe.

For the next few weeks, Cedric called Dianne quite frequently at night, resulting in some lengthy conversations. Dianne was amazed that a man should actually show such interest in her, especially after her experience with the unforgettable George several years earlier. Finally, Cedric worked up enough nerve to ask her out on a date.

"Have you ever seen *2001, a Space Odyssey*?" he inquired.

"No, I haven't," she replied.

"Well, it's showing at The Cinema, and I was wondering if you would like to go with me to see it Saturday night," he said.

"Yes, I think that would be very nice," she said.

"Okay, I'll pick you up at about 6:30 p.m."

Dianne nervously prepared for her date the next night, having trouble deciding on what to wear. "Can you believe it, Boo?" she said, addressing her cat. "I'm actually going out on a date."

Boo responded by rubbing against her legs as she studied the garments hanging in her closet.

"I know, I know. You think you're the only male in my life. It's just a trial date. I'll have to see how things work out. Now, if I could just decide what to wear. Too bad you can't talk. You could help me pick the right dress for this date."

Dianne finally settled on one of her favorite dresses, a red, white, and blue knit dress with a nautical print theme. *And the red shoes to go with it,* she decided.

After dressing carefully, she checked her hair and make-up in the mirror. *Well, this is it,* she thought jokingly. *I do the best I can with what I have to work with.*

Cedric arrived on time, and they headed out to the movie. I can't believe I'm going to the show on an actual normal date, she reflected as they got their tickets and headed inside. I have the feeling that something strange is going to happen, but what?

The movie itself was strange enough, and Dianne never did totally understand the plot. She was still mystified as they headed out to the car afterwards.

"What did you think of the movie?" Cedric asked.

"Well, I'm not exactly sure. Parts of it didn't make any sense to me," she admitted.

Before the conversation could continue, they were interrupted as two boys began yelling at them. "Mr. Johnson, Mr. Johnson, could you give us a ride home?" one of them asked. "My mom was supposed to pick us up, but she's not here. We don't have any way to get home."

Cedric looked at Dianne. "Well, I don't know. Dianne, do you mind?"

"No, I guess not," she replied. "I used to teach one of them at Ruby-Wise."

During the trip home, the boys kept up a continuous chatter.

"Boy, that was some movie. What did you think of it, Mr. Johnson?" one of them asked.

Dianne sat silently, listening to the conversation. Brother, I can't believe this. I finally get a real date, and it ends up being a taxi service. What's going to happen to me next?

The boys were dropped off at their respective homes, and Cedric and Dianne headed back to her apartment. She had left the front porch light on. Cedric escorted her up the steps to her front door.

"Thanks a lot, Cedric. I had a really nice time," she said. "I'll see you at church tomorrow."

Well, another date, another disaster, she meditated as she closed the door behind her. Cedric is a nice guy, but I will be truly surprised if he ever calls me again.

To her amazement, Cedric did continue calling her for the next few weeks. He tried to get her to go out to eat with him, but she kept putting him off. "I don't really like cafeteria food," she told him.

One night the tone of the conversations changed. "I'm thinking about moving out of town," he said. "I'm going to take the CPA test, and then I hope to get a higher paying job."

"Where are you going?" she asked.

"I don't know yet. It all depends on how I do on the test," he said.

That turned out to be their last conversation. Suddenly, the phone stopped ringing. Cedric was nowhere to be seen. He wasn't in church, and he didn't call anymore.

Well, I guess that's that, she concluded. My usual luck with men continues. My life is beginning to look like a soap opera.

Pets are definitely better than men. They love you unconditionally, and they don't run off and leave you, she decided. From now on, it's Boo and me.

Boo had actually proven to be quite entertaining. He had gotten himself into several scrapes, giving Dianne a good laugh every time she watched him try to get out of trouble.

Her bathroom had a small white space heater to complement the larger one in her living room. Being hot natured, she didn't light them too often. Boo wasn't used to having the bathroom heater lit, and he didn't quite know how to approach it. He liked to stay close to Dianne, and he often came into the bathroom as she was getting dressed.

One cold winter morning, Dianne was hurrying to get ready for school, as usual. Suddenly she noticed the odor of singed hair was beginning to penetrate the room. She looked down at Boo, whose tail was dangerously close to the heater. His tail began to smoke, and he glanced back at it, almost disdainfully. "Boo, you dumb cat. Your tail is on fire!" she exclaimed, as she quickly began to pat his tail against the floor. "Lucky for you I was close by, or you would have been minus a tail."

Another morning he jumped onto the heater to take his usual seat. Dianne had just turned it off, as she had gotten too hot. He sat there for a few seconds, and then he jumped off and scampered towards the bed. Perching himself in the middle of the bed, he began to lick his paws vigorously. "Burned yourself again, huh? When will you learn?" Dianne inquired laughingly.

Boo regarded her with reproachful eyes.

"Now don't go blaming me," she said. "You're the one who decided to jump onto a hot heater."

The bathroom again proved to be his nemesis when he had two unfortunate incidents with the bathtub. One occurred when he jumped onto the edge of the tub as Dianne was filling it with water, preparing to take a bath. Losing his footing on the slippery edge, he fell into the tub of water and got soaking wet. Once again, he appeared to place the blame on Dianne, giving her his most belligerent look, ears pinned back as she dried him with a towel. "Well, I guess you won't need to give yourself a bath tonight," she chided. "You have had enough baths to last a couple of days."

The next incident occurred several months later. Dianne had just finished reading *The Exorcist*, and she thought it was pretty scary. A couple of nights after reading the novel, she began hearing strange noises in the attic, some sort of scratching sounds. *What can it be?* she wondered. *Is the furniture going to begin moving around next?*

She reported the noises to her landlord, and he concluded that it must be rats or mice.

"I'll put out some poison for them," he told her.

A few days later she was getting dressed to go out, and Boo was sitting on the edge of the bathtub again. He jumped into the empty tub to get a drink of water from the faucet where it had dripped down into the tub. Suddenly, there was a terrible scratching and clawing as he scrambled to get out of the tub. He jumped out and took off running, shaking himself vigorously.

"What have you gotten yourself into now?" she inquired. "Is there something wrong with the tub?"

She peeked into the tub and was horrified to see that it was full of fleas. Fleas which were, by then, beginning to jump out of the tub and onto the floor.

"Oh, my God. My apartment is becoming infested with fleas from the dead rats! Boo, you poor thing! No wonder you were running," she exclaimed. "Now what am I going to do?"

She washed as many of them down the drain as she could. But she didn't have much time to deal with the situation, as she was already late for the event that she was scheduled to attend.

"Okay, Boo. You hold down the fort until I come back. I'll pick up some bug spray for the floor and some flea powder for you. Until then, you had better stay out of the bedroom," she remarked as she closed the door between the bedroom and kitchen.

Returning later that night armed with the promised insecticides, she sprayed the entire apartment floor and opened the windows to let the place air out. Boo, much to his consternation, was promptly doused with a heavy application of flea powder.

"Let's just hope that takes care of the fleas," she commented. "Otherwise, I'm going to think that this place is really haunted by some sort of demon."

She called the landlord the next day and told him about the fleas. He came over and sprayed around the outside of the apartment and underneath it with a heavy dose of insecticide. It was the last time that Dianne and Boo saw any fleas at their abode.

Although Boo was perfectly content to stay at home by himself, Dianne had to carry him with her whenever she left town. Cats were sometimes known to have ESP, and Boo was no exception. He would sit contentedly in the window or nap on the couch as Dianne loaded her car for the journeys. Then, as if by magic, whenever she placed the last load into the car trunk, he would be gone when she came back into the apartment. Somehow, he knew it was his turn, and he didn't want to be caught. Most of the time Dianne would find him hidden under the gas stove in the kitchen because there was a gap in the back which allowed him to slip in. It was his favorite hiding place. Unable to reach him from behind, the only way she could get him out was to turn on the oven and wait for him to emerge when he got too hot.

Dolores had given her a peach basket with a lid to use as a carrier. It was left over from the time that F. D. had briefly gone into the peach business during Dianne's teen years. She had padded it with a pet cushion. It worked, although it was a rather crude mode of transportation.

Boo's ride was upgraded when her uncle Sam Martin from El Dorado, Arkansas, made wooden carrier for him. Uncle Sam, who was married to F. D.'s sister, Berdelle, was an excellent carpenter, and he had made several things for the Hollises, including a bathroom stool for Dianne and Sallie's pink bathroom when they had moved into their new brick home in Rocky Branch.

Boo often glared at Dianne through the wire windows of his cage as they rode out of town. "Don't worry, Boo. I'll love you, no matter what," she always reassured him. "You'll always be the most important male in my life."

Chapter 18

When Dianne headed back to Carter C. Raymond the following fall, she felt a lot more confident about her situation. She knew her way around the school. She had met most of the faculty members, except for the new ones coming in. But, most importantly, she was better acquainted with the students and knew what they were capable of—both academically and otherwise.

Her science class had been moved to another classroom in the junior high wing because of the recess that had been held outside her room the previous year. It was still a long walk, and the new room was bare and uninviting. Dianne tried it out for a few days, but she just didn't like it at all. Then she had an idea.

She approached the assistant principal, Mr. Cowan, the next week. "Mr. Cowan, I have a tremendous favor to ask of you," she said. "That classroom over in the junior high wing is not very suitable to studying. I was wondering if we could have some desks moved to the vacant room in the home economics department. It is really supposed to be a lecture room, anyhow, because it has chalkboards."

"Well, I don't know. I will have to check with our principal before I can give you a final answer," he replied.

"It is really a lot of trouble for me to walk all the way over to the junior high wing," she said. "Besides that, it would really be helpful to me whenever we have cooking labs because sometimes the students don't get through exactly by bell time. I can't go off and leave them in the kitchen with no supervision. If I had the classroom close by, I could let the science students in and keep an eye on the kitchen at the same time."

"You've made a good case, so I'll see what I can do to help you," he promised.

True to his word, he had the desks moved into the vacant room the following week. The room was much smaller than a regular classroom, but Dianne didn't care. She had her own self-contained department, and she didn't have to make the dreaded walk to the junior high wing every day.

Dianne decided that it was time to make some changes in the curriculum of the home economics department. She had gone over only the basics with the students last year. Now it was time to expand on that background.

Of course, the curriculum for the General Science and the Home Economics I classes remained the same. What needed upgrading was the offerings for the older students, some of whom had been in the program for several years.

The Home Economics II and III classes would have more advanced cooking and sewing labs. Child Development would also be taught in Home Economics II, while the Home Economics III students would study a unit on Housing and Home Furnishings. It seemed like a good plan.

Getting the students to settle down at the beginning of each period for roll check proved to be a problem. Dianne's solution was to have a "Thought for the Day," which was written on the chalkboard. Each student was required to write a short paragraph on what they interpreted that thought to mean. It didn't really matter what they wrote, as long as they wrote something legible. The papers were taken up daily, and each student was given one grade for their collective writings during a six-week grading period.

The students appeared to enjoy having something different to study, although it was a lot more work for Dianne. Still, it was better than teaching science most of the day like she had been doing at Ruby-Wise, she decided. I don't know how much good I'm doing here, but at least I know that I'm trying, she reflected. The students really aren't so bad, once you get to know them. The main discipline problems aren't in the classroom. They're out in the halls at recess and lunchtime. If I can keep my classes under control, I've won at least half the battle.

Progressing from making biscuits, cornbread, and cookies in Home Ec. I, the Home Ec. II students tackled yeast breads, cinnamon rolls, and pound cakes. The Home Ec. III class made cream pies with meringues and chiffon cakes. Then Dianne decided that the students were ready to try something more advanced.

The Home Ec. II students were scheduled to have a lab on party foods that took them several days to prepare. Each group was allowed to invite one guest, and only those students who had received a written invitation would be allowed to come to the party. Word about the party soon spread through the school, and almost everybody was trying to get an invitation. Dianne stuck to her guns, though, allowing only those who had been invited to attend, much to the disappointment of many students.

"How come we can't come to your party, too?" one boy asked. "I hear you be havin' some good food."

"Sorry, but we have room for only so many people in the lab," Dianne replied. "Maybe you will get invited to the next one."

The Home Economics III students ended their foods unit with a lab that involved making a complete meal. They had a choice of either chicken or pork chops for the main course, complemented with vegetables, bread, and dessert. That also involved a two-day lab. On the second day, as the smells of the meal drifted down the hall, Dianne was, once again, shooing people away from the door. Even the two principals came by.

"I just wanted to see what you were cooking that smelled so good," Mr. Cowan told her.

"Would you like a sample of the food?" Dianne asked.

"Thank you, but, no. I'm on my way to the cafeteria for my lunchroom duty. Keep up the good work, though. It looks like they're doing a good job."

Dianne smiled to herself. Things had come a long way from that first time she had taken the students to the lab last year. Everyone had finally gotten it into their heads that they *would* wear an apron during lab; they *would* stay in their assigned lab group; they *would* work as quietly as possible without yelling and screaming during lab; they *would* use correct and safe cooking techniques; and eventually their turn would come where they *would* have to wash the dishes. Yes, cooking could be fun, but lab requirements must be met.

Things seemed to be moving along rather smoothly, or so she thought. Of course, there were always the day-to-day problems that had to be tackled, but overall she was pretty satisfied with her work and the students' accomplishments. She had, once again, settled into a routine.

Then one day she stepped out into the hall to close the door, as usual, just as the tardy bell rang. As she turned back to face the classroom, she was greeted with a most disturbing sight. Out of nowhere, a strange man had appeared, apparently jumping into the classroom through an open window. The obviously intoxicated man, drink in hand, began to yell out all sorts of obscenities and threats to the students.

"Go get one of the principals," Dianne quickly instructed one of the most dependable students.

The class sat spellbound by the narration of their uninvited visitor. Nobody said anything, and everybody was afraid to even move.

He continued ranting and waving his arms around to emphasize his nonsensical discourse, apparently thinking that he was, in some way, "educating" the students.

Just as the principal appeared in the doorway, the man took off, running down the hall and out of the building. The principal gave chase, followed closely by several students from Dianne's class. She let them go, rather than calling them back, hoping to find out what the outcome of the encounter might be.

They came back to the room a few minutes later.

"Well, what happened?" Dianne inquired.

"Oh, nothing much," one of them replied. "The man just ran off down the street."

"Did any of you know him?" she asked the class.

"No, we've never seen him before," several of them responded simultaneously.

"I don't know who he was, but let's just hope he doesn't ever come back. From now on, we'll keep the windows closed partway so that nobody else can jump in from the outside," she announced.

Later that day she reported the experience to Roy.

"You're lucky," he told her. "It could have been a lot worse. I was kidnapped and held at knifepoint in front of my class here last year by a young black female."

"You're kidding!"

"No, it really happened. And to make matters worse, she told me what she was going to do to me with that knife and exactly how she was going to do it."

"How did she get into your room?" Dianne asked.

"Apparently, she just wandered out of the street into the building. I think she was on drugs."

"Wow, that's really scary. How did you get rid of her?"

"Eventually, she decided that she'd had enough, so she just left through the classroom door."

"Did you report it to the police?"

"Yes, they were called, but she was gone before they got here. As far as I know, they never found her."

"It appears that we are in more danger from the "street people" than from the students. I'm going to be extra careful around here from now on!" Dianne declared.

Fall always brought the annual "faculty study," a required, but unpopular topic with most teachers. Dianne's previous experiences had always involved attending meetings that were held after school. Most of them lasted at least an hour or more. Most of them had also been totally useless to her. They were always about improving reading skills in the elementary grades.

"I'm not a reading teacher," she had often complained. "I have no skills or interest in teaching reading. I'm supposed to be teaching students how to cook and sew."

She was surprised to learn that the faculty study at Carter C. Raymond would be held during the regular school hours. Senior students were always assigned to watch over the classes while the teachers attended the meetings.

"I'm not going," she vowed as she and Roy discussed the plans for the meeting during their daily morning visit in the faculty lounge.

"First of all, it's illegal. They shouldn't be sending high school students in to keep teachers' classes. What if something happened to one of the other students? We could be sued. Besides that, there's just too much stuff in the home ec. department that people could get into if a teacher were not in the room. There's no way that I'm going off and leaving my department in the hands of a student!"

"Suit yourself," said Roy. "I don't want to go, either, but I guess I will. I'll give you a full report on what happens."

"If anybody asks, just tell them that I'm taking inventory in the department and I can't go off and leave all the equipment out," she said. It was true. She had gotten the students to take the equipment out of the kitchen cabinets and was inventorying to see if it was all still there after the summer break.

She didn't have a chance to talk to Roy again that day until after school had been dismissed.

"Boy, are you in hot water," he reported. "Some of those other teachers were really mad because you didn't come to the meeting."

"I wonder how they would like it if I called the Central Office and reported them for holding an illegal meeting in the middle of the school day," she retorted.

"You haven't heard the worst of it yet," he said. "Mrs. Byrd was especially ticked off. She made sure that you were appointed the head of one of the committees for the study."

Dianne laughed. "Is that all? Then the joke's on her! The chairman gets to delegate all the duties to other people on the committee. She actually just made life easier for me. I get to assign all the work to other people instead of having to do it myself."

"Hey, I hadn't thought of it that way. Good point!" exclaimed Roy.

It wasn't Dianne's first encounter with Mrs. Cassandra Byrd, one of the black elementary teachers. It had become clear to Dianne that Mrs. Byrd would never be the president of her fan club. It all began one morning when Dianne was sitting in the teachers' lounge before school started. She was deeply lost in thought, contemplating some of her family problems that had nothing to do with school. There were several members of her family who were ill, including her grandmother, Rose, who was in the hospital following a stroke.

Mrs. Byrd had entered the lounge and chirped out a cheery "Good morning" as she went over to the counter to sign in. Dianne had been so engrossed in her own private thoughts that she didn't even see or hear Mrs. Byrd.

Later that morning she had received a note that was hand delivered by an elementary student. Upon reading it, she was flabbergasted to see that Mrs. Byrd was accusing her of ignoring her in the lounge and further accusing her of being racially prejudiced. The note ended with the statement "In my opinion you are most unprofessional."

After thinking about it, Dianne had dashed off a reply. "I am sorry that you think I was ignoring you, but, in truth, I was thinking about my family problems and did not even see or hear you. In my opinion, it is unprofessional to write nasty notes to other teachers. Sincerely, Dianne Hollis."

She had reported the incident to Roy later that day.

"I was in there when she came in," he said. "I heard her say 'good morning,' but I wasn't aware that she was directing the remark to you. I thought it was just a general 'good morning' to everybody who was in the lounge at the time."

"I didn't even hear her," said Dianne. "I guess I'll have to try to be more alert from now on and think about my problems on my own time."

As the year went by, Dianne was soon assigned more duties in addition to teaching. The school needed a banner to carry in parades, and she was the logical person who was called on to design and make it. Mr. Hale, one of the math teachers, was somewhat artistic. He had drawn two figures of a ram, the school's mascot, on some white felt. Dianne was to make a banner in the school colors using red satin with white felt letters and white fringe trim. The rams were to be sewn onto each end of the banner. It would be fitted crosswise onto two pipes for parades. The top pipe would pass through a casing and extend one foot from each side of the banner in order for the carriers to be able to hold onto it as they marched. The bottom pipe was for weight only and would be totally enclosed in another casing.

She worked diligently on the project for an entire week. When she presented it to the principal, he was very pleased with the results.

"Miss Hollis, you are an excellent seamstress. We are going to have to think up some more projects for you," he commented.

"Thank you. I'm glad you like it," she replied, relieved to have the project completed and secretly hoping that no more were coming her way.

Such was not the case. As the Christmas holidays approached, Dianne was, once again, summoned to the principal's office. Christmas vacation was only a week away.

"Miss Hollis, I would like for you to prepare the food for a faculty Christmas party," he told her. "And I want a bowl of punch at each end of the table. I want one bowl of red punch and one bowl of green punch."

"It's pretty short notice, but I'll see what I can do," she reluctantly agreed. "However, there is one stipulation. There simply isn't enough time for us to make the food in the home economics department, so the cookies will have to be 'bought' ones."

"If it's 'bought' cookies it must be, then so be it," he replied. "The main thing is to have the party. I want to do something for the faculty."

Dianne walked back to her room slowly, racking her brain for punch recipes. How am I going to come up with two different colored punches in flavors that are compatible? she wondered. I have recipes for a red punch and a green punch, but they don't go together.

Finally, she decided on one of her old stand-by favorites—punch made with sherbet and ginger ale. I'll use raspberry sherbet for the red punch and lime sherbet for the green punch. That's a nice, simple solution to the problem.

Dianne bought the food and table decorations. Using the school's ditto machine, she ran off some red and green party invitations for the faculty. On the day of the reception, she had some of the senior girls set up the refreshment table. She was somewhat embarrassed to be serving cookies that were not homemade, but there was nothing she could do about it. There simply had not been enough advance notice to prepare the food from scratch.

Word that a party was being held in the department had, once again, spread throughout the school.

"How come you be fixin' food for all those teachers, but you don't fix none for us?" complained one boy in her sixth hour class.

"That's just the way life is," she replied. "You can't expect to eat every time there's food in the department."

Her sixth hour class filed out of the room as the final bell of the day sounded, greatly disappointed that they were not going to get any of the goodies.

She barely had time to turn around before the teachers started flocking in. They seemed somewhat surprised that a party was being held in their honor. Nobody mentioned that the goodies were all 'bought' cookies. Dianne had recruited several of the most reliable girls to stay after school and help with serving the refreshments. She breathed a silent sigh of relief when it all seemed to go off without a hitch.

It was almost an hour later by the time that the last teacher had left the party. Dianne and her helpers worked swiftly to store the leftovers. They were all ready to go home, too.

"Miss Hollis, may we have some of these cookies?" one girl inquired. "That was hard work serving all of those refreshments."

"Yes, you certainly may. You deserve it," Dianne agreed. "But remember, I promised the girls who set it up that they could eat the leftovers tomorrow, so be sure to leave some for them, too."

Dianne was just about at the end of her rope. She had been running on adrenaline for several days. Every winter, it seemed, she always caught a cold that she couldn't shake, and this year was no exception. She always managed to make it until the holidays, and then she collapsed into a state of exhaustion. For once, nothing important was scheduled on the day before the Christmas break began, so she decided to stay at home and recuperate.

She called in sick the day after the faculty party, leaving specific instructions for which class was to be treated to the leftover refreshments. Written assignments were given for the other students. Whether or not the plan actually worked, she never knew. And she really didn't care. All she knew was that she simply could not make it to work another day and she needed some rest.

Upon returning to school after the holidays she discovered that the punch ladle was missing. She never did find out what happened to it. A thorough search of all the kitchen cabinets turned up nothing. *That's the first thing that's gone missing from the department since I've been here, so I guess I should consider myself pretty lucky,* she decided. *I can always buy another punch ladle.*

The next few days were filled with reviews and midterm exams, as grades were due two weeks after the Christmas holidays. Dianne, as always, had spent part of her Christmas vacation catching up on her paper grading. She was relieved when the semester ended and it was time to start studying new topics. She soon found herself snowed under trying to complete new lesson plans and tests for the new units she had planned.

As if she weren't already busy enough, she was surprised to look up one morning during her free period to see Mr. Cowan knocking at the classroom door.

"Miss Hollis, you are so good with those sewing projects. I have another favor to ask of you," he said as he entered the room.

"What is that?" she asked.

"We need two coronation robes for our Valentine Sweetheart Court for one of the February basketball games," he replied. "Could you design and make them for us?"

"Well, I'll see what I can do," she replied. "What sort of material did you have in mind?"

"We would like the robes to be made of white satin material. We need one for the high school queen and one for the elementary queen."

"Okay, I'll do my best. However, I will need two students to use as models so that I can measure them and get the right lengths."

"I'll pick out two girls to send to you. When would you like to see them?"

"Let me work up a design first, and then I'll let you know."

"Sounds good to me. Just keep me posted on what you need."

Great, just great! Another project to complete. Just what I needed. Oh, well. I knew that pattern design class I took in graduate school might come in handy someday. I guess that day has finally come! she reflected.

She could hardly wait for the school day to end so that she could get started on the project. Even though it meant a lot of extra work, Dianne liked nothing better than a challenge. She started working on the design as soon as she got home that afternoon.

After drawing several sketches, she finally decided on a design.

The robes would have a ruffle at the neck and ties at the neck to keep them closed. They would be long and full, extending to a train that would hang down in the back. A sleeveless design would be best, she decided, so they would fit any size figure. They would be lined so that no seams would show on either side. It was going to take a lot of material.

The next morning she told Mr. Cowan that she was ready to measure the students.

"I'll send them down to your room the first thing this morning," he promised. "You just buy whatever materials you need and bring us the bill."

The girls showed up soon after the tardy bell rang. They seemed rather excited to be serving as models.

"I just need to get some measurements to determine how long to make these coronation robes for the Sweetheart Court," she told them. "Thanks for helping me out."

After school that day, she did some quick calculations to figure out how much material she was going to need.

Well, there's only one place to go that might have the kind of material I need in the quantity that I need, she decided. That would be Hancock Fabrics in Alexandria. They have all sorts of material for formal dresses and bridal dresses. If they don't have what I need, they can order it for me.

Luck was with her when she stopped in the store on her way home from school that same day. Not only did Hancock's have the exact material she needed, they also had large quantities of it. White satin was the most popular material for wedding dresses, so they always kept a good supply on hand.

Relieved to have obtained the materials she needed so easily, she soon set about working on the projects. She decided it would be easier to cut them out at school using the large cutting tables in the sewing lab. After that, sewing them together at home seemed to be the best plan.

She began working on assembling the projects during her spare time. Keeping the white satin off her kitchen floor and keeping her cat, Boo, off the white satin proved to be the main problems.

"No, Boo. I didn't buy this for you to sleep on," she scolded as he tried to step onto the large mass of flowing fabric. "Keep off the fabric, and that means you!"

Boo retreated to his usual place on the couch, twitching his tail to show his annoyance at being shooed away. He liked to stay close to Dianne and being rejected always put him in a bad mood.

After working on the projects for several weekends in a row, she draped the finished robes over two coat hangers and hung them over the bedroom door. *Not too bad, if I do say so,* she congratulated herself. *Dianne and her trusty "GoldenTouch and Sew Machine" to the rescue!*

She turned the robes over to the principals the next day. They viewed them appreciatively.

"Miss Hollis, you have come through for us again. You definitely have a talent for sewing," said Mr. Cowan. "We certainly thank you for all the extra work you have done for the school."

"You're welcome. I just hope the students enjoy the Sweetheart Court," she said.

With the sewing projects behind her, Dianne was free to concentrate on her classes again. The Home Ec. I and II classes were ready to sew. Each student was allowed to select their own pattern and materials. Dianne had obtained some copies of the discarded pattern books from Hancock's, and students looked through them to pick out their patterns. All patterns had to be approved by Dianne before they were purchased.

Most of the students elected to make spring garments, with shorts and tops being the most popular styles. Some of the girls in the advanced sewing class wanted to make their own prom dresses, and one girl wanted to make her own wedding dress. Dianne was a little skeptical that they would be able to complete the projects.

"Make your own wedding dress! Are you sure that you can sew that well?" she asked Beverly Dixon, one of her senior students.

"Yes, I promise you I can do it. I have been sewing ever since I was in the seventh grade," Beverly assured her.

"And Jackie wants to make a prom dress," Dianne exclaimed. "Those materials for formal dresses are really hard to work with. Are you sure you want to do that?" She directed the question to Jacqueline Metoyer, another senior girl.

"I can sew," Jackie replied. "You remember my blouse I made last year, don't you? It turned out pretty well."

"Okay, if you two girls think you can do it. But just be aware that it's going to be a lot of work. Once you start it, you have to follow through if you want to pass the course."

The sewing projects were proving to be more successful than they had been the previous year. For one thing, students now realized that they were not going to pass in home economics if they did not complete their assigned projects, and that included any and all sewing projects. Letting them pick out their own patterns also seemed to help. Dianne no longer had to listen to "Why do we have to make that? Can't we make something we like?" She was learning, along with the students.

At the end of the sewing unit, Dianne was so pleased with the results that she decided to put on a style show for the entire school. She contacted the art teacher, Mrs. Pamela Cripps, who agreed to have her art classes make the background decorations for the stage. Each student had to write up a description of their garment that they would model in the show.

Dianne edited the descriptions to come up with a script. Background music was selected and taped. Students who did not want to model their garments were assigned the duties of stage management and music monitoring. After all, somebody had to pull the curtains, she explained to them.

Students were given modeling tips during their home economics classes, and each student had to practice walking and turning. Dianne had gained some experience in modeling during style shows from her days in the 4-H club.

Since most of the students could not stay for after-school practice,

Dianne arranged for them to practice on stage during the last hour of the school day. It was pretty noisy because the stage was located in the school's gymnasium, but they managed. She had chosen the best reader from all the classes to be the narrator. Things seemed to be going rather well.

The next day the students were really excited and nervous about the show. Some of them wanted to back out, but Dianne wouldn't let them.

"You've come this far," she told them. "When you start a project, you need to finish it. Don't let me down now. I'm depending on you."

Things went off without a hitch. Everybody was on cue. The narrator did a spectacular job, and the music added the finishing touches to the program. They started out modeling the casual clothes and ended with the prom dresses. The grand finale occurred when Beverly stepped on stage wearing her wedding dress. It was a proud moment for Dianne. Things had come a long way from that first day she had walked into the classes, not knowing what fate had in store for her or the students.

Work in the other classes had also been progressing. The Home Economics III class was studying Housing and Home Furnishings, but there was a sad lack of materials to use as resources. Dianne decided to purchase a camera from Newcomb's Camera and Art Shop in Alexandria. Using it, she planned to create a series of slide presentations for the housing unit. She had quite a few magazines on homes and home furnishings, so she used those as reference materials. She was able to come up with over a dozen sets of slides for her classes. She also wrote the scripts and recorded the narrations for them on cassette tapes. It was a lot of work, and she paid for it with her own money, reasoning she would probably be able to use them in her later teaching years.

Towards the end of the unit, she decided that it was time for a field trip to Alexandria in order for the students to actually view some of the materials and furnishings they had been studying about. She made arrangements with several businesses and stores for an all-day trip for the girls. Just one problem remained—transportation. The group was too small to merit a bus and paying a bus driver for an all-day trip. Mr. Cowan came up with the solution.

"The school owns a van," he told her. "If you think you can drive it, I believe it will be just the right size for you and your class."

"How many people does it seat?" she asked.

"I'm not sure, but I think it probably seats about eleven," he told her.

"There are fifteen people in the class," she said. "How are we going to fit them all into the van?"

"Don't worry. I'll come up with something. You just worry about collecting the permission slips from everybody. Don't let anybody go who doesn't bring you a permission slip."

When the day for the field trip rolled around, Dianne gathered the students in the home economics department during first hour for roll check and final collection of permission slips. The students were eagerly anticipating the trip and missing a whole day of school to boot. Dianne's classes were assigned to go to the gym that day.

Mr. Cowan came down to the room to check on them. "I have the seating arranged for you," he said. "What I did was put some chairs in the van to provide the extra seats. Just be careful about starting and stopping because we don't want them to tip over."

The students traipsed out to the van, giggling and talking the whole time. They were arguing about who was going to get the back seats, always the favorite spot on field trips.

"Okay, girls, I guess we're about ready to go," Dianne announced as the last student climbed into place. "Remember to keep the noise down while we're traveling and be sure to stay with the group at all times whenever we get to one of our designated stops."

As she pulled out of the parking lot some of the girls began to squeal.

"Miss Hollis, these chairs are moving already. It's pretty scary!" one girl yelled.

"Stay calm. You're not going to tip over. I'll try to drive carefully," Dianne reassured them.

The van picked up speed as they entered the four-lane highway heading into Alexandria. Everyone quieted down, and Dianne grew more confident about handling the vehicle. She was silently congratulating herself on her driving skills when a garbage truck pulled up beside the van.

"Miss Hollis, those men are staring at us," complained another girl named Dinesha.

"Yeah, now they are waving at us," added a third girl named Sonya.

"Let's leave them behind, Miss Hollis. We don't want nothin' to do with them," declared still another student named Gerrilynn.

"First you want me to go slow. Now you want me to drag race. Make up your minds," teased Dianne.

"Go, Miss Hollis, go. We can outrun them!" exclaimed Gerrilynn.

"Okay, hold on. But I'm not drag racing, in case anybody asks. We're just going a little faster than usual," said Dianne as she mashed down on the accelerator to gain more speed.

"Go, go, go," came the chant from all the students. "Yeah, Miss Hollis, you did it," they yelled in unison and burst into applause as the van began to pull away from the garbage truck.

"You would make a good racecar driver," exclaimed Dinesha. "Way to go, Miss Hollis."

"I knew you had a wild streak in you," said Sonya. "Just wait until I tell the boys about this!"

"Remember, I said I wasn't really racing. We'd better keep this our little secret, or else we might all get into trouble," cautioned Dianne. "Let's just concentrate on learning what we're supposed to from this field trip."

The rest of the morning went by without incident as they visited several furniture stores, including Hemingway's and Downs' Furniture. They also stopped by the Sherwin Williams store to view paint and wallpaper samples. By then it was almost time for lunch.

Each student had been instructed to bring enough money to

buy at least a burger and a soft drink at Burger King. Food was always on their minds, and they didn't want to miss any meals, so everyone complied. They piled out of the van as soon as Dianne stopped the motor in the Burger King parking lot. She was feeling a little hungry herself.

They went through the line quickly and began finding a place to sit. Dianne picked up her tray and headed towards one of the tables the girls had selected. It was about that time she became aware that she was receiving some rather odd looks from the white people in the restaurant. To make matters worse, not all of the looks were that pleasant. It was becoming apparent that many people were wondering why a lone white person was choosing to sit and dine with a table full of black students.

Dianne felt somewhat uncomfortable, but she managed to totally ignore the stares. It's really too bad the people don't know my situation, she pondered as she slowly bit into her burger. I might have felt the same way a couple of years ago, but now these are my students, and I am not ashamed to be seen eating with them. I don't care what the old biddies and bigots think of me.

Fortunately, none of the students seemed to be aware of the unkind looks and obvious gossip about the situation. They finished off their food in short order and were ready to head out for the next destination.

The last place on their list was Sears, where they were to listen to a presentation on window treatments, draperies, and linens. Dianne knew Linda Winn, the clerk in that department, because she had taken a short course on home decoration under her through the Sears store.

The presentation ended a little earlier than Dianne had anticipated. Nobody wanted to get back to school early, so the students begged her to let them walk around in the mall.

"Okay, you may have exactly thirty minutes to look around," she agreed. "However, you must stay with at least one other person. Don't go anywhere by yourself. I'm going to park myself on one of these benches and rest. Be back on time, because we have to leave promptly in order to get back to school for you to catch the bus home."

Everyone showed up on time, as instructed, to board the van for the final leg of their journey. It had been a tiring, but happy day. Dianne sincerely hoped that they had learned something from the trip. They pulled up into the school's parking lot a short time later, just ahead of the final dismissal bell.

"That was fun, Miss Hollis," said Gerrilyn as she exited the van. "Thanks for taking us."

"Yeah, it was really fun. Let's do it again," said Dinesha.

"My favorite part was the drag racing," added Sonya.

"Remember, we weren't drag racing," instructed Dianne. "We were just driving a little faster than usual. Please, don't say 'drag racing'!"

Dianne had also continued to teach one class of General Science. They were a little calmer than the students she had encountered during her first semester at Carter C. Raymond. For starters, she was there from the beginning of the year, so she knew exactly what materials she needed to teach. Also, word had apparently gotten around through the student body that she expected students in her classes to come prepared to work, not to goof off. Notes would be given, and tests were a weekly requirement.

There had been a few problems, such as boys tussling before class began. One day two boys got into a shoving match and broke out one of the bottom window panes. She put in a request with the janitors for repairs, but they were slow in coming. She eventually patched up the broken pane with a large piece of bulletin board paper. She assigned the seat next to the broken window to Charles King, the boy who had broken it. When wintertime rolled around, he began to complain.

"Miss Hollis, it's cold back here by this broken window. Why can't I move somewhere else?"

"That's too bad, Charles. You should have thought of that before you broke it. Sorry, but you aren't moving anywhere. Let that be a lesson to you not to roughhouse with somebody in a classroom," she replied, secretly enjoying his discomfort.

She added as much interest to the class as she could by giving a few demonstrations and showing filmstrips and 16mm films. However, a classroom without a laboratory could only go so far. As the springtime months approached, she came up with an idea.

One of the favorite attractions in the Alexandria area was England Air Base. They often had air shows for the public, and field trips by school groups were always welcomed. Dianne decided that it would be a good experience for the students to see some of the things they had studied being put into practice. She arranged for an all-day field trip to the base for her science class along with the General Science class of her fellow teacher, Mr. Dwayne Turner.

This time there were enough students to take the bus, so Mr. Cowan arranged for one of the janitors to drive for them. "What we do is send a picnic lunch for them," he told her. "Just tell Mrs. Young, the lunchroom manager, how many students you have going, and they will prepare it for you."

"What about keeping the milk refrigerated?" she asked.

"What they usually do is freeze the milk. It is thawed out by the time the students get ready to eat it, so you don't have to worry about taking an ice chest," he informed her.

"And don't forget to collect permission slips from all the students, too," he added.

"Okay, great. Thanks for all the help and the advice," she said.

The students were ecstatic about going on a trip and missing a whole day of school. Dianne was a little worried about taking a group of almost sixty students but having Mr. Turner along as back-up for the discipline helped to soothe her nervous state.

On the day of the trip, they arrived at the base entrance gate and were given directions on where to go. The tour began without a hitch. One of their first stops was the flight control center, where they were given a demonstration on how incoming planes were directed in their landings. It was pretty exciting to be close to so much action.

Dianne had dressed especially well that day, wearing a beige pantsuit with a dark brown shell top. *After all,* she had reasoned, *there are a lot of eligible men on the base.*

As they left the flight control center, one of the girls whispered to her. "Miss Hollis, some of those men were asking us about you. They wanted to know if you were married."

"Oh, really?" Dianne replied. "That's very interesting."

"Yeah," added another student, "we told them you are engaged."

"Well, gee, thanks. If it's left up to you students I'll probably be single for the rest of my life!"

The tour continued around the base with the students getting a complete picture of everything that went on inside the Air Force. One of their favorite stops was at the flight simulator station. Several of the students got to actually try out the devices, although most of them crashed their "planes."

Following the tour, they ate their lunch at the base picnic grounds. Then it was time to head home.

"Don't drive too fast," Dianne instructed the bus driver. "We don't want to get back to school too early. Otherwise, we will all have to go back to class."

"Don't worry, Miss Hollis. If we get back early we'll just stay on the bus, and we can all sing campfire songs," said one of the students.

"Thanks for the suggestion, but I think I'd rather go back to class than hear you sing," Dianne retorted teasingly.

As the year drew to a close, Dianne reflected on some of the events that had transpired. Overall, I would have to say this year has been pretty successful. We managed to have some halfway decent cooking labs. The students did well with their sewing projects and even put on a style show for the entire school. I made my slides and lesson plans for the housing unit, and the girls in that class got to go on a field trip. The science class wasn't

too bad behavior wise, and I think they enjoyed their trip to the airbase. I made the school banner and the coronation robes for the Sweetheart Court. I sponsored the faculty Christmas tea and chaired a committee for the faculty study. What more could they want of me? Yes, I would say that I definitely earned my paycheck this year. Now if I could just get my social life on track, life would be grand!

Chapter 19

As the school year had progressed, Dianne had gone through some changes in her life outside the classroom. For starters, she and Roy had discussed carpooling to save on gasoline. The subject came up one day as they were sitting in the teachers' lounge.

"I've been thinking about how I could cut down on my expenses," Roy told her. "My wife and I are on a tight budget now that the new baby has arrived. We used to have two vehicles, but we had to sell the Camero, so now we just have the little Volkswagen station wagon."

"Doesn't it get good gas mileage?" Dianne inquired.

"Yes, but we still need to cut back. That's why I was wondering if you would be interested in carpooling with me, since we both live in Pineville."

"I don't know. I'll have to think about it. I've never been in a carpool, and I like my independence," she said.

"Oh, boy, carpool with Roy. You've got to be kidding!" Don Paulk interjected. "Let me tell you about my experiences carpooling with him."

"Oh, come on, it wasn't that bad," protested Roy.

"Not that bad! You're the reason I gave up smoking a pipe," Don continued. "You know, he never remembers to buy gasoline. His wife has to fasten notes on the sun visor reminding him that the car is about to run out of gas. He always thinks he has a few more miles to go on fumes. One day I was riding with him when we came to the south traffic circle. I was smoking my pipe at the time. He ran out of gas right in front of a semi, and I bit my pipe stem in half."

"You're kidding," exclaimed Dianne.

"No, it's true."

"Aw, come on, man," said Roy.

"And that's not the only time," added Don. "Another time I was smoking my pipe again when he ran out of gas just before we got to the gas station. We coasted in, barely missing the gas pumps, and I bit another pipe stem in half. That's when I decided to give up smoking a pipe for good."

"Well, I've already seen his tailgating in action. This is an entirely new angle," teased Dianne. "Let me think about it overnight, Roy, and I'll give you my decision."

Later that night she pondered over the situation. Roy's not the only one on a tight budget. I'm doing okay, money wise, but it never hurts to save a few dollars. The question is, would it be worth risking my safety to ride with Roy, considering his sometimes-unsafe driving techniques? I think I'll give it a try and pray that God will watch over me, as He always seems to do.

She broke the news to Roy the next day. It didn't take long for word to circulate around the school that they would soon be carpool partners.

"Don't tell me you're riding with 'Wild Man Roy,'" exclaimed Mrs. Cripps as they sat in the teachers' lounge during the lunch break. "Have you heard about his driving?"

"Yes, Paulk gave me a pretty good description of what to expect, but I decided to give it a try, anyhow. If it gets too wild, I can always quit," replied Dianne.

"Hello, I'm over here," interjected Roy. "If you want to talk about me, at least wait until I leave the room."

They began their carpool arrangement the following week, agreeing to alternate weeks on driving their vehicles. When it was

Roy's turn, he and his wife picked Dianne up at her apartment and then dropped his wife off at the school where she taught. During Dianne's week to drive, she picked Roy up at his house, leaving his wife free to use their station wagon.

There was a water leak at the edge of the road close to where Dianne had to back out every morning. She called the City of Pineville several times to report the problem, but nothing was done about it. It continued to leak, and the dirt around it grew softer and softer.

One morning she was backing out, as usual, but another car was sitting in the street close to the end of the driveway. She maneuvered carefully but misjudged the distance between her car and the water leak. One of her tires sank into the soft dirt. Try as she might, rocking the car proved to be of no avail in freeing the vehicle.

She traipsed back into her apartment and phoned Roy.

"You're not going to believe where I am right now," she told him.

"I'm no good at guessing, so just give it to me straight," he replied.

"My car is stuck in a mud hole at the end of the driveway. Phone the school and tell them that we are going to be late. I am going to walk up the street and get my uncle to see if he can pull me out. Otherwise, I'll have to call a tow truck."

Following the phone call, she walked briskly up the street and knocked on Uncle R. V. and Aunt Hazel's back door.

"Dianne, what are you doing up here at this time of morning?" her aunt inquired as she opened the door.

"My car is stuck in a mud hole at the end of my driveway, and I was wondering if Uncle V. could pull me out," she replied.

"I'll see what I can do, but I'm gonna use my old Kaiser, not the good car. Let me back it out and you can ride back down the street with me," said R. V.

When they arrived back at the stranded car, R. V. hopped out and quickly hooked a chain up to both vehicles.

"Okay, you get in and put the car in neutral," he directed. "I'm gonna pull you out backwards, so you steer. And don't hit my car when your car comes out of the mud hole!"

Dianne climbed back into her car feeling totally humiliated at getting herself into such a predicament. The other car was still parked by the end of the driveway, and the passengers seemed to be enjoying the side show.

R. V. put the Kaiser into gear and began pulling. Blue smoke billowed up from his spinning tires as the old Kaiser gave its all to the task at hand.

She felt a jolt as the wheel came free and rolled back onto the solid pavement.

"Girl, you're lucky," he told her. "I almost didn't get you out. Why didn't you report this leak to the city?"

"I did. Twice. But they never came to fix it," she replied.

"Well, I'm gonna call 'em when I get back home and tell 'em that they'd better get over here and fix it because one car got stuck and it's dangerous. Now, you'd better get on to school because I'll bet you're already late."

As Dianne and Roy carpooled for the rest of the school year, their friendship continued to grow. They shared many laughs, exchanging stories about their experiences with students during the school day. One day Dianne confided to Roy that she was thinking about getting a dog.

"We always had dogs as pets when I was growing up," she told him. "My little dog named Ruby was my best friend. My sister had a black cocker spaniel named Jettie, and I always wanted another cocker."

"Why don't you check the ads in the paper and see if you can find one for sale?" he advised.

A few weeks later she followed up on his advice, finding an ad featuring registered golden cocker spaniel puppies for sale. She called the number listed in the paper and got directions for finding the lady's house.

"The puppies are out in the back yard," the lady told her when she arrived. "Let's go out and you can see if you like them."

Always a lover of animals, Dianne was entranced with the cute puppies that were chasing each other around in playful fashion. "They're all cute. I can't make up my mind which one to pick," she said.

Just then she was approached by a friendly female puppy. "I think she likes me. This is the one I want," she decided.

After paying the fee and getting the AKC registration papers, Dianne deposited the puppy on her front seat and headed back to the apartment.

"You're cute, but I have a feeling that my cat, Boo, isn't going to like you," she told the puppy. "Maybe you'll grow on him. I have to think of a name for you, though. I can't just keep calling you 'puppy.'"

True to her prediction, Boo greeted the puppy by hissing and spitting as his tail fluffed up to twice its size. He immediately jumped up on the dining table and refused to come down as long as the puppy was in the room. It appeared that the two animals were not going to be friends.

Dianne went about her usual Saturday chores, leaving the puppy free to roam about the apartment. It had been a long time since she had owned a dog, and some of the problems she had faced with dogs had been forgotten. A short time later she walked into the bedroom and discovered a wet spot on the carpet.

"Oh, brother. I forgot that you probably haven't been housetrained," she commented to the puppy. "Guess I will just have to keep you off the carpet from now on."

She shooed the puppy back out into the kitchen and closed the door to the bedroom. That was only a temporary solution, though, because one of the two window air conditioners for the apartment was located in the bedroom. Closing the door would cut off too much cool air in the summertime.

What I need is some way to block the puppy from getting into the bedroom while still keeping the door open, she decided. *And I still have to think of a name for her. She reminds me of taffy, so I think that's what I'll call her—"Taffy." It's the perfect name!*

The following Monday she managed to corral the puppy in the kitchen, the only room in the apartment without carpeting. In addition to closing the bedroom door, she blocked off the living room by using a footlocker left over from her college days. Boo was content to lounge on the couch in the living room, out of range of the new puppy.

She mentioned the problem of needing something to block the doors to Roy as they drove to school that morning.

"I have a couple of pieces of plywood at my house," he told her. "They were left over from one of my carpentry projects. I think they would be just the size you need to block the doors."

"That would be great, if you don't mind bringing them by."

"Oh, no problem. I'll get them over to you this afternoon," he said.

A few days later she mentioned her problems with the puppy to her friend Margaret Paul as they were conversing on the phone.

"Yes, I already heard something about that," Margaret informed her. "I work with his wife, you know. She was complaining that she could never get Roy to do anything around the house, but when Dianne Hollis needs something, he's 'off like a shot.'"

Dianne laughed. "We're just friends," she commented. "All of the students think that we're 'dating' just because we carpool, but I would never get involved with a married man."

Roy had been enduring some teasing because of his carpooling arrangements. He was a ham radio operator, and he had a mobile radio unit in his car. Dianne enjoyed listening to him communicate with his radio buddies as they rode to and from school.

"Hey, Roy, who's that good-looking woman riding with you in the front seat?" one of his friends inquired one day. "How can you get away with that, being a married man?"

"Oh, that's my carpool partner. We're just friends," Roy commented.

"And be sure to tell him I'm a good girl," Dianne interjected.

"She said to tell you she's a 'good girl.'"

"Okay, Roy, if you say so. But you're one lucky guy."

"Don't I know it!"

As she continued to listen to Roy and his buddies exchanging friendly banter over the next few weeks, Dianne soon became familiar with their voices and call signs. They were almost like one big happy family.

Then one day an unfamiliar male voice came on. It immediately attracted Dianne's attention because of the pronounced Southern drawl.

"Hey, I've got to meet that guy. He talks just like I do," she told Roy.

"You know what, he's a single college student. His name is Rick Lundy. Maybe you should meet him," Roy commented.

"Oh, if he's a college student, just forget it. He's too young for me," she said.

"No, this guy's older. He just got back from serving time in the Navy."

"Really? Well, if that's the case, he might be okay then. Maybe I can meet him sometime."

A few days later as they were riding home from school, Roy made an announcement. "I've got to stop at a friend's house to pick up a radio part. I think Rick is going to be there. This is your big chance to meet him."

"Today! Oh, no, I can't meet him today. My hair's a mess," she said.

"It looks fine to me, but I know how you women are about your hair. You can just stay in the car and observe from a distance," he teased.

"That's him standing by the pickup truck," he observed as they pulled into the driveway. "I won't be long."

As Roy exited the vehicle, Dianne pulled down the sun visor on her side of the car, hoping that it would hide her from view. *Great, here's my chance to meet another eligible man, and it would have to be on a "bad hair day."*

"Well, what did you think? Roy inquired a few minutes later as he climbed back into the station wagon.

"I guess he's okay. He was too far away to tell."

"My radio club has a spring banquet coming up in a few weeks. I'm going to mention you to him and see if he wants to take you."

"Okay, we'll see if anything comes of that. Only time will tell."

"Has Rick called you yet?" Roy inquired a few days later. "I gave him your phone number, and he said he was going to call you."

"No, I haven't heard from him," Dianne replied.

"Well, he assured me he was going to call. I thought he would ask you to our banquet."

"No such luck. I haven't heard a peep."

What I need is an image change, she decided. Maybe a new hairdo would do the trick. I'm getting tired of this chin-length style with the side part. It's time to try something new.

She made an appointment for a haircut and permanent wave for the next Saturday.

On the night before her appointment, she was feeling pretty depressed. She decided to cheer herself up by ordering a pizza from Pizza Inn. *After all, today is payday, she had reasoned. I can afford to splurge a little.*

After picking up the pizza, she had just finished eating it when the phone rang. It was Rick.

"I was wondering if you would like to go to a movie with me tomorrow night," he said.

"Well, it's pretty short notice. I have an appointment tomorrow, but I think I will be through in time to go," she told him.

"I was also thinking that it might be a good idea if I came by tonight so that I would know exactly where you live. Would you like to go out to get a coke or something?" he asked.

"I guess I could do that. Sure, that would be okay," she replied. She then proceeded to give him the directions to her house on Payne Street in Pineville.

"Okay, here I go on another date, Boo. What shall I wear this time?" she wondered as she viewed the clothes hanging in her closet. "Something casual. A pantsuit would do, I think. Yes, this powder-blue pantsuit with the white collar would be just the thing," she decided.

A few minutes later Rick was knocking on the front door. "Now you two behave," she instructed Boo and Taffy as she answered the door.

"Hi, come in," she said. "These are my two pets. The cat is Boo and the dog is Taffy."

Boo regarded Rick suspiciously while Taffy barked out a friendly greeting, jumping up and down and wagging her stubby tail.

"Well, it looks like the dog likes me, but I don't know about the cat."

"Oh, he's just being a cat. It takes time for him to get used to a new person."

"Okay, if you're ready to go, let's head out. Where do you want to go?"

"I don't know. How about Hoppers? I used to stop there all the time when I lived in Lake Charles. It was about halfway home, so I stopped to get some food and stretch my legs."

"Nice car," she commented as they exited the apartment and headed towards his bronze-colored Firebird with a beige leather roof. "What year is it?"

"It's a 1970 model. I bought it just after I got out of the Navy with some of the money I had saved. They gave me a good deal on it because it was the last one on the lot, and they were getting ready for the newer models to come in."

A short time later they pulled into Hoppers.

"What do you want to order?" he inquired.

"Oh, I think I'll just have a Diet Coke," she said.

"I think I'll get a regular Coke," he said as he placed the order.

While they were waiting on the order, a blue Volkswagen station wagon pulled into the space beside them.

"Is that who I think it is?" he asked. "It looks like Roy and his wife."

"I think you're right!" Dianne exclaimed. "What a coincidence. I can't believe they ended up parking right beside us."

"Let me see if I can get him on my radio," said Rick. He and Roy were soon conversing.

"Man, I'm so sorry. I didn't realize it was you," Roy told him. "My wife told me not to park in this spot because your car reminded her of that Camero we had to sell."

"Yes, it just about broke my heart when we had to get rid of that car," his wife interjected.

"Looks like our orders are here. Talk to you later," said Rick.

"Okay, and I'll see you on Monday, Dianne," replied Roy.

They drove slowly back to Dianne's apartment, sipping their colas along the way.

When they arrived back at the apartment, Rick exited the vehicle and proceeded to open the door for Dianne. He walked her up the steps to her front door.

"Well, I guess I'll see you tomorrow. What movie do you want to see?" he inquired.

"I don't know what's playing. Did you have anything in mind?"

"How about *Papillion*? I've been wanting to see that one."

"It doesn't really matter to me. That will be fine if that's what you want to see."

"Okay, I'll pick you up about 6:30. See you tomorrow night."

Dianne let herself in and locked the door slowly. She hadn't mentioned the prospective new hairdo to Rick. Did I make the right decision about getting my hair cut? I don't know, but I'm going through with it anyhow. If I don't like it, I can always let it grow back out, she decided.

The next morning she was up bright and early preparing to go to her hair appointment. She had decided to have her hair cut into a short shag style because she liked the way it looked on one of her friends. It had been a long time since she had worn really short hair, almost back to the time of her college days.

At the beauty salon she endured several hours of snipping, perming, shampooing, rolling, and drying. It seemed almost like torture. *Will the results be worth it?* she wondered. *What have I gotten myself into? It's too late to back out. My hair is already cut and permed.*

"Well, what do you think? Do you like it?" the beautician inquired at the end of the session.

"It's different all right. I guess it will just take some getting used to," replied Dianne as she viewed the hairdo from all angles, taking a good look at what would turn out to be the worst hairstyle of her entire adult life.

After paying her fee, she quickly exited the salon and headed back to her apartment to prepare for her evening date. She ate a light supper and fed Boo and Taffy. Then came the task of, once again, deciding what to wear.

I'm going to stick with casual again for this date. Forget wearing dresses. I'm more comfortable in pantsuits, and that's what I'm going to wear. The question is—which one?

She flipped through the clothes hanging in her closet and finally made a selection. I think I'll go with the beige checked pantsuit. It always looks good on me, and it's not too dressy for a date to the show.

A short time later Rick was knocking on the front door. He looked slightly startled as she opened it.

"You look different," he commented. "You changed your hairstyle."

"Yes, and I'm not sure I like it, but I'm stuck with it now."

Rick escorted her out to the Firebird, and they headed across town to the Twin Cinema movie theater. Dianne was pretty nervous about the whole thing.

Here I am going on a date with a sailor. He's probably been with all kinds of girls. Somehow, I remember reading a story about a girl whose mother told her to always carry a quarter in her shoe whenever she went on a date. That way, she would have enough change to make a phone call if she needed somebody to come and pick her up. I don't know who I would call, though. I guess Uncle V. would be the logical person to call if I needed help.

A short time later they were sitting inside the theater, waiting for the picture to begin. Dianne had managed to carry on a fairly decent conversation during the duration, and she was feeling pretty proud of herself. Things seemed to be moving along smoothly.

The lights dimmed, and the feature began to play. All of a sudden, Dianne felt a hand on her knee. *Oh, dear. Looks like I might need that quarter, after all,* she thought. *What was I thinking, going out with a sailor?* She didn't move. Rick removed his hand and put his arm on the armrest. She breathed a sigh of relief, hoping that she could make it through the rest of the movie.

It contained some pretty raunchy scenes, including some with women flashing their bare breasts. Dianne could feel her cheeks burning in the dark. *Great, here I am looking at naked women while sitting next to a guy I don't even know.* She sent a silent prayer upstairs. *God, please give me the strength to get through this.*

When the movie ended almost two hours later, they headed for the lobby. Dianne was feeling rather self-conscious about her new hairdo.

"I hope I don't run into anybody I know," she told Rick. "I think I'll turn up my collar and try to hide behind it just in case I spot somebody who knows me."

Rick laughed. "I wouldn't worry about it too much. You look okay to me."

"You're lying! I know my hair looks horrible, but there's nothing I can do about it. I'll just have to wait for it to grow out."

They drove back to her apartment and Rick escorted her to the door.

"Thanks a lot, Rick. I enjoyed it," she told him.

"So did I. I'll call you soon," he promised.

Dianne unlocked the door and let herself in. "Oh, boy, Boo. That was some date. And here I am with the hairdo from hell. The guy said he would call me, but I'll bet I never hear from him again. Looks like you may still be the only male in my life."

A few days went by, and Dianne hadn't heard anything from Rick. In the meantime, she was enduring a lot of teasing about her new hairdo. The first comment came from Roy when she picked him up for school on the Monday after her date. After Dianne pulled into his driveway, he opened the car door to climb inside.

"Hi, how was your… whoa! What happened to your hair?" he inquired.

"I decided to change my image and got a new hairdo," she replied.

"Boy, I should say you changed it! Where did you get the idea for that hairstyle?"

"I saw it on one of my friends and thought it would look good on me."

"Well, I don't mean to criticize, but I think I liked the other style better."

"Oh, shut up, Roy! Sometimes you can be a real pain in the neck. Okay, okay, I get the message. The hairstyle didn't translate very well to me."

"Well, there's one consolation," he told her. "It will always grow back out again."

"That's true, but I may never hear from Rick again. I think this hairdo may have scared him off."

The reaction from the students wasn't much better.

"You cut your hair" was the first thing they said as soon as she met with each class.

"Whatever possessed you to pick that hairstyle?" some of them wanted to know.

The boldest comment came from a girl named Janet in her Home Economics III class.

"Miss Hollis, tell me where you got your hair cut," she said. "So I can be sure not to go there," she added before Dianne could reply.

"Okay, enough about my hairstyle. What's done is done, and I just have to live with it until it grows out," Dianne declared.

Dianne had about given up on hearing from Rick ever again. Almost two weeks had passed since their date to the movies. It was Valentine's Day, and she was all alone in her apartment. She had finished eating supper and was getting ready to type out a test when she heard a knock at her back door. Taffy began to bark, and Boo ran for cover behind the couch.

Who can be knocking at this time of night? she wondered. Should I even open the door?

She lifted the window curtain and looked outside. To her surprise, standing on her back doorstep was Rick.

"Hi, come in," she said as she opened the door.

He was holding an envelope in his hand. "I brought you a Valentine's Day card," he told her.

"Wow, this is a surprise. Thank you. I certainly wasn't expecting to see you tonight. Come into the living room and have a seat."

Taffy, as always, was delighted to see company once they were inside the house. Boo peeked out from behind the couch.

"Well, I see the dog is still glad to see me, but the cat is hiding," he commented.

"Oh, just give him some time. He'll come out in a minute when he gets used to you."

They sat on the couch conversing and watching T.V. A short time later, Boo emerged from his hiding place and jumped onto the couch beside Dianne.

"Hey, Boo," she said as she stroked his back. "We've got company."

Boo regarded Rick with distrusting eyes, his tail flicking.

"They say a cat is mad when its tail is moving," Rick commented.

"That's true," Dianne noted. "But, like I said, just give him some time. Cats don't take to people the way dogs do."

"I had a dog when I was growing up, but I never had much to do with cats," Rick admitted.

"They can be a lot of fun. They're actually more amusing to watch than dogs," said Dianne as she continued to pet Boo. "Look, I think he's getting more used to you now. His tail has stopped shaking. Why don't you try to pet him?"

"I don't want to get scratched."

"Oh, he can't scratch you. He doesn't have any front claws. I had to have him declawed after my landlady, Mrs. Oberia Price, redecorated my apartment one summer while I was out of town working on my master's degree. He was about to claw up that chair in the corner after she had it reupholstered. I couldn't let that happen."

"Hey, Boo. How are you doing?" Rick asked as he cautiously stroked the cat's back. "Ha! He didn't run away. Maybe he likes me after all."

"Consider it a compliment. Boo doesn't take to just anybody."

A couple of hours later Rick rose to leave. "Well, I guess I'd better be heading home."

"Do you have your own apartment?" Dianne inquired.

"No, I'm staying with my parents right now. I just got out of the Navy a few months ago, and they just moved back here from Pine Bluff, Arkansas. They're renting an apartment on Vance Street in Alexandria, but we're probably moving back to Colfax pretty soon. We have a house there. They were leasing it out, and they just have to wait for the people to move out before we can move back in."

"What kind of work does your father do?" she asked.

"He's in the restaurant business. He's managed all kinds of restaurants and cafeterias. We moved around a lot while I was growing up. Right now he's managing the cafe in the Montgomery Ward's store in Alexandria."

"Does your mother work?"

"No, not anymore. She's a licensed beautician, but right now she's just a housewife. She worked a lot when my brother and I were growing up."

"Just about everybody in my family is a teacher," said Dianne.

"I'm talking aunts, uncles, and cousins, in addition to me and my parents. We're a teaching family. That's what we do best."

"That's why I'd better go," he said. "You need your rest to deal with all of those students you'll be facing tomorrow."

"There's just one more thing before I leave," he added.

"What's that?" she inquired.

"This," he replied as he bent down and placed a gentle kiss on her lips.

"You know, I almost didn't come back," he told her laughingly. "I took one look at you in that new hairdo, and it almost scared me away."

"Oh, please, not the hairdo again!" she protested. "I'm letting it grow out again."

"Okay, I'm gone this time. I'll call you."

"Good night, and thanks for the Valentine's Day card."

Dianne closed and locked the door behind him.

"Well, Boo, can you believe it? A guy actually showed up after a second date. I don't know what's going to develop from this relationship. Only time will tell. Who knows? Maybe this time you won't be the only male in my life."

Chapter 20

"**Y**ou seem unusually chipper today," Roy commented as he climbed into Dianne's vehicle the following morning. "What's up?"

"Oh, nothing much," Dianne replied as she backed her car out of the driveway. "You'll never guess who came by my apartment last night."

"Gee, let me think. Could it have been Rick?"

"Yes, he showed up unexpectedly right after I finished eating supper. And he brought me a valentine, too."

"Really? That guy is just full of surprises!"

"And."

"What? Don't keep me in suspense."

"I think Boo likes him."

"Whoa! Boo likes him, huh? Well, that means he's in."

Roy had met Boo when he had helped Dianne carry some of her school supplies into her apartment on several occasions. He knew that anybody who passed the "Boo test" would be okay in Dianne's eyes. She had often mentioned that she thought animals were usually good judges of character. Anybody who wanted to be friends with Dianne had to make friends with Boo and Taffy, too.

Rick continued to come over to Dianne's apartment during the next few weeks. They went out on several dates, usually to the movies. She learned more about him each time they conversed.

"I found out I was about to be drafted," he told her. "That's why I joined the Naval Reserve. They gave me some tests and found out I am good at sending Morse Code. I have been an amateur radio operator since I was fifteen years old."

"What happened after you joined the Navy?" she asked.

"First I went to boot camp. Then they sent me to radioman school up in Bainbridge, Maryland. I could already send code, so they let me play the tapes for the other guys to learn. When I graduated, I got a special 'Golden Key' from the captain because I could send the code at over thirty words a minute."

"In fact," he continued, "our class was full of college graduates. We made one of the highest overall scores of any graduating class that had ever been through the academy. They let us out of class early on Fridays, and all the other guys were jealous."

"You were probably glad to get finished," she commented.

"Yes, I got to go home to see my parents. Then they shipped me off to Australia for the two years I was in the reserve."

"Australia! Why in the world would they send somebody who was in the Navy to Australia in the middle of the Vietnam War?"

"There was a radio station on the coast at the Northwest Cape, and we had to run it. I had to have a 'top secret clearance' to be able to pass the radio messages. We mostly stayed on base, but we did go into town once in a while. We were warned to stay away from the women because there are ten women for every man there. A lot of them were just looking for some guy to marry so they could get into the United States."

"I'll bet the guys really heeded that warning!"

"Most of us did, but there were some who ended up marrying girls from over there."

He laughed. "Also, the only time I ever got drunk was when I was stationed over there."

"What happened?"

"Well, it was Christmas, and we were depressed about not being at home with our folks. A bunch of us went out to the bars and started drinking on a dare. I was drinking rum. I drank so much I got sick when we got back to the base. Then the next day I had one heck of a hangover. That's the first and last time I ever got drunk!"

"I guess you don't care for rum anymore."

"No, I really don't care for alcohol at all. Some of the dark beer is pretty good, but I mostly stay away from alcoholic beverages."

That's good, Dianne thought. I really couldn't keep dating a guy who drinks, because I don't believe in drinking alcoholic beverages. It's against my religion, and it's not good for people's health, either. He doesn't drink and he doesn't smoke, so that's two points in his favor. Besides that, Boo and Taffy like him. I guess the next step is for me to meet his parents and for him to meet mine.

One night after they had been to a movie, Rick took Dianne over to meet his parents. The door to their apartment opened to a steep stairway that led to their upstairs apartment.

"Hey, are y'all up?" he yelled. "I'm bringing some company upstairs."

"I have to give them some warning," he told Dianne, "because my dad sometimes sits around in his underwear after supper."

Dianne climbed the steep stairway, not knowing what to expect. She was pretty nervous about meeting Rick's parents.

"Mom and Dad, this is Dianne Hollis, the girl I've been telling you about," Rick said.

"Dianne, these are my parents, Rosa and Sonny Lundy."

"Hellos" were exchanged, and Dianne was offered a seat on their sofa. She looked around the immaculate apartment. It was evident that Mrs. Lundy was an excellent housekeeper.

It was also evident that Rick had inherited his looks from his mother's side of the family. Mrs. Lundy, a full-blooded Italian, was a very small and petite person with sparkling brown eyes and an outgoing personality. Rick, likewise, was short with a stocky build. He had a dark complexion, brown eyes, a prominent nose, and dark curly hair.

His dad, on the other hand, was tall and had blue eyes and wavy gray hair that was thinning on the top. He had a ready smile and hearty greeting for anybody who came his way. Meeting and greeting people was one of his talents, and it had served him well in the restaurant business.

Dianne was soon feeling at ease among such pleasant folks. They were easy to talk to, and they seemed to be very down-to-earth people with no airs about them. Mr. Lundy always had a funny story or two to amuse their company. Mrs. Lundy, who was an excellent cook, usually had some type of refreshments prepared for guests. Entertaining people was their specialty, and they were very good at it.

———

"My mother wants to invite you over to supper sometime," Rick told Dianne a few weeks later. "She wants to know when the best time for you would be."

"Well, I'm pretty busy during the week, so I think sometime during the weekend would be best," Dianne replied.

"Okay, how about this coming Saturday night?" he asked.

"That would be good," she said.

"Let me check with my mother to be sure, but I'm fairly certain that date will be fine with her. She said to make it for your convenience because she doesn't work."

Rick picked her up on Saturday evening and they headed for the Lundys' apartment. "I think my mother has prepared one of her favorites for you—fried chicken," he told her.

"Whatever she has cooked, I'm sure it will be good," Dianne replied. "I'm looking forward to eating someone else's cooking for a change."

A short time later Dianne found herself seated at the Lundys' dining table with a delicious meal in front of her.

"I have a special way of cooking chicken," Mrs. Lundy commented as they began to pass the food around the table after Mr. Lundy had offered thanks. "I use a little something extra in the coating to make it crispy."

"You'll have to share your recipe with me some time," said Dianne as she helped herself to the chicken, mashed potatoes with gravy, and broccoli. "This tossed salad looks really good, too. I don't think I've ever seen such crisp lettuce."

"That's another one of her secrets," Rick noted. "She knows just how to prepare the lettuce to make it crisp. Plus she makes her own Italian salad dressing, too."

"It's all delicious," said Dianne as she sampled the food. "You are a very good cook, Mrs. Lundy."

"Thank you. I enjoy cooking. It has always been one of my hobbies," Mrs. Lundy replied.

"And eating has always been one of mine, so we make a perfect couple," teased Mr. Lundy. "Working in the restaurant business so many years has taught me to appreciate good cooking, no matter who does it."

"Can you cook?" Dianne inquired.

"Yes, I can, but I'm usually working, so I let her do most of the cooking."

"The only thing I didn't make for this meal is the rolls," added Mrs. Lundy.

"Believe it or not, making rolls used to be one of my specialties," commented Dianne. "I went to the 4-H Short Course in Baton Rouge twice in roll-making."

"Did you win?" inquired Mr. Lundy.

"No," replied Dianne laughingly. "By the time all of us got through with the rolls, our feet were hurting from standing up so long, and we just wanted to get it over with. We stuck as many pans of rolls as we could into the oven and mine ended up burning on the bottom both times. When the 4-H agents asked me to go the third year, I turned them down."

"Do you still make rolls?" Mrs. Lundy asked.

"No, I prefer to just buy them now. I got burned out on that!" Dianne exclaimed.

"Be sure to save room for dessert," Rick interjected. "I think she made another one of her specialties, lemon icebox pie."

"It's been a long time since I had lemon icebox pie. I used to make it all the time when I was growing up," said Dianne. "My mother depended on me to make the desserts after I learned how to cook. I started cooking when I was in the fifth grade in the 4-H club. My mother didn't want me to be like she was. She didn't know anything about cooking when she got married. My daddy said she didn't even know how to boil water. He had to teach her how to cook."

"Is that what inspired you to be a home economics teacher?" asked Mr. Lundy.

"Well, partly, I suppose. But I had a lot influences in my life regarding cooking and sewing. Of course, I think I inherited some of my talents from my grandmother Rose. She was an excellent cook and seamstress. However, I had some really good teachers when I was in high school. I'll never forget my two home economics teachers at Farmerville High. I had Mrs. Mary Louise Rabun in the eighth grade. Then I had Mrs. Lucille Stewart for the other four years of home economics. And I can't forget the home demonstration agents in Union Parish, especially Mrs. Bonnie Gaddis. They were all great."

"And maybe someday your former students will say the same thing about you," said Mrs. Lundy.

"I don't know. Retirement's a long way off. Right now I just have to think about what I'm doing from one day to the next and hope it all works out for the best," said Dianne. "At any rate, this has been a really delicious meal, and I thank you both for inviting me."

Dianne decided it was time to build a small yard for Taffy. There was an alley between her apartment and the garage where she parked her car. It was the perfect size to allow Taffy to get out and get some exercise. She ordered a roll of picket-type fencing and some steel fence posts from the J. C. Penney's catalog. Since she needed a way to get out of her back door, she also ordered a gate to go along with the fence.

After they arrived, she was faced with the problem of installing them. She was pretty sure she could do it herself, having grown up on a farm. However, she was greatly relieved when Rick offered to help. He was scheduled to come over on a Saturday morning to tackle the job.

In addition to putting up the fence, some wire had to be installed along the bottom side of the apartment because it sat up above ground level. Dianne had purchased some chicken wire and staples from one of the local hardware stores.

"You're definitely a privileged character," Rick told her several times as he worked diligently, trying to finish the job before dark. His neck was starting to turn red from exposure to the sun, and Dianne was starting to feel guilty about accepting his help. It had become evident during the course of the day that Rick was mechanically inclined. He seemed to be able to fix almost anything and putting up the fence had turned out to be a major project.

They let Taffy out in the yard when it was finished. She ran to and fro, excited to finally be allowed outside without being on a leash.

"She seems to like it," said Dianne. "Thank you so much for helping me. I don't think I could have done it by myself."

To show her appreciation, she treated him to a home cooked meal of broiled pork chops, baked potatoes, and broccoli. It was the first time he had sampled any of her cooking.

"These pork chops are really good," he commented. "I've never seen anybody cook them on a little grill like that. What kind of outfit is that, anyhow?"

"It's called a smokeless grill. I got it free when I bought a set of stainless-steel cookware," she replied. "The water in the bottom keeps the drippings from smoking. It's pretty neat because it's electric and you don't have to worry about going outside and starting up a charcoal barbeque grill."

"I guess I should have known that you are a good cook, you being a home ec. teacher," he said. "Everything is delicious."

"Thanks, I'm glad you are enjoying it. It's the least I can do after you spent your whole Saturday helping me install the fence."

Dianne began introducing Rick to some of her friends. The first ones to meet him were Barbara and Bill Hare. They drove over to the Hares' house one Saturday afternoon. After the introductions were made, Rick and Bill went out into the back yard to view some tomato plants Bill had set out. That left Dianne and Barbara by themselves in the living room.

"Well, what do you think?" Dianne posed the question to Barbara.

"I think you should set a wedding date," replied Barbara.

"I guess that means he passes inspection then," said Dianne. "Actually, we haven't talked about getting married. We're just dating right now."

"Oh, I can just tell. I think he's the one," Barbara told her.

"Your opinion means a lot to me. So far, we're hitting it off, but we haven't been dating that long. We'll just have to wait and see what develops," said Dianne.

The next on the list were Margaret Paul and her husband, Leslie. Dianne knew that Margaret was an excellent judge of character, and she was rarely wrong in her evaluation of people.

Rick and Leslie hit it off right away. They quickly found out they knew a lot of the same people. Leslie even knew one of Rick's uncles, W. K. Brown, who had been a Louisiana State Representative.

Margaret gave Rick her stamp of approval. "He seems like a really nice guy. I would say he's a 'keeper.'"

"We're just in the 'get acquainted stage' right now," Dianne told her. "I'm not sure how much I really like him. I know that he's a nice guy, but I think he likes me more than I like him."

"My advice to you is to just keep dating and see what happens.

You never can tell about relationships. Sometimes the ones that start out slowly are the best kind," Margaret replied.

"Okay, thanks for the advice. I think that's what I'll do."

Dianne decided it was also time for him to meet Aunt Hazel and Uncle R. V. After all, they had practically adopted her as their fourth child. They were the ones she always turned to whenever she needed help.

"When are we gonna meet that new boyfriend of yours?" R. V. asked her one afternoon when she stopped in for a quick visit. "Are you hiding him from us?"

"No, Uncle V. I've just been so busy that we haven't had time to come by," Dianne replied.

"Girl, you'd better make time to bring him by here! I want to see what kind of guy you're going out with."

"Yes, why don't you bring him by one Saturday afternoon?" commented Hazel. "I'll have a little something for you to eat, some cake or cookies."

"Okay, I'll see what I can do. He has to work half a day on Saturdays, though."

"Where does he work?" asked R. V.

"His family owns a wholesale business up in Colfax, and he works there. He just got out of the Navy a few months ago."

Dianne and Rick stopped by the Fultons' a few days later. Rick and R. V. were soon conversing like old friends. R. V. was delighted to learn that Rick knew a lot about repairing vehicles. Anybody who could discuss cars with him was okay in his book.

Aunt Hazel, likewise, soon put her stamp of approval on Rick. "He's such a pleasant person," she commented to Dianne. "I can see I've lost my movie partner. Looks like I'll have to find somebody else to go to the show with me from now on."

Chapter 21

hile Dianne's relationship with Rick had been moving along on a positive note, things weren't going as well with the rest of her life. Problems had developed with her family back on the home front of Rocky Branch.

It all started one weekend when her mother, Dolores, and her sister, Sallie, came to Pineville for a visit with Dianne. They had planned to spend the night, but a phone call from F. D. had changed everything.

"I just got a call from your sister, Nina, in Junction City, Arkansas," he told Dolores during their phone conversation. "Your mamma has had a bad stroke and is in the hospital."

"Oh, dear! I guess we had better head back home instead of staying here for the weekend," Dolores commented after hanging up the phone. "Gather up our belongings, Sallie. We need to get going as soon as possible."

"Gee, I'm really sorry you have to leave, but I understand. Please call and let me know how our she is doing," said Dianne as they headed out the door of her apartment.

"Okay, I'm sorry we can't stay, but I'm really worried about her. This is her second stroke, you know. We put her in the nursing home after she had the first one, and she got better. I don't know what is going to happen this time," replied Dolores.

"Well, just keep me posted. And drive carefully."

For the next few weeks, Dianne was in a constant state of nervous tension. In addition to dealing with school, she had to worry about her grandmother Rose's health. Dolores, she learned, had been driving to Bernice after work to check on Rose and also to sit with her some at night. The extended days and long drives were taking their toll on Dolores's health, too.

Dianne decided to go home one weekend to check up on the ailing family members. Dolores appeared to be especially tired and was having trouble catching her breath every time she walked across the room. One of her legs was swollen and red, but she refused to go to the doctor.

"I have a doctor's appointment next week," she told her family. "I'm not going until then."

"You really need to go," Dianne told her.

"There's no use arguing with her," said Sallie. "Once she has made up her mind about something, there's no changing it. I just hope she's okay."

Dianne and Sallie helped out as best they could while they were both at home for the weekend. They did most of the cooking and housecleaning, letting their mother rest.

Dolores was still worried about Rose's condition, so they volunteered to go over and sit with her one night during the weekend.

They were greeted at the hospital door by their aunt, Nina Bolen, who was known to them by the nickname "Auntie."

"It's really sweet of you two to come over here tonight," she told them. "There is a sitter who comes in at ten o'clock every night. I have been staying until then. I won't know what to do with myself, having a night off."

"We wanted to do it," Dianne reassured her. "Mother would have come, but she isn't feeling too well, so we volunteered to come in her place."

They went into the room where their grandmother lay upon the hospital bed. She was looking small and frail, unlike her old energetic self. Rose had grown up on a farm with a large number of brothers and sisters. After her two older sisters had married, she had stayed at home to help out with raising the younger children. She was no stranger to long days and hard work.

One of her sisters, Sallie, had married a man named Albert Gunter. Sallie had passed away shortly after the birth of their son, Otho, leaving Albert with a baby to raise. He had then married Rose and moved in with her family on their farm near Beech Grove in Union Parish. Otho had later died from pneumonia when he was only two years old. Albert and Rose had two daughters, Dolores and Nina, with Nina being the oldest by seven years.

Dianne and Sallie had visited the Gunters at their home place many times while they were growing up. In the summers Dolores would drive them up to spend a few days with Rose and Albert. Nina, who lived close by in Junction City, would come over and pick them up so they could stay with her for a few days to visit with their cousins, Albert and Rosemary Bolen.

It was the visits to the Gunter farm that had given Dianne a real picture of what old-timey country living was like. Rose and Albert still lived much like they did before the times of modern conveniences. Their house had no running water and no indoor toilets. Water had to be drawn from a well in their front yard, and they had what was considered a deluxe outhouse, it being a "two-seater."

Dianne liked to help Albert feed the chickens. During her younger years she had been assigned the task of feeding the chickens and gathering eggs at the Hollis farm. When she was only seven years old, her mother had arranged for one of the ladies in their church, Mrs. Mittie Ann Laster, to buy two dozen eggs from her every two weeks for fifty cents. That was a lot of money to a seven-year-old. Her favorite chore, however, was helping Rose milk the cows, although she wasn't very good at milking. She also liked to churn butter from the number four blue-and-white stone churn that Rose always left filled with milk and sitting by the fireplace.

Sometimes Albert would hitch their two mules, Jim and Joe, onto the wagon to take the girls for a ride. Their farm was a large spread consisting of two hundred and nineteen acres, so they had plenty of room for an outing. Once he even took them on a back road through their woods to a country store owned by their great-aunt Melissa Shinpoch and her husband, Jim.

While they did have electricity, Rose didn't like to burn the lights during the daytime. Dianne remembered the scolding she got one day when Rose came into a room where Dianne had the light turned on.

"Oh, honey, don't burn that light now," Rose had told her. "You're going to run my electric bill up to five dollars this month!"

Dianne also liked to play Rose's old pump organ every time she went to visit. She had taken piano lessons for three years, so reading music came easily to her. With stacks of church hymnals and old sheet music sitting on the organ, she had plenty of material to choose from. She loved that old organ, and Rose had promised it would be hers someday. That was a promise Dianne never forgot.

"A man offered to buy the old organ from me," Rose told her one time, "but I wouldn't sell it to him, because I had already promised it to you."

"Don't sell it, Ma," Dianne had pleaded. "Please don't ever sell it."

Rose's days of living on the old home place had come to an end when Albert passed away at age eighty-nine in 1967. She had moved in with Nina and her family. Her days of sewing, quilting, working in the garden, canning, cooking, and making jellies and preserves were over. It had been a good life, but it was time for her to move on.

Now here she lay in the hospital bed, eyes wide open, but unable to speak or communicate with the outside world. Dianne and Sallie were rather nervous about staying with her, but they felt they had no choice. Dolores simply wasn't up to making the trip. They didn't know what might happen while they were sitting there with Rose. Dealing with sick folks was something entirely new to them, because their family had been blessed with good health for most of their lives.

Dianne, as always, had some papers to grade, so she had brought them with her to the hospital. As she and Sallie settled in for their watch, Rose raised her head and looked like she was attempting to sit up.

"What's she doing?" Dianne wondered. "Do you think something is wrong?"

"No, I don't think so," Sallie replied. "I think she's just trying to see what you're doing."

"I'm grading papers, Ma," Dianne said. "Teachers always have lots of papers to grade."

"Maybe we should try talking to her," she added. "She seems to want to know what's going on. Do you think she knows who we are?"

"Probably," answered Sallie. "I can't think of anything to say, though."

"Maybe I should tell her I have a boyfriend. She was always worried that I wouldn't get married. She thinks I'm going to be an old maid," Dianne commented.

Dianne then proceeded to tell her grandmother about some of the events in her life during the past few weeks. "And you'll be happy to hear I have a boyfriend," she concluded at the end of her oration. "Maybe I won't be an old maid after all."

Sallie and Dianne's watch ended when the ten o'clock sitter arrived. They were relieved to be leaving, but sad to see their grandmother in such bad health.

"There's just not much we can do about it," Dianne told Sallie as they walked out to their car. "She's ninety-two years old, so her chances of recovering aren't very good.

The next morning they discovered Dolores's leg was worse, and she was still having trouble breathing. She had sat up all night, propped up in the bed with Dianne's backrest. Dianne decided that she should stay in Rocky Branch and take Dolores to her doctor's appointment on Monday. She phoned Mr. Cowan and asked him to get her a substitute.

On Monday morning Dolores's school was out for a holiday. Sallie headed back to Louisiana Tech, where she was a student, and F. D. headed to his teaching job in Junction City, Arkansas. That left Dianne totally responsible for getting Dolores to her appointment on time.

Shortly after they arrived at the doctor's office, Dolores was called to the back. Dianne decided to stay in the waiting room. She was looking through the magazines when Dolores came back into the waiting area.

"Take me to the hospital," she told Dianne breathlessly.

"The hospital! Are you sure?" Dianne asked nervously.

"Yes, the doctor said for me to go to the emergency room. I have a blood clot in my lung, and it is making my heart beat too fast. That's why I have been having trouble breathing."

They made it to the emergency room in short order. Dolores was immediately admitted because the doctor had phoned ahead that she was coming. Dianne muddled through all the insurance information in Dolores's wallet but was unable to come up with exactly what was needed for the hospital records.

"I'll have to go home and phone the Union Parish School Board Office," she told the admitting clerk. "I don't know very much about her insurance policies."

"We're going to go ahead and admit her because it is an emergency. You just phone me when you have all the information we need," the clerk replied.

Shortly afterwards, Dolores was settled into a hospital room. Dianne stayed to make sure that she was comfortable. Then she had to leave to check on the insurance policies.

"Mother, I'm going to go now," she told Dolores. "I'll be back to see you later."

"Okay," Dolores replied weakly. "I'll be all right. The nurses will take care of me."

Dianne drove back to Rocky Branch in a daze. Her mother being sick was something entirely new to her. Dolores had always been the tower of strength in the family, the one that could always be depended on, no matter what might happen. Now here she was, unable to help herself.

Please, God, take care of her, she silently prayed as she drove on the familiar road, crossing the D'Arbonne bridge and passing through the swamp area.

As soon as she arrived at home, she phoned the school board office. She explained the situation to them and got the necessary information about Dolores's policies. Then she phoned the hospital and relayed the information to them.

The next task facing her was to get in touch with her father. She called Junction City High School and asked to speak to F. D.

"He's in class now. We can't get him out of class for a phone call," the office secretary told her.

"This is his daughter, and this is an emergency," said Dianne.

"Well, if it's an emergency, we'll try to get him to the phone," replied the secretary. "Just hold on."

A short time later Dianne was conversing with F. D.

"Mother's in the hospital," she told him. "The doctor says it's her heart. The blood clot has gone to one of her lungs, and it's making her heart beat too fast."

"Her heart!" F. D. exclaimed unbelievingly. "That's hard to comprehend."

"Well, that's what the doctor said. I'm going to try to notify Sallie. Then I'm going to have to go back to Pineville because I can't miss too much school. I can't do anything else for her while she's in the hospital."

After phoning Sallie in Ruston, one more task befell Dianne. She had to find somebody to substitute for Dolores because she wouldn't be able to go back to school for some time, if ever.

The logical person to call was the school board member from Rocky Branch, Mr. Raymond Chapman.

He was shocked to learn Dolores was in the hospital.

"How long do you think it will be before she is able to come back to work?" he asked.

"Frankly, I don't think she will be back for the rest of the year," Dianne informed him. "You'll have to find somebody to take her place because I don't know what to do. She's the principal, so she's the one who is normally in charge of getting substitutes. Now we have to get a substitute for her."

"Don't worry. I'll take care of it," he reassured her. "I just hope she'll be okay."

"Me, too," replied Dianne. "All we can do is wait and see."

Back home in Pineville, Dianne could scarcely concentrate on her schoolwork. Her mother's and grandmother's illnesses were constantly on her mind. Her weeks became one constant merry-go-round.

On Friday mornings she would drop Taffy and Boo off at the vet's office for weekend boarding. Then as soon as school let out on Friday afternoons, she rushed home, packed a few belongings, and headed to Rocky Branch. On the way home she usually stopped at the hospital to visit Dolores, who was in for a long haul.

The rest of the weekend was spent cooking, cleaning her parents' house, and doing F. D.'s laundry. She also had to pick up any groceries that were needed. Actually, the grocery list proved to be rather short because Dolores always kept a full pantry. She had canned and frozen foods from F. D.'s plentiful annual garden. They had their own beef, so the freezer was always full of meat. The main decision Dianne had to make was what to cook from the bountiful supply.

One weekend she decided to thaw and cook some T-bone steaks. F. D., who had been living mostly on sandwiches and canned foods, was happy to get a home cooked meal again.

"I'm going to pay you a compliment," he told Dianne as he dug into a dinner of tossed salad, steak, and French fries. "You can cook as good as your mamma. She couldn't cook when we first got married, but now she's a really good cook."

"Thanks, Daddy. I'm glad you like it," replied Dianne. *Good old 4-H training to the rescue again,* she thought.

On Sunday afternoons she always headed back to Pineville, stopping by the hospital for another visit with Dolores. Boo and Taffy had to remain at the vet's office until Monday afternoons, when she would pick them up on the way home from school.

Keeping up with her schoolwork and keeping up the Hollis household at the same time was a formidable task. But Dianne was always a trooper, never afraid to pitch in to do her fair share of the work, a trait inbred from her days of growing up on a farm. Still, she was tired most of the time, being unable to catch up on her rest on the weekends. She was beginning to wonder how much longer she could keep up the pace.

Then more tragedy struck. Her grandmother Rose was unable to recover from the stroke and passed away quietly one night. Dolores, still in the hospital, was unable to attend the funeral. Dianne, Sallie, and F. D. represented the family at the sad affair. The services were held at the Beech Grove Methodist Church, just down the hill from the old Gunter homestead. It was appropriate because Rose, who was not a Methodist, used to play the piano for them on Sundays.

"I would play the songs in whatever key they wanted," she had told Dianne one time.

Rose was buried alongside Albert in the Beech Grove cemetery. Land for the cemetery had been sold to the church for thirty-five dollars by her father, Nathan Dettenheim, who had also provided the Union Parish School Board with an acre of land for the Beech Grove Elementary School.

Their aunt Nina invited them to come and eat at her house because people had sent all kinds of food. They declined the offer and headed back to their house in Rocky Branch.

Dolores was heartbroken because she was unable to attend her beloved mother's funeral. Dianne stopped by, once again, to visit her on the way back to Pineville.

"How did she look?" Dolores asked.

"She looked good, really good, Mother. It was a beautiful funeral. She got some pretty flowers, too."

"She always loved flowers," said Dolores. "I remember our yard being full of all kinds of flowers. We had gardenia bushes and roses of all colors, pink, red, and yellow."

"Yes, I especially loved the pink rose bush that grew by the back door," Dianne commented. "And don't forget the watermelon-colored crape myrtles that grew in front of the chicken yard. Those things were as big as trees."

"Then there were the red and yellow cannas that grew all the way across the house by the edge of the front porch. And there were always yellow daffodils and white narcissuses. The yellow forsythias and the white bridal wreaths were pretty, too." Dolores added. "I'm glad I got some cuttings from some of the roses and also the hydrangea that grew by the back door."

"Yes, I remember it was pink and ours is blue," observed Dianne.

"That was because we always threw the soapy water out the back door, and the soap turned it pink," Dolores explained.

"I got some cuttings from the old pear tree, too, and I finally got one to grow in my back yard. That tree was set out by your great-grandfather, Nathan Dettenheim," she continued.

"I remember those pears. I have never tasted any others like them. They were always soft and good, not like the hard pears in the grocery stores today. I also remember gathering the scuppernongs and muscadines from the vines that grew on her back fence. I used to eat them right off the vine," said Dianne.

"Yes, we got a lot of good jelly from those vines, and a lot of good, canned pears and pear preserves from the old tree. We had peach and apple trees in the back, too."

"She also had a lot of four o'clock vines growing on the back fence. She taught me how to make ballerinas from the flowers, and I taught Sallie how to make them. We had lots of fun with that when we were up there visiting during the summer. I remember there were a lot of good places to hide Easter eggs when we were growing up, too. I always loved to go up there to visit on holidays. And I'll never forget the big old pecan tree that was in the pasture in front of the house. It was the only one I could climb because it had a low limb. Our cousin Rosemary could climb all kinds of trees, but Sallie and I just weren't that athletic." Dianne reminisced.

"No, you and Sallie never were very good at climbing. I remember what happened one time when Sallie was little. She climbed on top of the monkey bars at the Rocky Branch school and got scared. She grabbed my hair and almost pulled it out before I could get her down!"

Dianne laughed. "We might not be athletic, but at least we're good at cooking and sewing. I think we inherited some of that from Ma."

"Yes, I suspect you did. I wish I had gotten some of her recipes, but she never wrote any of them down. And speaking of food, I'm about tired of this hospital food. I just can't eat the stuff. It has gotten where it just turns my stomach to even look at it or smell it. I'll be glad when I get out of this place. I'm ready to go home."

"Well, maybe it won't be too much longer. I think you've been here for a month now. The doctor says you're getting better, so he'll probably let you go home soon."

"I hope so."

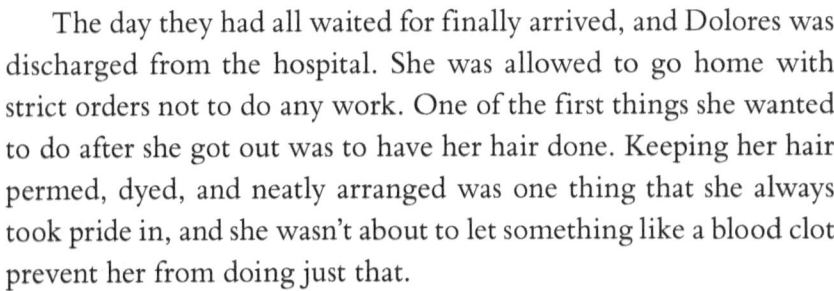

The day they had all waited for finally arrived, and Dolores was discharged from the hospital. She was allowed to go home with strict orders not to do any work. One of the first things she wanted to do after she got out was to have her hair done. Keeping her hair permed, dyed, and neatly arranged was one thing that she always took pride in, and she wasn't about to let something like a blood clot prevent her from doing just that.

"I don't want to have gray hair," she always told her family. "I intend to go to my grave with my hair dyed."

At that time, teasing hair and adding to its volume with hairpieces was in style, and Dolores was no exception to the rule. She had bought a little hairpiece to add to the top of her hair, and she wouldn't be caught anywhere without it.

Dianne decided it was time for Rick to meet her family. So as soon as Dolores got out of the hospital, she began making plans to that effect. They were scheduled to drive up one Sunday for a visit.

"Don't worry about food, Mother," she told Dolores as they conversed on the phone. "There's a Kentucky Fried Chicken place in West Monroe on the way home. We'll just stop there and pick up everything we need for the Sunday meal."

"Okay, that will be good," replied Dolores. "The doctor doesn't want me to do any kind of housework or cooking right now."

Dianne and Rick made the trip in his Firebird, stopping to pick up the chicken dinner, as promised.

Dianne deposited the chicken in the kitchen when they arrived and began making introductions all around.

"Daddy and Sallie, this is the guy I've been telling you about, Rick Lundy. Rick this is my dad, F. D. Hollis, and my sister, Sallie."

"Pleased to meet you" and handshakes were exchanged.

"Where's Mother?" Dianne asked.

"She's sitting up in bed in your bedroom," Sallie replied. "You can go on back and see her."

"Okay, come on Rick, and I'll introduce you to her," said Dianne.

Rick followed her back to the bedroom. Through the open door they could see Dolores, who was smiling as she awaited the introduction.

"Mother, this is Rick, and Rick this is my mom, Dolores Hollis."

"It's nice to finally meet you, Rick," said Dolores. "I've heard a lot about you."

"And I've heard a lot about you too," replied Rick. "Can I ask you one question?"

"What's that?" inquired Dolores.

"Is all that your real hair?"

"No, I have a hairpiece on the top of my head," admitted Dolores.

"I thought that looked like a lot of hair," he commented.

They all chuckled. "Enough about the hair. Let me see about getting the food on the table," said Dianne. "Rick, why don't you sit in the den and talk to my father while Sallie and I set up the table," she suggested.

"Well, what do you think?" she asked Sallie as they set out paper plates and prepared the glasses for the iced tea. "Does he pass inspection?"

"He's pretty cute, and he seems nice. If you like him, I guess he's okay," replied Sallie.

Rick and F. D. hit it off immediately. F. D., who would have rivaled Mark Twain as a storyteller, could converse on almost any topic. Reminiscing about his war experiences was one of his favorite pastimes. Rick, he soon discovered, was a big fan of history. The family had heard the war stories over and over, so he was glad to have a new person to appreciate his colorful narrations.

A few minutes later they sat down at the dinner table.

"Tell him the story about the gypsies, Daddy," said Dianne as they passed the fried chicken around the table.

"Yes, that was always one of our favorites," added Sallie.

"Well, I was a communications officer stationed in a one-man radio shack off the coast of England," F. D. began his tale. "The soldiers all made friends with the children there because we got chocolate bars in our rations. We used to pass them out to the children whenever we got a chance. One day I went into town, and I was handing out my chocolate bars, as usual. Some of the boys came up to me and said, 'There are some men in town who say they are coming up to your radio station tonight. They say they are going to kill you.'"

"Did that scare you?" Rick asked.

"Well, it was a warning I took pretty seriously," replied F. D. "I decided I was going to be ready for them. I got out my machine gun. As nightfall approached, I was just sitting there waiting for them to show up. It wasn't long before I heard somebody outside the door. They knocked, and I asked, 'Who's there?'"

"'A friend,'" came the reply in a voice with a strange accent."

"'If you're a friend, then you should be able to give me a name,' I told them."

"I listened, and they didn't say anything else, so I decided that I would fire one shot over their heads, just to scare them. I opened the door's peephole hatch and pulled the trigger. Instead of shooting off just one round, I accidentally hit the automatic button. Machine gun fire started spraying all over the place. I turned on the flood lights. All the men out there, who were apparently gypsies from the way they were dressed, were on their knees, crawling, crying, praying, and begging for mercy."

"Then what happened?" asked Rick.

"I yelled 'You men better get out of here right now,' and they took off running. After they left, I discovered that I had not only shot at them, I had blown a hole clear through the ceiling."

"Did you get in trouble for that?" inquired Rick.

"No, the general came by a couple of days later. He asked me how the hole got in the ceiling. When I told him, he just laughed and said he would send somebody out to fix it."

"And that was the end of the gypsies," said Dianne laughingly.

"Yes, they never bothered me again," added F. D.

Dolores, who had joined the family at the table for the meal, chimed in with an additional comment. "When he was stationed there, he used to ride a bicycle a lot. He kept writing me to send him watches, saying that he had broken his in a bicycle wreck. After sending him several watches, I found out he was selling them for a profit."

"Well, I did break one of them," F. D. interjected.

"Anyhow, after I found out what he was doing with them, I stopped sending them," she noted.

After the meal Dianne and Sallie made quick work of tidying up the kitchen. Then it was time to pose for pictures. Dolores always wanted to make pictures whenever the family gathered for a special occasion, and she considered her discharge from the hospital to be one of those occasions. Dianne and Rick posed for their first picture together standing outside in front of the shrubs. Afterwards it was time for them to head back to Pineville.

"It's been good to visit with all of you, but we need to be leaving. I have to go back to school in the morning," Dianne announced.

"Yes, it was good to meet all of you, finally," Rick said.

"And we were glad to meet you, too," added Dolores. "Thanks for bringing the food, Dianne. Maybe I'll be able to cook something for you the next time you come."

"Well, just be careful and don't overdo it. We don't want you back in the hospital again," said Dianne.

Sallie and F. D. followed them out to Rick's Firebird and waved goodbye as they drove down the winding driveway that had once been a cow path before the house was built in the middle of the pasture.

"Well, that's my family. What did you think?" Dianne asked.

"I liked them," replied Rick. "Your dad is really entertaining. He has a lot of stories about the war. And he's really good at talking about history, too."

"Yes, he's a great storyteller, and a history teacher, to boot. The people at the Rocky Branch Church of Christ have commented frequently that he's probably the best Sunday school teacher they've ever had for the adult class."

"I believe it," said Rick.

Back home in Pineville, Dianne was soon wrapping up the school year, while her relationship with Rick continued to develop. Although she had given her best effort at Carter C. Raymond, she still wanted to transfer to a school that was closer to home. She made her yearly phone calls to all the Rapides Parish high school principals, inquiring if there were any openings for home economics teachers at their schools. She was met with the usual negative replies, but she was determined not to give up in her quest to eventually get transferred.

God, I don't know what you have in mind for me as far as the future is concerned, but you have always looked out for me, so I am going to trust you to do so this time. I don't know where this relationship with Rick is going, either. I hope I will make the right decision about that, too. Please continue to guide me in all the phases of my life, she prayed silently as she pondered over her situation. She realized the summer break would give her a chance to catch up on some much-needed rest. She also knew it would be the turning point for her relationship with Rick. Whatever happened, her life would never be the same again.

Chapter 22

*A*s soon as school was out, Dianne and Rick began spending more and more time together. He came over to her apartment almost every night after he got off work. They watched television on weeknights and often went to the movies on weekends. One of their favorite pastimes was driving to the Dairy Queen in Alexandria to pick up dip cones.

They discovered they were quite compatible, both having easy-going personalities. They even shared the same sense of humor about most things. He appreciated Dianne's cooking, and she appreciated his ability to be able to fix almost anything.

Her Torino was getting older, and it was at the stage where it required some maintenance. One day Rick noticed the car was beginning to leak some kind of fluid between the rear wheels. She told Uncle R. V. about it, and he quickly diagnosed the problem.

"What you have is a problem with the rear seal," he told her. "I can fix it for you if Rick will help me. A mechanic is going to charge you a lot of money to do that."

Rick agreed to help R. V. with the job, and they tackled it one weekend. After leaving her car at her aunt and uncle's house, she walked back to her apartment to prepare a meal for Rick that night.

Boy, I'm really lucky to have Uncle V. to help me out whenever I have trouble with my car, she reflected. I remember the time my water hose sprang a leak when I went to the downtown Pineville Dairy Queen to get a burger. I managed to make it back home. He came down to my apartment and changed the hose for me. Then there was the time my car stalled right in the middle of the street on the way to the mall. I had to coast over to the curb and walk back to a pay phone at the service station by Texada Meats. I remember being startled by a talking parrot the owner kept there. When I walked in, I heard a wolf whistle. Then somebody yelled, "Hey, good looking!" It was the bird! Uncle V. showed up a few minutes later with his Kaiser and towed me home. The problem turned out to be a bad ignition switch, which he replaced for me. Yes, Uncle V. has certainly saved me a lot of money over the years, and I am truly thankful to him.

She had to smile when she recalled his lecture on buying parts for her car.

"I never buy new parts," he had told her. "I always get rebuilt ones. They cost a lot less and last just as long. Remember that from now on whenever you need any parts for your car."

Back at the apartment, Dianne set about preparing the meal for herself and Rick. She decided on pineapple salad, Irish stew, green beans, and cornbread. It was something that would keep indefinitely because she wasn't sure of exactly what time Rick and Uncle R. V. would be finished with her car. While she was waiting for the food to finish cooking, she busied herself with tidying up the apartment and doing some laundry. Everything smelled delicious, and she was getting really hungry.

I'm not going to eat anything until Rick gets here, she vowed, no matter how hungry I get.

Shortly after 7:00 p.m. she heard her Torino pulling up in the driveway. She peeked out the back door just in time to see Rick exiting the car.

"Boy, that was some job, but we got it done," Rick told her as he headed into the apartment. "Your uncle sure saved you some money on that one!"

"Yes, I know he did. He always looks after me," Dianne replied. "I have some food for you."

"I already ate. Your aunt came flying out the back door just as I was leaving. She wouldn't let me leave until she fed me."

"Great! I've been sitting here all this time about to starve to death, and you already ate."

"It's okay. I didn't eat that much. I can eat some of your food, too."

"Well, all right, if you're sure you can eat more food. I know I'm going to eat it, because I'm plenty hungry."

"This looks really good. You're definitely a good cook," he commented as she dished up the food.

Dianne had a feeling things were moving too smoothly. Somewhere along the line there had to be a bump in the road. It came unexpectedly one night when Rick came by for one of his visits.

"I have something to tell you," he said. "You may not like it very much."

"What is it?" Dianne asked.

"I'll be gone for a couple of weeks starting next week. I have to report for my two weeks of active duty in the Naval Reserve. I'm being sent to one of the bases on the California coast."

"Well, I'm going to miss you," she admitted, "but at least the Vietnam War is over now, thank goodness."

"Yes, I'm grateful for that. I know a lot of our guys got killed during the war. I'm just glad I was never in active combat. I heard a lot of stories from some of the guys I knew. One of my cousins, Buddy Tumminello, had some bad experiences over there. I believe he caught malaria. He also told me there was a snake on his chest heading right for his face when he woke up one night. He jumped up, but it bit him on the lip."

"That sounds really painful."

"Yes, I think it made him sick. His mother, my aunt Edna, went to church to pray for him every day while he was in Vietnam. I also had a roommate over at Louisiana College who was a veteran. We had both been in the military, so they put us in a room together."

"What was his name?"

"His name was Tee Clifford. He was a sniper. He told me to never touch him if I wanted to wake him up. He said to get a broom or something to poke him with.

Otherwise, he might attack me, thinking I was somebody trying to kill him. He was tough, too, because he had also been a Marine drill instructor. We had the quietest wing in the dorm. If the guys started making too much noise, he just stuck his head out the door and yelled for them to keep it down. He didn't have to tell them twice."

"Some of the guys I went to school with ended up in Vietnam, too," Dianne commented. "Johnny Albritton, the guy I walked down with the aisle with at my high school graduation, was killed over there. My mother sent me a news clipping with his picture in it. There had been an AP news story about him, along with a picture of him hanging his ammo out to dry while he was on combat duty. He was killed a day or two after that story was printed. That made me pretty sad."

"Well, at least that's all behind us now," said Rick. "Not only have I never been in combat, but I've never been out to sea. I hope one of these days while I'm on duty I get stationed on a ship that actually sails for a while."

"Keep hoping and maybe your dream will come true," said Dianne teasingly.

They say the way to a man's heart is through his stomach. So, I think I'll give Rick a big send-off by cooking him a really great meal. That will keep me on his mind while he's off on his two weeks of Navy duty, Dianne decided. After that, what happens is anybody's guess.

She settled on a dinner featuring one of her special dishes, baked chicken with Creole rice. That, along with some of F. D.'s frozen purple-hull peas, a tossed salad, and some brown-and-serve dinner rolls would make a pretty good meal. For dessert, her mother's old-fashioned egg custard pie with apple filling would be just the right complement. And Dolores had taught her and Sallie the secret for making a perfect pot of tea. All in all, it promised to be a mouthwatering affair.

She issued a dinner invitation to Rick, planning for it to fall on the Friday just before he left for his Navy duty. He showed up on time, just as she was about ready to pop the rolls into the oven.

"Boy, everything smells really good," he exclaimed as he came through the front door.

"Thanks. It should be smelling good, considering I've spent most of the afternoon cooking," Dianne replied. "I'm going to go ahead and start putting the food on the plates while we wait for the rolls to cook. I hope you like this chicken-and-rice dish. It's something I learned to make while I was in college."

"If you cooked it, I'm sure it will be good. I haven't tasted anything bad from your cooking so far."

And let's hope you never do, Dianne vowed silently.

They were soon enjoying the meal that turned out to be as good as they had anticipated. Afterwards the kitchen was cleaned up in short order. Then they retired to the living room to chat.

"I hate to leave so soon, but I have to get back home to finish packing," Rick told her. "I'll be flying out to California tomorrow afternoon."

"I hope you have a safe trip. Just be careful," commented Dianne.

"Oh, there's nothing to worry about. The Navy always makes sure I get there and back safely," Rick reassured her. "And at least I don't have to pay for the transportation."

He leaned over and kissed her softly. "Well. I guess I'd better go. Goodnight. I'll probably call you from California."

"Goodbye. I'll miss you," she said as Rick rose and exited the apartment. She closed the door slowly behind him.

"Well, Boo. He's really gone. Guess we'll see what life is like without him around for a couple of weeks. Now you and Taffy will get all of my attention."

Boo regarded her with unblinking eyes from his usual place on the couch. It was almost as if he knew he had no competition for her affections for the next few days. He curled up into a ball and prepared for his evening nap as Dianne returned to the kitchen to feed Taffy.

Taffy was waiting in the kitchen, hoping for a handout of the supper leftovers. She wagged her tail expectantly as Dianne entered the room.

"No, Taffy. I told you, no table scraps. I learned that from Uncle R. V. He told me as long as you feed a dog just dog food the dog will eat it. But it you ever feed it table scraps, it will want table scraps from then on and won't like the dog food anymore. Besides, dog food is better for you anyhow," she said as she plopped a spoonful of it into Taffy's bowl.

Taffy dug hungrily into the heap of food.

"Wow, I guess you really were hungry," observed Dianne. "I didn't realize it was so late. I'd better get ready for bed now that you've had something to eat."

The end of summer was fast approaching, and Dianne's days were filled with activities in preparation for returning to school. One break from the tedious work did occur, however. The Hollis clan was scheduled to hold their annual reunion at the Colvin Memorial Center located in Dubach. There were seventy-three first cousins who descended from the union of George and Sallie Jacobs Hollis. Dianne was always amazed at both the similarities and differences between the cousins and her dad, F. D.

They had all grown up in the farming community of Spearsville, Louisiana, in northern Union Parish. Many of the families had lived on adjoining farms, and the children were constantly visiting each other. As a result, they seemed almost like one big family. F. D. had been very close to one set of cousins in particular. His father, Claude, had married Sallie Webb. Claude's brother, John, had married Sallie's sister, Ellen. The resulting children from the two unions were classified as "double first-cousins" and were as close as regular brothers and sisters.

Dianne had traveled back to Rocky Branch while Rick was gone in order to attend the reunion with her parents and Sallie. Dolores bustled around in the kitchen getting the food ready for the trip. She usually took fried chicken, deviled eggs, potato salad, purple-hull peas from F. D.'s garden, rolls, pineapple pudding, and iced tea. Everybody always brought a complete meal. The food was spread on a long table and served buffet style so they could sample each other's cooking.

Sallie and Dianne began to wrap and secure the food for the trip. F. D., impatient as usual, didn't feel they were getting the job done fast enough.

"Let's go if we're going," he fumed, spouting off one of his favorite sayings. "We're going to be late."

"Okay, Daddy, we're just about ready," replied Dianne. "I think we have everything now."

"Yes, finally," said Dolores. "I'm about worn out, but it's all done. I guess we're all ready to go."

Dianne wasn't looking forward to traveling in a car with F. D. and his cigarette smoke, but she could see no way around it. *Maybe he won't light a cigarette until we get there,* she thought hopefully.

The family loaded the food into their green Ford Galaxy and headed for Dubach. It was a sunny day, beautiful weather for an outdoor gathering.

"At least there's one air-conditioned room in the facility," Dianne noted. "It will be nice to go in there if we get too hot."

They arrived at the memorial site a short time later. To Dianne's relief, F. D. had managed to make the trip without lighting up. Cars were piling in from all over. Dianne always liked to observe the cousins as they descended on the place. It was fun to see who she recognized and what new faces might appear.

One of the most jovial of the bunch was F. D.'s cousin Stanley. He was the most musically talented person in the group. He loved to sing and play his electronic organ.

In fact, he had devised a way to accompany himself on tape in four-part harmony and had even produced some tapes to sell commercially. There was never a dull moment whenever Stanley was around. Stanley's wife, Marcelle, always brought lemon chess pie. Dianne and Sallie never missed a chance to nab a piece before it was all gone.

One of Stanley's sisters, Lois Heard, pulled in just behind him. Lois never went to a family gathering without bringing along two things—her famous barbequed chicken and her third husband, George. Lois, who had outlived her first two husbands, had a brood of six children, most of whom had already married and left home. Dianne usually spent most of the day with Frances, one of Lois's daughters who was about her age.

Lois and Stanley's other brothers and sisters soon began arriving. There was Millard, a mechanic who lived in Ruston, and his wife, Lorene. Another brother, Dalton, and his wife, Eva, surprised everybody by riding up on two motorcycles. Dianne always had a hard time keeping Millard and Dalton straight, because they looked so much alike.

Two more of their brothers, Brooks and Earl, drove up. Brooks was accompanied by his wife, Olive. Dianne had once asked F. D. why their cousin Brooks had such an unusual name.

"He was the baby of the family," F. D. had explained. "With eleven children, Aunt Ellen had run out of names, so they just called him 'Baby.' When he got old enough to talk, they asked him what he wanted his name to be. He said 'Brooks,' which was the name of a Church of Christ preacher they knew, so 'Brooks' it was from then on."

People were coming in so fast Dianne could scarcely keep up with the flow. Some she knew and some she didn't. F. D.'s brothers and sisters were always there, along with their spouses. She counted them off as they arrived. His sister Berdelle drove up in the little Ford Falcon that belonged to her and her husband, Sammy. Berdelle had just recently learned to drive after Sammy was incapacitated with a heart attack. A talented seamstress and excellent cook, she could always be counted on to bring some mouth-watering food. The dish she was most known for was her fresh coconut layer cake with pineapple filling and seven-minute frosting. That was another dish Dianne never failed to sample.

His sister Corrie and her husband, Mina, were close behind. Corrie, a home economics teacher, always brought an array of food.

"I wonder what kind of food Aunt Corrie brought today," Dianne commented to Sallie as they watched them exit their vehicle. "Maybe her chicken cacciatore and coconut pie. Look, here come Aunt Hazel and Uncle R. V. I'd know that gray Oldsmobile anywhere. Aunt Hazel always brings something good, too. They're both great cooks. She usually brings her three-bean salad."

"Don't forget about Uncle Donald and Aunt Euline. Here they come. She's a home economics teacher, so we know her food will be tasty," Sallie added. "I hope she brought that sweet potato casserole she always makes."

"Well, that accounts for the five brothers and sisters in our immediate family. Geez, to hear us talk, you'd think we came just to eat. I guess we'd better start circulating around and visiting with some of these people," said Dianne.

"I hope we eat before too long," complained Sallie. "I didn't eat much breakfast, and I'm really hungry."

"Don't be in too much of a hurry. You know that Faye, one of Lois's sisters, is always late. We have to wait on her every time. We can't start until she gets here, no matter how hungry we are."

More and more cousins continued to arrive. By the time they and their descendants all got there, the crowd was quite huge. The Hollises were talkers with hardly a shy one amongst them. All in all, it was enough to overwhelm any newcomer to the clan.

Faye eventually straggled in just behind her sisters Georgia and Lottie Mae. Georgia had married a man named Otha Brown, so her name became Georgia Brown. It took all of Dianne's self-control in order not to burst into a chorus of "Sweet Georgia Brown" every time she encountered that particular cousin.

Faye's arrival usually signaled the end of the parade of cousins, so the blessing was recited and the famished crowd then dug eagerly into the scrumptious feast. Dianne and Sallie wasted no time in helping their plates, enjoying a chance to sample other people's cooking. One thing of Dolores's that they were always sure to get, however, was her tea.

"Nobody makes tea as good as Mother, do they?" asked Dianne as they poured the beverage into the colorful aluminum cups that Dolores always brought to such occasions.

Sometime later, with everyone fed and the leftovers tucked safely away, the real visitations began. The grown-ups were feeling fat, full, and lazy from such bountiful eats. About the only people moving around were the youngsters, who had their usual games of tag and hide-and-seek going. It was then the storytelling began. Dianne and Sallie were always amused to learn some new facts about their parents' adventures when they were younger.

"You know, F. D. was a pretty tough character when he was growing up," said his cousin Dalton. "The other boys used to put him up to fighting and then bet money on him. He fought and beat just about every boy in the community until there was only one left. That was Clyde Cherry."

F. D. chuckled. "Yes, they finally let me fight him, but they never would let either one of us win. They always pulled us apart just before one of us could whip the other one. Otherwise, they wouldn't have had anybody left to bet on. Old Clyde and I still joke about that, wondering which one of us would have won."

"I can tell you a couple of stories that top that," chimed in his cousin Josh, who was one of Uncle Joe Hollis's children. "A creek we called Little Corny ran through Aunt Sallie and Uncle Claude's property. It was a pretty popular swimming hole in the summertime. Of course, when it was just us boys, we went skinny dipping. We would put our clothes on some bushes by the bank. F. D. always mudded Donald whenever they went swimming. Donald got tired of it, so one day he left and took F. D.'s clothes with him. When F. D. got back to the house, he could see they had company, so he had to run and hide in the barn. He hollered for help until he was hoarse, but he finally got somebody to come and bring him some more clothes."

"That's not the only time Donald got the best of F. D.," added Josh's brother, Warner. "One time F. D. chewed Donald out because he didn't like the way Donald had plowed a field. Just about that time, Stanley came by with one of their mules. Donald asked Stanley if he could borrow the single tree the mule was hitched up to. Stanley said, 'Sure,' not knowing what Donald wanted it for. Donald unhitched it and then took the single tree and knocked F. D. out cold. He hitched it back up and left and went to the house, leaving F. D. lying there."

"Yes, I did," admitted Donald. "And when he came back to the house, he didn't say a word about it."

"And speaking of mules," said Stanley, "those two mules of Aunt Sallie's, Charlie and Coley, were something else. Charlie was real smart. In fact, he was just about as smart as a man. There wasn't a latch of any kind that he couldn't open. The only way to keep him fastened in was to put a lock and chain on the gate or door. One day I was walking up to their barn, looking for old Charlie. I didn't see him anywhere. I heard a noise coming from the hayloft, so I crept up the ladder real slowly and softly, trying not to make any sound. I poked my head up through the opening just enough for my eyes to go up over the edge. I saw Charlie and he saw me. There he was up in the hayloft, helping himself to the hay. I knew that I had better get down pretty quick, so I hurried down. I had barely gotten to the floor when there came old Charlie right behind me, sliding down the hay ramp on all fours."

"Aunt Sallie could handle those mules, though. She could handle 'em as good as any man," commented Josh.

"Okay, if y'all are gonna tell all those stories on me, I have to tell one on Dolores," said F. D. "Did I ever tell you about the time I was teaching her how to drive on the back roads close to our house? She seemed to be getting the hang of it, so I let her take the wheel. As soon as I let go, she ran the car straddle of a log in the woods. She jumped out and ran down the road to Uncle Lloyd's house, crying the whole way. She said that she was never going to drive again. Aunt Wadie told her, 'Girl, you go right back and get into that car and drive it!' We finally got it off the log, and she did try it again. Otherwise, she probably never would have learned how to drive."

"I can still remember Dolores walking to school," said Josh. "She had a big dog that came to school with her every day. I'd see that big dog coming down the road, and I knew that she would be coming in right behind him."

"Yes, I took him partly for protection," Dolores interjected. "I had to pass a house where some black children lived. They used to throw rocks at me and call me 'honkey' whenever I passed by."

"And since you want to talk about me, Josh," she added, "I'm going to tell some tales on you, too. I know that F. D.'s mother didn't like to let him go off from home very often. However, you were the one person she trusted him to be with. One time y'all almost got in trouble anyhow. You boys always thought you had to steal a watermelon from old Mr. McFinney's melon patch every year. It just wasn't officially summertime until that watermelon was stolen. One night he was with you and some other boys when y'all decided to sneak up and swipe one of the melons. Old Mr. McFinney heard you and got his shotgun after you."

"Aw, he just shot up in the air," protested F. D. "He didn't really want to hurt us. It was just a harmless prank."

"You know, that melon we stole tasted better than any other melon we got that summer," added Josh. Everybody laughed appreciatively.

Several other cousins sauntered up to the group and began to join in on the conversation. The first two were Grady and his wife, Celeste. Grady was one of Uncle Howard Hollis's sons.

"I remember that your dad used to pick on me a lot," he told Dianne and Sallie. "I wasn't too fond of school and didn't like to study. One of the favorite tricks the boys had was to heat an eraser on the old wood stove in the winter time and then stick it onto somebody's neck. I was often the unlucky victim of that prank."

"Yes, I guess that was pretty mean of me," admitted F. D. "And even though you didn't like school, that didn't keep you from being a brilliant inventor. We cousins all know that you invented those 'grabbers' they advertise on T.V. all the time. I remember when you and Celeste used to make them out in your back yard."

"Yes, we did," replied Grady. "But I sold my patent. I never dreamed those grabbers would be so famous all over the country."

"He invented some other things, too," added Josh. "I know that he invented a planter for cotton seeds that would plant each seed just as far apart as you wanted."

"I think he has a total of five patents," said Celeste. "That's counting his mole trap, one of his most recent inventions."

"The talent for inventing things must run in our family," observed F. D. "Don't forget that our cousin Homer Hollis invented the terrace plow. It's too bad he got killed in a wreck down in south Louisiana. He was down there working on another invention."

A hush fell over the crowd as they remembered the tragic death of their cousin many years ago. Several men nodded in agreement. Another cousin, Millard, puffed on his pipe with a thoughtful look on his face.

Dolores broke the silence. "Well, I'm not really much of a matchmaker, but I guess I can take the credit for getting Grady and Celeste together. I remember they spent their honeymoon night on a mattress in our living room."

"That doesn't sound like much of a honeymoon," Dianne observed amid laughter and guffaws as the jovial mood returned to the group.

"We didn't start out with much, but we've done okay," said Grady. "And we have four wonderful children—Howard, Calvin, Mary Olla, and Bonnie."

"At least you got some boys out of the deal. Donald and I ended up with all girls," lamented F. D.

"Ain't nothin' wrong with girls," said Stanley. "Nothin' a' tall!"

Earl Hollis walked up just in time to catch that last remark. "What's that y'all are talking about? Did I hear something about girls?" he inquired.

"Nah, we're just sitting around telling tales on each other. You'd better watch out or we just might start telling something on you," joked Stanley.

"Don't do that. Please, don't do that," begged Earl.

"It's too late. You've already joined the crowd, and everybody's fair game today," said F. D.

"Okay, I know one on Earl," declared Josh. "Let me tell you about the time he had the run-in with the sheriff in Spearsville."

"Oh, no, not that again. Anything but that," Earl implored.

"Earl and his wife had a little spat, so Earl left home and didn't want to go back. His wife started looking for him but couldn't find him anywhere. She finally called the sheriff and reported him missing. Earl was sitting in a store in Spearsville when the sheriff walked in. He told Earl, 'I'm looking for Earl Hollis. Have you seen him anywhere?'

"Earl said, 'No, but if I see him, I'll tell him you were looking for him.' Then he took off for Aunt Ellen's house in Bernice as soon as the sheriff left."

"Well, it never did work out between us after that," Earl admitted. "She found out where I was. Then she called me and said she wanted a divorce. I told her to put my clothes out on the porch, so she put them out in a paper bag. I went by and picked them up and that was that. I like living by myself now. I don't have to worry about anybody else. I eat when I'm hungry and sleep when I'm tired."

"And he likes to cook, too," noted Dianne. "Say, Earl, I remember the last time I saw you. You were down at our house watching me make fried apple pies using canned biscuits for the crust. You wanted to know if canned biscuits would work as a regular pie crust. I told you I thought it wouldn't work, but you said you might try it anyhow. Whatever happened with that idea?"

"I tried it, and you were right. It rose up too much," replied Earl.

"Ha! I knew that would happen! Well, everybody, it's been really fun hearing about all of these adventures from your younger days, but I guess we girls had better circulate among the women for a while and see what new gossip we can learn," Dianne announced to the crowd. "Come on, Sallie and Frances. Let's go visit with our female cousins for a while. Mother, why don't you come, too?"

"Yes, I think I will," said Dolores. "Let me leave before F. D. thinks up some more stories about me."

The men were sitting out under the covered patio so they could smoke. As soon as they lost their female audience the conversation quickly turned to topics such as sports, cars, and gardening. Donald, who was a county agent in Caldwell Parish, was always willing to offer anybody advice on how to handle problems with their plants or farm animals.

"Your Uncle Donald is a good county agent, a real good one," R. V. had once commented to Dianne. "But your daddy is one of the best people I've ever seen when it comes to growing things. I don't care what it is, plant or animal. Give it to him, and he can make it grow. He's just one of those people who has a natural talent for that sort of thing."

"Maybe you're right," Dianne had replied. "I remember that peach orchard we had when I was growing up. Ruston is supposed to be the peach capital of Louisiana, but people drove from Ruston to Rocky Branch to buy our peaches. People kept coming even years after we had uprooted all the trees. They were really disappointed to learn we didn't have any more peaches for sale."

All the women had retreated to the one air-conditioned room in the facility as soon as the food was cleaned up and stored away. Dianne and her group were actually glad to head inside to get out of the heat.

"Well, we were wondering when y'all were going to come in and join us," Berdelle exclaimed as they came through the door. "We thought you were going to stay out there with the men all day."

"They were telling us some tales about their younger days, and we just had to listen," replied Sallie.

"Yes, we thought we might get some ammunition for future use," joked Dianne. "Especially on Daddy. He was quite a character."

"Oh, I could tell you some stories myself," Corrie told her. "Did

I ever tell you about the time he bought me a Christmas present and then took it away?"

"No, I don't think I've heard that one," said Dianne.

"Well, we didn't have much, you know. Our daddy died when we were young children. Mamma had to bring up all of us five children by herself on a farm during the depression. We just didn't get very many presents. F. D. finally got a little money when he went away to college. He paid his way through college by working as a janitor. He swept a lot of floors at Louisiana Tech. Somehow he managed to get enough money to buy a few Christmas presents. Mine was wrapped up in some brown paper, and I couldn't wait to find out what it was. I tore a little hole in the paper and peeked. It was a sweater and skirt set, and I was so excited. F. D. found out what I had done and took it back to the store."

"That wasn't very nice of him," said Sallie.

"No, but that's how he was. I never did get that sweater and skirt back, either. I guess he thought he was teaching me a lesson."

"Well, that's enough about all of that," interjected Peggy, one of Lois's daughters. "I heard Dianne has a new boyfriend. I want to hear about him. Why didn't you bring him with you today, Dianne?"

"He's out in California. He had to go to his two weeks of active duty in the Navy," replied Dianne.

"Make sure you bring him along next time. We all want to meet him," said Sue, one of Peggy's sisters.

"Well, I've met him, and I like him. I like him a lot," said Hazel.

"The next thing we know you and Frances will be married off and have two or three kids like our younger sister Ruthie," commented Peggy laughingly.

"Don't marry us off too fast," Frances protested. "And I don't know if I want to have any kids, either."

"Yes, let us get engaged first," added Dianne.

The conversation then turned to more general topics that women usually like to discuss such as recipes, jobs, and children. All in all, it was a pleasant way to spend a Saturday afternoon. Dianne always enjoyed visiting with her cousins and considered them to be quite entertaining.

As the sun began to sink in the west, people gathered up their leftover food and their children in preparation for leaving. A hat was passed among the men to collect donations to pay for the use of the facilities. Hugs and kisses were exchanged as everyone headed for their vehicles in anticipation of their trips back home.

When Dianne climbed into the Hollises' car, her thoughts turned to Rick. She wondered what he might be doing to pass the time on a Saturday afternoon in California. And she wondered if he might be thinking of her, just as she was thinking of him.

Chapter 23

The next day was Sunday, and the Hollis family always attended the Sunday church services at the Rocky Branch Church of Christ. The congregation was literally bursting at the seams in their newer building, which was located on Louisiana Highway 143 between the Rocky Branch Elementary School and the Rocky Branch Community Store. One of their elders, Mr. Albert Smith, who was a carpenter, had been one of the main builders of the new facility. His wife, Miss Annis Smith, had taken care of Sallie before she started school, and Sallie had often accompanied Albert out to the building site during construction.

"I guess I can say I helped build the new church," Sallie had told her family.

Dianne could still remember when the church was literally a church in the wildwood. The original old white wooden building had been located behind the Rocky Branch Cemetery nestled amongst the trees and thickets. A simple building with wooden floors and no indoor toilets, its only ventilation had been open windows and the fans all the ladies carried with them to the spring and summer worship services.

The church had no baptistery, so whenever anybody needed to be baptized, someone from the congregation would volunteer the use of their pond. F. D. sometimes allowed them to use his pond.

Several members, however, became skeptical about using it because they feared it was infested with alligators.

The rumor had started when F. D. brought home a baby alligator during his tenure with the Louisiana Wildlife and Fisheries Department. Dianne had wanted to keep it as a pet, but Dolores wouldn't let her. F. D. had carried it to church in his pocket on a Wednesday night. One of the members, Kelton Howard, had scared his wife, Jerry, half to death chasing her around the outside of the church while pretending he had the alligator in his possession. F. D. had later taken it over to his pond and released it. Although the alligator was never seen again, the rumors still persisted.

Dianne could also recall attending church there as a very young child. She was the oddball of the group of youngsters, with nobody her own age attending. All the other children had been older than Dianne, and she was put into a Sunday school class with Flo Smith, who was Mr. Albert and Miss Annis's youngest daughter; Katie Anne Laster, who was the daughter of Mr. Shady and Miss Mittie Anne Laster; Pete Freeman, who was the oldest son of her cousins, Bennie and Bessie Freeman; and Billy Keith Wisecarver, Miss Annis's nephew. She had felt completely out of place and very lonely.

The one bright spot in her Sunday mornings had been sitting by Miss Corine Howard. Before Dianne learned how to count or read, Miss Corine would help her find the correct pages in the songbook for each song. Dianne usually sat by her until Dolores arrived for the worship services.

The Howards were the next-door neighbors of the Hollises. F. D. had purchased the land for his homestead from them. They were a farming family who had led a simple life, but they had taught their children well. Their oldest son, V. E. Howard, who was the first boy in Rocky Branch to receive a high school diploma, had attended Abilene Christian College and eventually had become a preacher. His simple sermons and country ways had soon brought him recognition. His favorite phrase, "Are you listening?" had become his trademark. He and his wife, Ruth, had moved to Texas where he had become known worldwide through his "International Gospel

Hour" radio program that aired every Sunday. Another son, Jack, had gone into politics and had been elected the mayor of Monroe, Louisiana, where his tenure had lasted a number of years. V. E. and Jack, together with their brother Alton and their sister Euphra Terry, and her husband, Lartis, had pooled their money to buy a franchise in what later became the chain of Howard Discount Stores.

Gradually, over a period of time, other children closer to her age began attending. She became friends with Karen, Pam, and Suzanne Howard, Kelton and Jerry's offspring, who were frequent playmates for her and Sallie as they were growing up. The Richardson children, Bianca (B.B.), Phyllis, and Sybil, grandchildren of Albert and Annis, were also their friends. Dianne always enjoyed seeing them again at the church services whenever she was back in Rocky Branch.

One thing that had remained constant in the congregation was the excellent singing. They were lucky to have several talented song leaders including Mr. Broadus Smith and Kelton, who was Miss Corine and Mr. Hardy Howard's youngest son. All the Howards were musically talented. Mr. Hardy was a country singing school teacher and had once won third place in a statewide fiddling contest. His nephew, Robert L. Howard, was one of the song leaders for the Pleasant Hill Baptist Church in Rocky Branch. Broadus, who was Miss Corine's brother, was a trained singer and music teacher and had traveled all over northern Louisiana teaching other Church of Christ congregations how to sing. Dianne had often accompanied him and his wife, Esther, to the singing schools. There was never a lack of good a cappella singing during the worship services at the little Rocky Branch congregation.

Broadus was particularly fond of songs with either bass or alto leads. He knew that he could always count on Jake Richardson, Wendell Parks, and Bob Hodge for the bass. Dolores, Erma Jean Richardson, and Kelton's sister Cassyle McMurray sang beautiful alto. Kelton and Cassyle's husband, Homer, never missed a note on the tenor. And everybody else, young and old, chimed in on the soprano.

The rafters practically rang as they sang out on the old songs such as "Just a Closer Walk With Thee," "Jesus, Hold My Hand,"

"Just a Little Talk With Jesus," "On the Jericho Road," "Kneel at the Cross," "Sing to Me of Heaven," "The Rainbow of Love," "Did You Repent?" and "Home of the Soul."

Broadus was well known for slipping in an extra song or two. "Good singing, really good singing! It's so good I have to get in an extra song. I hope you will all forgive me," he would announce to the congregation. And forgive him they did because they all loved to sing.

Dianne could have listened to Kelton's wonderful tenor voice all day. "He sounds like an angel when he sings," she had once remarked to Dolores. "I'm glad we have people like him and Mr. Broadus to help out with the singing."

The congregation had been through its share of preachers during the time Dianne was growing up. The first preacher she could recall was Brother Meredith Johnson who preached when the congregation met in the old wooden building. He and his brothers were also barbers, and Dolores had frequently carried Dianne to their shop in Monroe for a haircut during her younger days.

Some of the other memorable preachers included Graham Hale and Sonny Ferguson. Sonny, who was married to Dianne's cousin Delma, had been the victim of a heart attack one Sunday night when he was delivering the sermon. The congregation began praying for him, and they were relieved when he made a full recovery.

Jurd Brantley was another preacher Dianne would never forget. He had followed in his dad's footsteps in deciding to become a preacher. He was known for illustrating his sermons with handmade slides, which he often showed on a large white sheet that was hung behind the pulpit. Dolores had once invited Jurd and his family to their home for Sunday dinner. After the dinner was over Jurd had remarked, "Mrs. Hollis, I've had some delicious dinners in my time, but I believe your roast is the best one I've ever eaten."

Another preacher who stood out in Dianne's mind was Jerry Lee. His wife, Ann, was a niece of Meredith Johnson. Jerry had also been the principal at Neville High School in Monroe during his tenure as the pastor of the Rocky Branch congregation. He and Dianne had often exchanged friendly banter about who had the better football team, Neville or Farmerville. The Neville fans had been really shocked when the Farmerville Farmers, who were the underdogs, beat out Neville one year. Dianne had attended that game as a part of the Farmerville pep squad, and she had a lot of fun teasing Jerry the following Sunday.

"Our team was just over confident," he had lamented. "They were just so sure they were going to win that they let Farmerville slip by them."

One of the youngest preachers the congregation ever had was Don Delukie. Don was a student at the White's Ferry Road Church of Christ Preachers' School. With a family to support, Don was short on money, and his shoes had become noticeably worn. F. D. had stopped by one of his favorite stores, Smith's Shoe Store in West Monroe, and paid for a new pair of shoes for Don. He instructed them to call Don and let him know about the shoes but not to tell him who had paid for them. Don had sported the new shoes the following Sunday commenting on how much he appreciated his anonymous benefactor.

Yes, this congregation has seen its share of preachers, Dianne reflected, as she and the Hollis family entered the church auditorium took their seats in their favorite pew. Today, however, there was a preacher whom Dianne had not seen before. His name was Earnest West. He and his wife drove from West Monroe to attend the Rocky Branch church. Although he was an older man, his hair had not turned gray. Dolores had reported to Dianne that once a girl in the congregation had asked, "Mrs. Hollis, why are you and Brother West the only two grown-ups in the church who don't have any gray hair?"

"I didn't know what to tell her," said Dolores, "so I just said, 'I guess we're just like Ronald Reagan.'"

Dianne sat through the service, watching the people she had known while she was growing up and noting how much some of them had changed over the years. Despite the changes in their appearance, their personalities had remained the same. Everybody was always glad to see one of their own return to the fold, and Dianne was no exception. The Hollises were among the last to leave that day by the time everybody had finished talking to Dianne and finding out what she had been doing since her last visit.

Later that afternoon Dolores reminded Dianne there was one more person she needed to call on before returning to Pineville.

"Miss Laura Dodd has been asking about you and wanting to know when you were coming back to see her again," Dolores told Dianne.

"Yes, I do want to see her before I leave. She was almost like another grandmother to me while I was growing up," Dianne replied. "I think I'll go by to see her tomorrow."

Mrs. Laura Dodd, affectionately known as Miss Laura to most people in Rocky Branch, was a widow and had owned and operated a country grocery store until she was well into her eighties. Dianne had frequented the store when she was growing up, and she and Miss Laura had held some lengthy conversations about times past and also about life in general. Miss Laura was a well-respected member of the community and a staunch Baptist.

The store, which was just across the highway from the Rocky Branch School, consisted of a large room in the front with living quarters in the back. She shared her home with her sister, Miss Emma, who had never married.

Dolores had become friends with both ladies over the years. She often invited Miss Emma to attend the Church of Christ with her and would pick her up for the services. One night Miss Emma decided she wanted to be baptized into the Church of Christ. She was worried that her sister might get mad about it, so Dolores offered to go home with her to break the news to Miss Laura. To their surprise, Miss Laura took the news pretty well and seemed to accept the fact that her sister had chosen to belong to a church other than the Baptist church that she had attended for a number of years.

"Miss Emma is the one star in my crown," Dolores had told

Dianne and Sallie afterwards. "Whether you're going to heaven or hell after this life, you're going to take somebody with you. I'm hoping Miss Emma and I both make it to heaven."

That statement had remained implanted in Dianne's mind. After that day, whenever she heard the old hymn "Will There Be Any Stars in My Crown?" she always thought of her mother and Miss Emma.

The following day, true to her word, she made it a special point to visit Miss Laura. By that time the little store had been closed for several years. Miss Laura had converted the store's floor space into a large den, and she wanted Dianne to see it.

"Some people made fun of me spending my money on fixing up this place at my age, but I don't care," she told Dianne. "It's my money, and I intend to spend it the way I want to."

"The den is really nice," Dianne told her. "I'm with you. You're absolutely right! Spend the money the way you want to and don't worry about what anybody else thinks or says."

After the visit, Dianne returned to her parents' home and began to pack her belongings.

"Well, I guess it's about time for me to leave," she informed her family.

"Leave? Why do you want to leave so soon?" F. D. inquired. "I thought you were a Nip 'n' Tuck girl."

"I'll always be a Nip 'n' Tuck girl, Daddy, but now I live in Pineville. The summer is almost over, and I have to be getting back home," she explained. "Besides, I have a lot to do before school starts, and there's not much time left to get it done. I guess I will leave tomorrow morning and head back to Pineville. I've been to the family reunion and visited with all the relatives. I talked to almost everybody at church on Sunday, and I went to see Miss Laura and her new den. It was all fun, but Boo, Taffy, and I really must hit the road tomorrow."

Plus Rick will be coming home from California soon, and I want to see him, too, she reflected. So, look out Pineville, here I come!

Chapter 24

Dianne was glad to get back to her little three-room apartment on Payne Street. It was small, but it was home. Boo and Taffy were apparently glad to be back in familiar surroundings, too. They both immediately headed for their favorite spots in the apartment and flopped down for a long rest.

"Okay, I see how it's going to be," she informed them. "I do all the work while you two do all the napping. I wish I had time to rest, but I have to finish getting these lesson plans ready for the first week of school. Besides, Rick will be back in town before long, and I want to have all of the schoolwork finished before he comes over."

Rick arrived a couple of days later. He called Dianne from his parents' home the same night he returned.

"It was an interesting trip, and I'm pretty tired, but I'll be over to see you tomorrow," he told her. "I thought about you while I was gone. They had some really good food, but it wasn't as good as your cooking."

Wow, I guess that chicken-and-rice dish did the trick, Dianne thought.

"I know my cooking is good, but I didn't know it was that good," she said.

"The Navy has the best food in the service, but it's still not home cooking," he replied. "Anyhow, your cooking wasn't all I was thinking about when I was thinking about you."

"Oh, really?"

"Really. I'll tell you more about it when I come over."

"Okay, I guess I'll see you tomorrow night, then."

"I'll be there."

The following day Dianne rushed around cleaning and straightening up the apartment. She wanted everything to be just right whenever Rick arrived. When she was satisfied with that project, she decided to do everything she could to make herself presentable to Rick after his two-week absence.

After all, it never hurts to look your best whenever an eligible man is around, she reminded herself.

Almost two hours later after a leisurely bubble bath, with her hair freshly washed, dried, and brushed, makeup carefully applied, and cologne adding the final touch, she was ready to greet Rick whenever he showed up on her doorstep. Since it was almost 7:00 p.m., they both would have already eaten, so food would not be an issue during this visit.

It wasn't long before she heard his knock on the front door. Taffy barked out a warning, and Boo ran for cover, their usual reaction to a visitor until they found out who it was.

"Oh, for pity's sake, be quiet, Taffy. It's just Rick. Boo, there's no need to hide. You like him, too," she said as she made her way to the door.

"Hi, come in. I've been wondering when you would get here," she told Rick as she opened the door to let him enter.

"Well, you know how it is. All the relatives had to check up on me to make sure I got back safely. I had a hard time getting away," Rick replied. "Give me a kiss. I missed you."

"Wow, I've been thinking about that all day," he added after kissing her softly on the lips.

"I've been thinking about you all day, too," she admitted. "I'm glad you're back from California."

"Me, too. It's hard to try to learn the routine of wherever you get stationed. Just about the time you get it down pat, it's time to leave. Of course, I always work in the communications department since I'm a Radioman. I don't have to do anything too hard, just send and receive messages."

"Boy, I can't believe my summer vacation is almost over," she commented. "School starts in just a few days. I've been working on lesson plans and bulletin board materials, trying to get everything ready to go. Looks like I'll be back at Carter C. Raymond for at least another year."

"I thought you were going to try to get moved from that school."

"I did try. I called all the high school principals in the parish, but nobody had any openings for a home economics teacher. Anyhow, I'm used to it now, and I know the students, so it really isn't so bad. I just do the best I can, and that's all I can do. They need qualified teachers in that school, just like they do anywhere else."

"Well, that's enough talk about school. Let's talk about something else," said Rick.

"Okay, what do you want to talk about?" inquired Dianne.

"Let's talk about how much I missed you while I was gone. I thought about you every day. I just couldn't get you off my mind," he admitted.

"Really?"

"So, I have made a decision. I think it's time we started talking about getting married."

"Married? Are you sure that's what you want to do?"

"I'll show you how sure I am," he replied as he slid off the couch and dropped to one knee. "Dianne, I love you. Will you marry me?"

Dianne sat in stunned silence with thoughts racing through her mind. I can't believe I have tried to find the right man for twenty-seven years, and now he's finally here.

"Well, say something," Rick prodded.

"Yes! Yes, I will marry you!" she almost croaked out as her voice finally returned. "Do I get a ring?"

"I didn't buy a ring yet because I wanted you to pick out the one you really want. I know how particular you are, and I didn't want to get the wrong one. Let's go tomorrow and look for one. I want you to have it before you go back to school."

"And aren't most engagements sealed with a kiss?" he asked.

"Yes, I believe they are," she said as Rick planted another kiss on her lips.

The following day they headed out to look for a ring, just as Rick had promised. They had a hard time making up their minds just which jewelry store to choose.

"I don't know which store would be the best," Rick mused. "What do you think?"

"Why don't we try Wilson's? They sell all kinds of jewelry there," responded Dianne.

When they arrived at Wilson's they were immediately waited on by one of the sales representatives. Dianne tried on several rings but couldn't make up her mind.

"They are nice, but somehow they're just not what I'm looking for," she told the clerk. "I think we might look around some more before deciding."

"Okay, what's your next suggestion?" Rick inquired after the clerk had left to wait on other customers.

"Why don't we try Schnack's? They have one of the best jewelry stores in town. I thought of them first, but they are probably more expensive. I was trying to save you some money," Dianne replied.

"Oh, don't worry about the money. I have some saved from my Navy checks. Anyhow, I want you to have the ring you really like, not just some cheap kind."

"Are you saying money is no object?" Dianne teased. "In that case, I might have to upgrade my thinking."

The trip to Schnack's proved to be the right decision, and they ended up with what both considered a perfect ring. To top it all off, the ring had come as part of a set, so they also had the wedding ring to boot.

A few days later Dianne headed back to Carter C. Raymond with the ring prominently displayed on her left hand. The first person to notice was her car pool partner, Roy.

"Engaged! You don't mean it!" he had exclaimed.

"Yes, it's true, and I guess I can say I have you to thank for getting us together, Roy."

"Oh, no! Please don't say that. I don't want to take any credit whatsoever for being responsible for anybody getting married. That way I can avoid the blame if it doesn't work out!"

"You should have more confidence in yourself, Roy. Don't worry. I have a feeling everything's going to work out just fine. After all, we're both old enough to know what we're getting into. We're not just a couple of kids, you know."

"When's the wedding going to be?"

"We haven't decided yet, but probably next summer. It's too hard to get married while school is going on. Besides, it takes time to plan a wedding, you know."

"Why don't you two just elope and avoid all the fuss of a big wedding?"

"Are you kidding? It's every girl's dream to walk down the aisle in a white wedding dress, and I'm not about to let that dream escape me."

It didn't take the students long to spot the ring, either. Word quickly spread around the school, and many of the girls made a beeline for the home economics department to check out the rumor and the ring.

"It's a nice ring, but I thought you would have a really big diamond," lamented one girl.

"I didn't want one that was too big," Dianne explained. "I would worry about losing it or catching it on my clothing."

"Or maybe getting it stolen," added another student. "Ha! I'll bet you thought about that, too."

"Actually, that thought never crossed my mind, but it might be something to consider," admitted Dianne.

"Are you going to be leaving us now that you're getting married?" inquired another student. "That's what happens to all of our good teachers. They get married, and then they quit teaching, and we have to get used to somebody else."

"No, I have no plans to quit teaching. I'm in it for the long haul," said Dianne. "Don't worry. I know I'll be here until the end of this school year."

The school year quickly settled into a routine once the excitement of the engagement ring had worn off. There had been some changes in the high school faculty. The social studies teacher, Don Paulk, had been replaced with another white male teacher, William Payne, who was a bachelor.

Mr. Payne was the one of the most organized teachers Dianne had ever met. His outlines of his lesson plans written on transparencies were so neatly and evenly spaced that they resembled formally printed materials. Dianne had once asked him how he managed to get them so neat, and he showed her a grid that he used to space the letters. He also used a timer to keep students on schedule during his lessons.

"When I tell them they have two minutes to copy something from a transparency, I mean exactly two minutes," he explained. "If they waste time and don't get it done, they don't get a second chance."

Mr. Payne had traveled all over the world, and he had an extensive slide collection that he used to add interest to his classes.

"I wouldn't mind sitting in on some his lectures myself," Dianne commented to Roy one day as they were sitting in the teachers' lounge. "The students are really lucky to have someone with such a wealth of knowledge to share with them."

He also kept a bottle of disinfectant in one of his desk drawers and constantly cleaned his hands during the day.

"You don't know what kind of germs some of these kids have," he told her. "I have one student who smells so strongly of disinfectant that I know he must have some kind of contagious disease. I don't even let him get close to my desk."

"Who is that?" Dianne inquired.

"Bernard Milton."

"Oh, brother. I have him for homeroom. I think I'll keep a close eye on him from now on."

There was also a new addition to the English department. Betty Cross, who had attended Louisiana Tech with Dianne's sister, Sallie, replaced one of the teachers who had been transferred. Betty had an outgoing personality and wasn't afraid of hard work, so Dianne felt that she would fit in just fine with the Carter C. Raymond faculty. In addition to her other talents, she was also an experienced cake decorator, Dianne had learned. She stored that bit of information away for future use, thinking it might come in handy during her home economics classes.

The business teacher had been replaced with a fairly young man, David Barton, who lived in the community. Unlike the previous business teacher who had vowed to leave as soon as she could, he seemed to actually enjoy his job, and the students took to him immediately.

The P. E. teacher, Jannia Easley, a black teacher who had been at the school for years, had also requested a transfer. Her replacement was a black female named Miss Vontrecia Chew. Miss Chew, who didn't have an ounce of fat on her body, declared that she was going to "whip the girls of the school into shape." She wasted no time in carrying out her program, and soon the girls were complaining about the routine.

"Boy, Miss Hollis, that Miss Chew is something else," one of them commented as she flopped down tiredly into a chair in the home economics department. "She's about to work us to death. We have to do calisthenics all hour."

"Every day?" Dianne asked.

"Yep, every day. All hour every day. That's all we do."

Several days later Mr. Cowan stopped by the home economics department to speak to Dianne.

"Miss Hollis, may I have a word with you privately outside your room?" he inquired.

"What's going on?" Dianne asked as she stepped out into the hall and closed the door.

"I'm coming by to warn you to keep a close eye on your car. Somebody slashed all the tires on Miss Chew's car this morning."

"Wow, thanks for the warning. It sounds like Miss Chew's plan backfired on her. I believe I'll start parking right outside my room! That way I can watch my car through the windows all day long."

Since it was the third year Dianne had been assigned to the school, things moved along rather smoothly. She had her lesson plans done for each unit, and she knew most of the students. That made for a much easier time in the classroom.

However, there were still a few problems in the day-to-day operations. Dianne had stuck to her guns in assigning five-hundred-word reports to students who caused discipline problems in class. One student who received such an assignment was a boy named Daniel Antoine. Although Daniel usually didn't cause any trouble, he persisted in talking one day after being corrected several times by Dianne.

"Okay, Daniel, that's it. You've had enough warnings about

talking. Tomorrow you are to bring me a five-hundred-word report on today's topic, nutrition."

"Man, that's not fair. I ain't gonna do no report," he retorted.

"It's up to you, Daniel, but if you don't do the report, you will be sent to the office," she responded.

The following day Daniel shuffled up to her desk sheepishly and handed her a rumpled-looking paper.

"Here's the report," he said.

"Thank you, Daniel. You may take your seat," Dianne instructed.

Daniel's handwriting was so bad Dianne usually couldn't read half of what he wrote on anything he handed in. She mostly had to read between the lines to make any sense of his work. Something told her she had better examine his report rather carefully.

Later that day during her lunch period she decided to see if she could make heads or tails of the messy-looking paper. As she read through the report, suddenly her name jumped out of the badly-scribbled text.

What's this? she wondered. Why is he writing about me when the report is supposed to be on nutrition?

As she struggled to read that particular paragraph, she was able to decipher Daniel's hidden message embedded in the report.

Miss Hollis is ugly and she stinks like a dog.

Dianne retrieved her yellow highlighter from her desk drawer and proceeded to highlight that particular sentence. *I think Mr. Cowan just might be interested in seeing this,* she thought.

After school that day she carried the report down to the office and explained the situation to Mr. Cowan.

"I will call that young man into my office the first thing tomorrow morning," he promised. "He will be writing that report over and writing it correctly."

As the year progressed, Dianne continued to try to come up with ways to add interest to her classes. The local electric company, CLECO, had home economists who would come and give demonstrations to home economics classes on the use of electric appliances and how to conserve energy. Their visits were a favorite activity for the students because they always got something to eat when the demonstrations were finished.

One day Dianne had arranged for such a demonstration to be given to her Home Economics II class. The agent was in the middle of her demonstration when someone knocked on the door. Dianne instructed Monique Hammond, one of her most reliable students, to answer the door, which was around the corner from the kitchen.

As the demonstration continued, Monique failed to reappear, and suddenly Dianne could hear loud voices coming from the doorway.

Guess I'd better see what's going on, she thought, as she unobtrusively slipped away during the middle of the demonstration.

As she rounded the corner, it was obvious that Monique was in the middle of an argument with Tiffany Booze, a student from another one of Dianne's classes.

"What's the problem, girls?" she inquired. "You are making noise and disturbing class while we have a guest speaker!"

"Ain't nothin', Miss Hollis. Tiffany was just leaving," said Monique.

"That sounds like a good idea," Dianne declared, reaching over to close the door.

"Girl, I'll show you nothin'," retorted Tiffany before the door closed. She reached past Dianne and began to pummel Monique with her fists. Monique responded in kind. Dianne attempted to break up the fight and was accidentally slugged by Tiffany in the process.

"Oh, God, Miss Hollis. I'm so sorry. I didn't mean to hit you," insisted a totally mortified Tiffany.

"It's too late to be sorry, Tiffany. I'm going to have to report this to the office after school. Now I suggest you go back to class. You'll be hearing more about this tomorrow," Dianne told her.

Monique and Dianne headed back into the classroom and managed to catch the end of the demonstration. The agent, totally oblivious to the situation, had continued with her lecture.

That class was the last one of the day, so Dianne had to wait until school was out and the busses had left before conferring with Mr. Cowan.

"You don't mean it! One of the girls actually hit you?" he asked.

"Well, it was an accident. I don't know what they were fighting about," said Dianne.

"I'll guarantee you, it was over some boy. It had to be about a boy," he exclaimed. "Don't worry. I'll call them both in tomorrow and get to the bottom of the problem."

As the year progressed, Dianne continued to go about her daily routine with very few problems. She had apparently been accepted by the students at the school, and some of them had even begun to confide in her. One day one of her brightest and most outstanding students came to her with a problem.

Dianne was surprised to see Delandria Piper knocking on her door during her planning period.

"Miss Hollis, there's something I need to talk to you about," said Delandria as Dianne opened the door to let her in.

"What seems to be the problem, Delandria?" inquired Dianne.

"Some girls have started a rumor that I'm pregnant. I don't know what to do about it."

"Well, Delandria, the best advice I can give you is to ignore it. They will get tired of talking about it and find something else to gossip about."

"Okay, I guess that's what I will do. Thanks for your help."

It never occurred to Dianne to ask Delandria if the rumor happened to be true. Surely not, she had thought. Of all the students I teach, Delandria has the most common sense. I can't believe that she would set herself up for anything like that.

Unfortunately, the rumor did turn out to be more than just a rumor, and Delandria ended up missing the large part of one semester of school. However, being a good student, she managed to catch up with all the work she had missed and even made better grades than the rest of her classmates in her home economics class.

"Well, I guess that will teach me a thing or two," Dianne later lamented to Roy. "I just never believed that Delandria would let herself get pregnant. I thought she wanted to make something of herself."

Despite being accepted by the majority of the students, there were still some who did not like Dianne. They did cause some discipline problems in class, and one day the problems evolved into an incident between classes. At the end of her planning period Dianne was heading back to her room before the bell rang. Suddenly, almost out of nowhere, one of her most troublesome students, Darrieus Ellis, appeared beside her. He attempted to put his arm around her, but she managed to brush him off.

"Cut it out, Darrieus," she warned.

If I can just make it into my room, I'll be okay, she thought.

She managed to reach the door of the home economics department and got it unlocked. As she attempted to slip inside and shut the door, Darrieus forced his way in behind her.

Before she could defend herself, he grabbed her by both arms and pinned her up against the chalkboard.

"Why are you doing this, Darrieus? You don't even like me," she protested.

"I love you," he said as he leaned down in an attempt to kiss her.

She managed to push him back and turned her head away just in time to avoid being kissed on the lips. The kiss, however, did hit her left earlobe.

"Get off me this instant," she demanded. "And get out of this room now!"

Darrieus appeared to be taken back by her rebuffs, so he dropped her arms and headed for the door just as the bell rang.

Now that's what I call being saved by the bell, she thought, as relief flowed through her veins.

It was lunchtime before she could go down and report the incident to the office. The other teachers were incensed when no apparent disciplinary action was taken against the student. Some of them felt that Dianne should report it to the school board office, but she decided not to.

On the ride home that afternoon she described the incident to Roy.

"Kissed you on the ear. Oh, my God! Rick lost an ear!" he exclaimed.

The following morning Dianne was called into the principal's office. Darrieus and his mother were both present. The principal had apparently discussed the situation with them.

"Miss Hollis, Mrs. Ellis has requested that I call you in to confirm the story about Darrieus attacking you yesterday," he stated.

"Yes, it's true. Darrieus shoved me up against the chalkboard and tried to kiss me," Dianne told her.

"Miss Hollis, I am so very sorry. I just couldn't believe it until I heard it from your lips. Darrieus's father passed away last year, and I am trying to raise him by myself. It's been hard, really hard, but I'm doing the best I can."

Darrieus had remained stonily silent during the interview, apparently feeling little regret for his actions.

"Well, Darrieus, do you have anything to say for yourself?" inquired the principal.

"I'm sorry," he mumbled with his head down and eyes focused onto the floor.

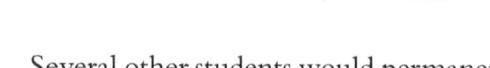

Several other students would permanently embed themselves into Dianne's memory as the school year continued. One such student was Augustin Clark. Dianne always kept a box of pink Kleenex on her desk for students who might have a runny nose. Every day, without fail, Augustin would stroll casually up to her desk and take one of the tissues. Dianne noticed that he never used them. One day her curiosity got the best of her.

"Tell me something, Augustin. Why do you keep getting a tissue every day but you never use them?" she inquired.

He smiled shyly as he replied, "Oh, I don't know. I just like to get them."

"Well, I bought those Kleenex for students who really need them, so I would appreciate it if you don't take them unless you need them, too," she said.

"Okay, but I'm going to keep the last one I got today."

Dianne taught a number of students who were brothers and sisters. One such family was the Milton family, of which Bernard was a member. Each of them had a different personality. The oldest girl, Louise, was a heavy-set girl who was always quiet in class and made fairly good grades. The youngest girl, Bonita, was just the opposite. She sported a thin frame and was a constant talker, a regular bundle of energy.

"You know, my mamma never cooks for us," she told Dianne one day. "We all have to take turns cooking and washing the dishes. When it's my turn, I always pick the easiest thing to cook."

Dianne had Bernard in one of her classes, as well as for her homeroom. He, too, was usually quiet and rarely caused any problems. That all changed one day when the entire school was involved in standardized testing.

The faculty had been instructed to keep students in their classrooms during the tests.

"Whatever you do, don't let anybody out for any reason," the principal had told them.

As much as she hated administering the standardized tests, Dianne was doing her best to comply with the guidelines. After the students had been working on their tests for over an hour, some of them began to complain that they needed a break to go to the restroom.

"I'm sorry, but we have been told not to let anybody out of the room," she stated firmly.

"Oh, man, I really need to go," Bernard pleaded.

"Well, Bernard, I guess you'll just have to use the trash can," she joked.

She gave them a five-minute break between tests to stand up and stretch their legs and to resharpen their pencils. Then it was time to begin the next segment of the test.

"Miss Hollis, something in this room stinks," one of the girls told her.

"I know what it is," announced another student. "You told Bernard to go in the trash can, and that's just what he did!"

"You've got to be kidding," Dianne exclaimed. "Bernard, I was just joking. I didn't think you would really do it."

"Told you I had to go," he said.

"I can't concentrate with that smell in here," complained another girl.

"Okay, we'll just set the trash can out into the hall for now. As for you, Bernard, I will have to report this incident to the office after the testing is over."

Well, I guess that's the last time I'll use that joke. I might just have to borrow some of Mr. Payne's disinfectant after this, she thought.

———

At the beginning of the year Dianne had been assigned a seventh-grade exploratory class of Family Living. Some of the students were not happy to be in a home economics class. One white boy, Bobby Moody, was especially outspoken.

"Home economics classes are for girls! I don't want to take home ec. I'm going to go down to the office and complain," he told Dianne.

"Go right ahead, Bobby," she replied. "There's nothing I can do about your being in here, but maybe you can get transferred to another class."

A few days later Mr. Cowan came down to see Dianne during her planning period.

"I've got some good news for you," he said.

"What's that?" she inquired.

"We are going to transfer that seventh-grade exploratory class to another department. You can have another regular home economics class provided you can find at least ten students who want to take home ec."

"Well, I guess Bobby Moody will be glad to hear that. He has really been fussing about being in here.

"Yes, he came down to my office, and he was just like a little lawyer, listing all the reasons why he should not have to take home ec."

When Dianne informed the class later that day they were to be transferred, some of the students didn't take the news very well. They couldn't understand why they had to change to another subject.

"I didn't have anything to do with it," Dianne informed them. "The decision was made by the principals."

"I don't want to leave now," said Bobby. "I'm going back down to the office to register another complaint."

The next day Dianne walked down the hall during her planning period, asking students in every class if anybody wanted to take home economics. She managed to round up just enough students to form the class, much to her relief. She reported the results to Mr. Cowan.

"Those junior high students are all right, but I'd rather work with high school students," she told him. "You won't believe this, but Bobby Moody is now unhappy about being taken out of home ec."

"Yes, I know. He was down here again," said Mr. Cowan. "I asked him what changed his mind, and he said, 'I think she's cute.'"

Carter C. Raymond was a small high school assigned to the Class C division of sports. Their basketball team was one of the best ones around, and this was the year that proved it. They had worked their way up to the district play-offs and were hoping to make it to the Louisiana state basketball tournament, which was known as "The Top Twenty."

The gym was always packed with fans during their home games, and many of the people also followed the team whenever it traveled. Plans were made to take several busses to the play-off games, and teachers were asked to help chaperone.

The white math teacher, Mr. Bob Hale, was still at the school, and he volunteered to go along with the team. A big pep rally was held the afternoon of the first play-off game. The entire student body was bursting with pride and excitement for their team's accomplishments.

Dianne thought they had a pretty good shot at making it to the finals. She tuned into the sports report later that night to see how they had fared. They won their first game in the play-off tournament, so she knew there would be little concentration on academic matters the next day.

Upon arriving at school the following morning, she was shocked to learn Mr. Hale had been attacked and beaten by some fans of the opposing team when he was attempting to get back on the bus after the game. The attack resulted in his nose being broken, so he came to school sporting a large bandage over the affected area.

"Did you hear about Bob getting beaten up last night?" Roy asked her.

"Yes, I did hear something about it when I got here this morning. What happened?" inquired Dianne.

"Some of the fans from the other team were mad because we won. They jumped on Bob and started beating him up and calling him a 'nigger lover.'"

"Poor Bob. I just can't believe it. He works so hard and then this happens to him."

The team went on to play another game later in the week, but they were not victorious in their efforts that time. Dianne, as well as the rest of the school, was quite disappointed.

"What went wrong?" she asked Roy. "They were doing so well."

"Oh, they could just see their names in lights at The Top Twenty. That's all they could think about, and they lost their concentration on the game," he told her.

Academically, the rest of the year went rather routinely. Dianne managed to snag several faculty members to come to her classes for demonstrations and lectures. Betty Cross agreed to demonstrate cake decorating to the advanced home economics classes. Roy gave a talk on ham radio to the General Science class one day and on another occasion let them look at his car engine to see how all the parts worked together. Mr. Cowan, who also sold insurance, made a presentation to the senior class on life and health insurance. Dianne was glad she had such local talents available.

After midterm Roy had surprised her one day with an announcement.

"I have something to tell you," he said. "I'm getting a new vehicle, a little sports car. It's a convertible."

"You've got to be kidding! You in a convertible. What were you thinking?"

"It's just something I've always wanted, and I had a chance to get it at a good price. Besides, that will free up the station wagon for my wife."

"Well, Roy, in that case, I've got some news for you. There's no way I'm riding around with you in a little tin can. I guess that means the end of our car-pooling days."

"Aw, you haven't even given it a try yet."

"And I'm not about to! You know your driving habits—tailgating, speeding, passing on a wing and a prayer with barely enough room to get by. Need I go on?"

"Okay, if that's really the way you feel. It was fun while it lasted."

Dianne was also called on several more times to use her sewing skills to help out other departments. Mr. Sanders, the industrial arts teacher, asked her to repair the ties on his shop aprons. He sent a student over to relay the request, aprons in hand. Dianne made a deal to repair the aprons in exchange for getting some of the kitchen cabinet drawers fixed.

The baseball coach asked her if she could sew the letters on the team's caps.

"I would really, really appreciate it if you could help us out," he told her.

"Okay, I can do it, but I will have to sew them on by hand. I don't think I can get the caps up under the sewing machine needle," she responded.

Later that day she took the dozen or so caps home and started working on them. The job turned out to be harder than she thought, so she convinced Rick to give her a hand.

"I wouldn't do this for anybody else," he declared. "You are definitely a privileged character."

"I believe I heard that comment once before when you were helping me build that yard for Taffy," she said. "Besides, you're supposed to help me out now that we're engaged!"

One of the final decisions she had to make during the year was picking a senior student to receive the home economics departmental award at graduation. Delandria Piper, the girl who had gotten pregnant, had by far the best grades of any senior she taught. This presented a dilemma.

"I don't know what to do about the home ec. award this year," she told Roy.

"Delandria has the best grades, but she had an out-of-wedlock baby. What kind of message would it send to people if I gave her the award?"

"It's up to you, but if she has the best grades, maybe she deserves it," he replied.

"I'm going to have to think about it some more before I make up my mind. They want a name by tomorrow."

Sitting at home later that night Dianne pondered over the situation. Then she reached a decision. Delandria, it will be. She made all "A's" on her work, and she is the smartest senior student I teach. Maybe she will be able to turn her life around some day and make something of herself in the long run.

If Dianne could have looked into the future at that moment she would have seen that Delandria would, indeed, go on to better things. She would eventually graduate from the Central Louisiana Vocational Technical School as a certified LPN.

But Dianne did not know what was to transpire in Delandria's life. All she could do was to give her the award and hope for brighter days ahead.

All I can do in the lives of all my students is teach them what I can and then hope for the best. I had faith God would send me the right person to marry, and He sent me Rick. Now I can only pray I will find the school where I really belong. Teaching at Pineville High School is still my dream, but I don't know if I will ever get a chance to be transferred there or not. I will put it in God's hands and trust Him to lead me along the right path.

Chapter 25

A large part of Dianne's time during that school year had been devoted to planning the wedding. Since she and Rick had both been financially independent from their parents for several years, they decided to pay for everything themselves. It would be a small, modest wedding.

Having taught a unit on how to plan a wedding, Dianne knew pretty much what she had to do and how to go about it. She and Rick started discussing matters shortly after she had settled in for the school year.

"The first thing we need to do is pick a date for the wedding. Then we have to decide on a place and time. After that we can select our attendants. So, do you have any preferences?" she asked him.

"No, whatever you want to do will be fine with me. Let's just keep it within reason financially," he replied.

"Okay, I think we should wait until school is out. I don't want to have to worry about carrying out a wedding during school. I think June is the best time. It's supposed to be the traditional month for brides and weddings."

"Sounds good to me."

"Also, I think a Saturday is best. It's hard to do weddings on weekdays or on Sunday afternoons. I see that one of the Saturdays in June is my grandfather Albert Gunter's birthday—June 14th. I think

I would like to get married then. That way my mother can have something happy to remember about that day instead of being sad because her papa is dead, and I will always think of my grandfather whenever we have an anniversary."

"June 14th it is, if we can get a church then."

"Traditionally, the bride gets to pick the church. Since I am a member of the Pineville Church of Christ, I prefer to have it there."

"Okay by me."

"Fine. I'll call them and see if we can get it on the calendar. I think an early afternoon time is best, something like 2:00 p.m. That way we can travel for a while on our honeymoon before it gets dark," she said.

Several days later she reported the results of her phone call to Rick.

"They had that date open on the calendar, so I signed us up for 2:00 p.m. Now there's the matter of getting a preacher. You won't believe this, but one of the preachers I grew up listening to is now preaching for the Alexandria Church of Christ. His name is Jerry Lee. I would really, really like him to conduct the ceremony for us."

"Pick whoever you want. It doesn't matter as long as we get married."

"I'll try to find his number in the phone book," she said. "If I can't, Aunt Hazel and Uncle R. V. attend that church, so I'm sure they can get it for me."

Dianne was able to get in touch with Jerry a few days later. She wasn't sure if he would remember her or not from his days of preaching at the Rocky Branch Church of Christ.

"Dianne, of course I know who you are," he had reassured her when she identified herself over the phone. "I would be honored to perform the wedding ceremony for you."

"Now that we have the church and the preacher settled, we need to pick our attendants," she told Rick. "I really don't have a lot of close friends, so I will have to think about who the best ones would be to ask."

"What about Barbara Hare?" he inquired. "Didn't you two used to be pretty good friends?"

"Yes, we were friends when I taught with her at Ruby-Wise. That seems like ages ago, but maybe she would do it. Then there's my old friend from my days of working on my master's degree at Northeast, Martha Bass."

"Did you say 'Bass?' I know some Basses from Colfax. I wonder if she is kin to them."

"I don't know, but I'm pretty sure she would do it. That leaves my sister, Sallie. I want her to be my maid-of-honor."

"Okay, if you are having three attendants, I need to think of three, too. I believe I'll ask my cousin Buddy Tumminello and one of my friends from the Navy, Bruce Shockley, to be groomsmen. My brother, Jimmy, is the logical choice for best man."

"What about a flower girl and ring bearer?" she wondered. "Do you know any little kids?"

"Well, my cousin Jean Rambo has a real cute little girl named Karen. She would be a great flower girl. I don't know any little boys, though," he replied.

"Neither do I, so I guess we'll just go with a flower girl. We don't have to have a ring bearer. That's about it, I guess. Oh, I almost forgot. What about somebody for the candle lighters? Sometimes the ushers do it, but I had rather have some girls if we can think of any. Hey, I've got it! Two of the girls I taught at Ruby-Wise still write to me all the time. They were two of my favorite students, and I think they would be perfect for the candle lighters."

"Who are they?"

"Their names are Regenia and Marlene Quattlebaum. That about settles it. Now all we have to do is ask all these people and see what they say. I'll call my people, and you can call yours."

Rick suddenly began laughing.

"What's so funny?" she demanded to know.

"You sound just like a drill sergeant!"

"Years of practice, m' lad. Years of practice You try keeping thirty teenagers all under control at the same time, and you might just start to sound like one, too!"

———

Several weeks later Dianne and Rick conferred on the results of their missions. All the people in question had agreed to be in the wedding.

"Now I suppose I had better start looking for a wedding dress," she told him. "I think I will go by myself and look first. Then I need to get somebody to come with me for a second opinion."

The following Saturday she headed for some of the most upscale stores that sold wedding dresses in the Alexandria area. First she tried on several dresses at Aileen's Bridal Boutique. Then she went to Gus Kaplan's and finally ended up at Wellan's. It was really hard to decide because the dresses were all beautiful. However, she managed to narrow the choices down to one or two dresses at each store.

I'm going to ask Rick's mother and Aunt Hazel to come with me one day to look at the dresses. They both have good taste, and I trust their judgment. Besides, it would be too far for Mother to travel for just one day, she decided.

She made arrangements to take a day off from school shortly after that. Mrs. Lundy met her at her apartment, and they picked up Hazel on the way to their first stop. Dianne had really liked the dress at Aileen's the best, so she saved that one for last on the tour.

Hazel and Mrs. Lundy agreed that all the dresses were pretty, but when Dianne put on the dress at Aileen's it was like an instant transformation. Suddenly she *was* a bride, a real honest-to-goodness bride!

"That's the dress," they both said, almost in unison.

"You can always tell when a girl has picked the right dress. She just lights up when she puts that dress on," Aileen observed.

"Well, I guess that settles it then," said Dianne. "Now I need a veil or headpiece to match."

After further consultation the veil was selected, and Dianne put a down payment on the dress with a promise to come back with some of the bridesmaids to pick out their dresses.

They went to lunch at the Piccadilly Cafeteria afterwards. Hazel and Mrs. Lundy insisted on paying for Dianne's lunch.

"I've really enjoyed it. You just let this be our little treat," said Hazel.

Barbara Hare agreed to meet Dianne at Aileen's on a Saturday to pick out the bridesmaids dresses. She tried on and modeled quite a few of them for Dianne, but it was still hard to choose. Suddenly a mint green chiffon dress caught Dianne's eye.

"I love this color," she declared. "It's perfect for a summer wedding, and I know it would look fabulous on Martha, too, with her red hair. I think this is the one."

For the candle lighters she decided to pick out a pattern and fabric at Hancock's fabric store. She settled on a soft yellow for the color. Regenia and Marlene would be able to make their own dresses, she was sure, after all that 4-H training they had in their early years.

Aileen informed her she could order the same material as the bridesmaids' dresses for the flower girl's dress. Dianne decided to make it herself, as Jean told her she couldn't sew. She chose yellow as the color for that dress, also.

That left just the men's clothes to consider. The logical choice for tuxedos was Randall's Formal Wear. It was one of the best-known places in town for renting tuxedos. Dianne and Rick decided on a dark gray for early afternoon, with the groomsmen wearing ruffled shirts in a soft yellow and the groom wearing a white one.

"That pretty much completes the color scheme. Now we have to pick out the flowers," she told Rick. "I think I will go with yellow flowers for the attendants, yellow boutonnieres for the groomsmen, and a white boutonniere for you. Since it will be in the early summer,

I think a mixed bouquet would be best for the bridal bouquet and also mixed flowers at the altar."

One of the town's bakeries most famous for making wedding cakes was Atwood's Bakery. Dianne decided to use it, picking out a simple three-tiered white cake with white frosting topped with yellow confectioners' sugar flowers.

"I can't stand the little brides and grooms they put on the top of cakes," she said. "That's why I'm going to decorate ours with just flowers."

"What about the music?" asked Rick.

"Well, we don't have instrumental music in the Church of Christ, so I suppose we will have to have some kind of recorded music. I think the church has some records and tapes we can select from. I'll see if I can borrow them."

"Okay, I think Bruce has a pretty sophisticated tape recorder. We can pick out what songs we want, and he can transfer them to just one tape. Then I have a friend named George Brandis who is a ham operator. He is pretty good at electronics, so I think I will ask him to operate the sound for us."

"That sounds great. I think that pretty much takes care of everything except for picking out the invitations, choosing a photographer, and deciding on the places for the reception and the rehearsal dinner."

"Another one of my ham operator friends, Eddie Auewaeter, is a professional photographer. We could probably get him to make the pictures for us," said Rick.

"Okay, I'll let you ask him, since he's your friend."

"And, you know, I'll bet my cousin Jean Rambo would let us use her house for the reception. She lives in Charles Park, and she and her husband, Sam, have a really nice house."

"That would be good because the Pineville church isn't really set up for receptions. Since she's your cousin, you can ask her, too."

Eddie put them on his calendar for the pictures, and Jean agreed to let them have the reception at her house. That left just the decision on where to have the rehearsal dinner. They picked the Holiday Inn on MacArthur Drive, as it was a popular place for buffet meals.

Everything moved along on schedule. All the attendants managed to show up for their fittings, and Dianne had the final fitting of her wedding gown. F. D. had informed her he was not going to wear a tuxedo.

"There's no way I'm wearing a monkey suit for anybody," he told her.

"That's fine, Daddy. You can just wear a regular suit. That means that Mr. Lundy and the preacher won't need tuxedos, either," she said.

The last few weeks before the wedding flew by like a whirlwind. Dianne was caught up in all the bridal showers and luncheons she had to attend. Her cousin Jerrine Harrell and one of Jerrine's friends, Spud Henry, sponsored a shower for the ladies of Dianne's church. Barbara Hare and Martha Bass, along with Marion Sullivan, hosted one for the friends from Alexandria. Dianne was flabbergasted during a monthly meeting of Kappa Kappa Iota, a teachers' sorority she belonged to, when they brought out a cake and wedding presents.

"Tell us now, didn't you get the least bit suspicious?" they teased.

"No, I really had no idea. This shower is a total surprise to me," she exclaimed.

Not to be outdone, a group of ladies from the Rocky Branch Church of Christ held a shower for Dianne's friends from Union Parish. One of Dianne's friends from college days, Kaye Hayhurst, whose father had once been a preacher at the Rocky Branch Church of Christ, made the cake for that shower.

Jean Rambo had the rice bag party at her house. Two of Rick's aunts, Estelle Anders and Lena Sorey, wanted to have another shower. However, Dianne told them she really couldn't think of any new people to invite, and she didn't want to keep asking the same people for presents, so they volunteered to sponsor the bridesmaids' luncheon.

By then Dianne's little apartment was about to overflow with all the presents along with the paraphernalia for the wedding.

"Looks like we won't need to buy any towels or linens for about five years," she observed.

"Wow, I can't believe we got so much stuff," said Rick. "Where are we going to put it all?"

"I don't know. We'll find someplace for it. This is really nothing compared to what a lot of people get. I'm sure we'll find a use for it all sooner or later."

There was one more important matter Dianne had to attend to before the wedding. It was something she was most reluctant to do.

"I don't like animals in the house," Rick had told her. "My parents never allowed them in the house when I was growing up. We had to keep all our pets outside. I really don't want to live with a dog in that little apartment of yours."

"Okay, I'll sell Taffy," she had agreed. "She's AKC registered, so it won't be hard to find a buyer. But Boo is my baby, and I'm never going to get rid of him. He and I have been through a lot together. Boo and I are a package deal."

"Well, I guess I can live with that. I'm not too crazy about it, but I can live with it."

She placed an ad in *The Alexandria Town Talk* the following week. The phone began ringing almost immediately, and Taffy was soon dispensed to a new home where the owner planned to breed her with a black male cocker spaniel. A follow-up call by Dianne a week later had found Taffy to be well and happy. That marked the end of Dianne's dog ownership days.

Dianne and Rick made it through the frenzy of activities that surrounded the final weeks before the wedding. School was out for the year, so that was one less thing Dianne had to worry about. All that remained was making it through the wedding rehearsal and then the wedding itself.

Everything had fallen into place nicely. Dianne was a born organizer, and she had planned everything down to the last detail. The rehearsal went smoothly and everyone enjoyed relaxing afterwards at the rehearsal dinner. Dianne was too nervous to eat much, and Rick didn't appear to have his usual appetite, either. She was surprised to see Samuel Dixon, one of her former students from Carter C. Raymond, serving food at the buffet cart.

Well, I guess word of my wedding will get back to the students now, she thought.

Following the rehearsal dinner, everyone headed back to their respective lodgings to bed down for the night. Dianne's parents were staying in a motel, while Sallie was spending the night with Dianne at her apartment. Dianne still had several details to finish up before the wedding the next day.

Boo had been boarded at the vet's office until she and Rick returned from their honeymoon. That left the last-minute packing to complete and any other loose ends to tie up. Rick and Dianne had decided to take some sandwiches and snacks to eat on the road, so she had to prepare those and ice down the colas. Aside from that, little remained to be done.

She and Sallie managed to get to bed shortly after midnight, but they were too nervous to sleep much. Dianne spent most of the night tossing and turning as she mentally reviewed the wedding details. Drat it all, I can't go to sleep. I wonder what Rick's doing. Knowing him, he's probably sleeping like a baby. He never gets upset or nervous about anything. Oh, well, tomorrow's the big day, the day I've been waiting for most of my adult life. I just hope everything goes off as planned and that God continues to watch over me in my life and blesses me and Rick in this marriage.

As morning broke, Dianne and Sallie rolled out of bed, both tired from getting little rest, but knowing they had to make it through the day somehow. Although it seemed like they had all the time in the world, the hours passed quickly with the 2:00 p.m. deadline drawing near. They gathered their belongings for the wedding and headed to the church to get dressed in one of the rooms near the back of the building.

The flowers arrived just as they got there. All the attendants made it on time, and everything seemed to be moving along according to schedule. Thanks to Dianne's precise planning, nothing had been left out or forgotten. There were no last-minute changes, nor was anybody running around trying to find lost items.

The mothers were more nervous than the people in the wedding party. Dianne had ordered white corsages for them to match any color dress they happened to choose. Both walked in wearing dresses of soft turquoise.

"Dianne, do you have your something old, something new, something borrowed, and something blue?" inquired Mrs. Lundy.

"I think so," replied Dianne. "I have my new wedding dress and a blue garter. There's my gold cross necklace Mother gave me when I was in high school for the something old. That just leaves something borrowed. I didn't think of that."

"Here, let me loan you this white tissue. Tuck it up in your sleeve. You may need it if you start crying. You need a penny to put in your shoe, too. Who has a penny she can use?" said Mrs. Lundy.

Dolores found a penny in her purse. It was then inserted into one of Dianne's shoes. The mothers, satisfied that everything was taken care of, strolled towards the front entrance of the church to await being escorted down the aisle.

"It's time, Dianne," Martha announced.

"Is everybody set?" asked Barbara.

Everyone murmured in agreement they were ready as they picked up their wedding bouquets.

"Okay, let's head out the side door and around to the front of the church. This is it," said Dianne.

They could hear the faint strains of the Harding Acappella Chorus's taped recording of "Because" and "O, Promise Me" as they walked down the hall towards the outer doors.

When they reached the front of the church, F. D. was standing alone, as everyone else had already been escorted in. They listened for their musical cue of the traditional "Faithful and True" to begin, and then the bridesmaids and flower girl headed down the aisle.

Dianne and F. D. reached the entrance, awaiting their turn to march in. *What do brides think about as they are going down the aisle?* Dianne wondered. *Guess I'm about to find out!*

Everyone stood as they entered the church. Dianne managed to glance at the crowd as she walked towards the altar, recognizing many familiar faces. Still, it was all just a blur with Rick waiting at the front of the altar.

F. D. handed her over to Rick and took his seat beside Dolores, his part in the ceremony completed. Dianne and Rick climbed the steps and joined the rest of the wedding party. The all-too-familiar words of the ceremony were soon flowing with Dianne and Rick responding in the appropriate places. Everything was moving along according to plan. It was perfect, just perfect, or so Dianne thought.

Then came the one glitch in the proceedings. Following a prayer, Dianne had planned to have a recorded version of "Father, Hear the Prayer We Offer" played. Instead of the sound coming out of the speakers, it began spewing forth directly from the tape recorder itself. Dianne looked over towards the source of the sound. To her horror, she noticed someone had opened the doors to the hallway, exposing George Brandis and the tape machine.

Oh, God. It's the just like "The Wizard of Oz," and we can see the little man behind the curtain. Why didn't I think to tell him to be sure to keep the doors closed? she bemoaned silently. So much for having the perfect wedding!

Nevertheless, the remainder of the ceremony went off smoothly, much to Dianne's relief. The wedding party marched briskly down the aisle to the tune of Mendelssohn's "Wedding March" as they exited the church. Hugs and kisses were exchanged all around, and then it was time to pose for photos. Thanks to Eddie's expertise, that task was handled in short order, and everyone headed towards the Rambo house in Charles Park for the reception.

By the time the wedding party arrived at the scene, the guests had mixed and mingled and were anticipating the cutting of the cake. F. D., always at his best in a crowd, had been entertaining them with some of the stories he was so well-known for narrating.

"Your daddy says please don't make him stand in a line. He's having too much fun talking to everybody," said Dianne's cousin Joyce Watson.

"Well, I'm sorry, but I did plan a short receiving line. It will just be the parents, the bride and groom, and Sallie," Dianne told her. "Maybe he won't have to stand in line very long."

Following the cutting of the cake, Dianne managed to round up everybody to form the receiving line. She basked in the compliments she received as the guests moved through the line.

"You know, I think this wedding had the prettiest colors of any wedding I have attended in our church," said Cherry Holsomback, one of the church members. "Everything was just beautiful."

Dianne had planned for the color scheme of the reception to mirror that of the wedding. A bouquet of mixed flowers accented the refreshment table. The punch was a lime sherbet and ginger ale mixture, forming the same mint green as the bridesmaids' dresses. The cake was decorated with yellow roses made from confectioners' sugar. Mixed nuts and assorted dinner mints completed the menu, keeping the cost within their budget.

The candle lighters, Regenia and Marlene, presided over the bride's book with the bridesmaids' bouquets framing the background on that table. Martha and Barbara served the punch, while Dianne's aunt Hazel and Rick's aunt Lena doled out the cake. Rick's niece, Denise, and Jerrine's youngest daughter, Becky, had been chosen to act as tea girls. Denise sported a long yellow frock, while Becky's was mint green, both dresses having been made by their mothers.

"I suppose we had better make this marriage official," announced the preacher, Jerry Lee, sometime later. "It's time for the couple to sign the marriage license."

"Too late to back out now, old buddy," teased Bruce, one of the groomsmen.

"Yeah, sign your life away on the dotted line," added his brother, Jimmy.

Amid much jesting and joking, they managed to get the task completed. They then went outside for Dianne to throw the bouquet. The wind carried it high into the air as it headed towards the unmarried females in the bridal party. Sallie and Martha tussled over it, with Sallie coming out the winner, much to Martha's disgust.

After that, it was time to change clothes before leaving for their honeymoon. Dianne went to the master bedroom and was assisted by the bridesmaids as she thankfully shed the wedding attire for more comfortable clothes. She had made her own going-away dress. It was a hot pink princess-style sleeveless dress with an A-line skirt and a multi-colored jacket that featured miniature pink, yellow, and green flowers. She had managed to find a pair of hot pink sandals to match the dress. A corsage of multi-colored flowers completed the outfit.

Rick, who was getting dressed in another room, had chosen tan slacks with a checked sports coat, both of which Dianne had helped him pick out. They emerged from the dressing rooms at the same time.

"Are you ready?" he inquired.

"I guess so," she replied.

"Okay, let's go get pelted with some rice!" he exclaimed.

The crowd had assembled on the front sidewalk as they waited for the couple to leave through the front door. Everybody had their rice bag in hand, ready to douse the couple with a cloud of the white stuff.

Dianne was wearing her older eyeglasses, as her newest pair changed color whenever a flashbulb went off. The eyeglasses were slightly tilted on her face, and as they ran towards the car, the lenses filled up with the rice so generously tossed by the guests.

"I'm blinded. I can't see a thing," she shouted as she was forced to remove the eyeglasses in order to dump the offending rice, running as she spoke. Suddenly, she felt a jolt in the back of her head, somewhat akin to being hit in the head by a rock. Somebody had thrown an entire rice bag intact without removing the rice. *It had to be one of those kids,* she thought. *What a great way to start my honeymoon with a knot on the back of my head!*

A few people had saved their rice, waiting for the couple to get into their car. The pelting continued as Rick and Dianne quickly climbed into Dianne's Torino that had been traditionally decorated with white shoe polish by the trusted groomsmen.

"Hurry up and close the door, Rick," she pleaded. "They're throwing rice into the car. I hope they didn't do something like put sardines on the motor."

"No, I told them not to do anything like that," he said.

"That doesn't mean they didn't do it. Let's just hope we don't start smelling something putrid a few miles down the road."

Dianne insisted on stopping by Robo Carwash on the way out of town. She was too embarrassed to ride around in a car decked out with white shoe polish. The attendant almost fell over laughing as he pre-hosed the car.

"Well, at least they didn't tie any tin cans on the back," Rick noted.

They had decided on Florida as their honeymoon destination. Rick and his family had lived there for several years when he was growing up, but Dianne had never set foot in the state. They made their headquarters in Gulf Breeze at a motel where Rick's family had often held their large Tumminello family reunions.

"My grandfather, James Tumminello, used to rent the whole motel for a week," he told Dianne.

After a week of sightseeing and swimming in the ocean, they were both ready to take their sunburned bodies back home to Dianne's little apartment. As soon as they arrived back in Pineville and unloaded the car, Rick wanted to head to Colfax to retrieve his Firebird, but Dianne was determined to run by the vet's office to pick up Boo.

"It won't be home until I get Boo back," she said. "Let's go get him first before the vet's office closes. Then we can go pick up your car."

Dianne's one regret about the trip to Florida was not visiting Disney World. So, she and Rick decided to go back in July before she had to start back to school. Seeing Disney World had always been one of her dreams, and she couldn't believe she was actually getting to go to Florida twice in one summer. They booked a motel room at a Holiday Inn about thirty miles out of Orlando. Dianne was more excited about the trip to Disney World than she had been about going on her honeymoon.

Upon arriving at Disney World, they purchased some two-day tickets at the front gate. Then they made their way into the facility. When they stepped onto Main Street, Dianne stood in stunned silence, turning around and around, taking it all in.

"It's just like something out of a fairytale! It makes you feel just like a child again," she finally exclaimed.

They put in two full days, visiting as many exhibits as they could and going on all the rides, including Space Mountain. That was one ride they would never forget, and one they would never go on a second time, either!

"I can't believe we were dumb enough to go on that ride," Rick lamented.

"I guess we should have paid more attention to the warning signs posted on the way up during the hour-long wait—the ones that said pregnant women and people with heart problems should not go on the ride," agreed Dianne.

They caught the bicentennial parade on their first day. On their final night, they stayed for the bicentennial fireworks display. It was the most spectacular one either of them had ever witnessed. Tired, but happy, they headed back to their motel for a night's rest before driving back to Pineville.

"We got to see everything but the Haunted House," Rick commented.

"Yes, the lines for it were just too long. Maybe we can return someday and see that, too. I'm just glad I finally got to go. I think everyone should visit Disney World. It is truly the most fascinating place I have ever seen. If you're not young at heart when you get there, you will be when you leave!"

When they returned to Pineville, Dianne had a letter from the Rapides Parish School Board in the mailbox.

"I wonder what they want now," she said, as she opened the envelope.

She was surprised to read she had an offer to transfer to Pineville High School to teach home economics. She was instructed to call the principal, Mr. Eugene Millet, to set up an appointment for a job interview.

"It's been so long since I went on a job interview I've forgotten how to act. I don't know what to wear, either," she told Rick.

"Why don't you just wear one of your pantsuits?" he asked.

"Yes, I think I will. I think I'll wear the apricot-colored pantsuit I made for our honeymoon," she decided.

Several days later Dianne found herself sitting in Mr. Millet's office, facing her possible future boss. She couldn't remember when she had been so nervous.

Don't blow this, Dianne, she told herself. This is your big chance, your biggest dream come true. All the years you've been in Rapides Parish you've driven by Pineville High School and wished you could teach there. You asked

God to guide you, and now He's given you the opportunity. Think before you speak and try to give the right answers.

Mr. Millet proceeded to go over the basics of the job with Dianne, including what her schedule would be, should she decide to take the job. She would have one class of Home Economics II, one class of Home and Family Living, one class of Handicrafts, and two classes of General Science. It would actually be a step backwards from the job she presently held, as she would be, once again, teaching more science classes. *Would the move be worth it?* she wondered.

"Well, Mrs. Lundy, it's up to you to decide whether or not you want the job. According to Mr. Harold Parks, the Rapides Parish Personnel Director, the job is yours because you are a displaced teacher due to the desegregation lawsuit."

Dianne almost looked around when she heard him say "Mrs. Lundy." Then she realized that she *was* Mrs. Lundy. It was a title she had not yet gotten used to.

"Yes, I do want the job. I'll take it," she said, sitting up a little straighter in her chair.

"Very well, then. I'll notify Mr. Parks, and you will be receiving a letter assigning you to Pineville High School for the coming school year."

"Thank you very much, Mr. Millet. I'm looking forward to working with you," said Dianne as they both rose and shook hands to seal the agreement.

"Well, did you get the job?" Rick inquired when she walked back into the apartment.

"You won't believe it, but Mr. Millet said that the job is mine if I want it, and I do. So, I told him I would take it. Now I have to go to Lecompte and break the news to Mr. Cowan that I'll be leaving Carter C. Raymond."

They drove down to Lecompte the next day. Dianne needed to get some of her personal items from the home economics department, as well as let Mr. Cowan know that he would have to find another home economics teacher.

"I surely do hate that you are leaving. I don't know how we are going to replace you, but I can't blame you for wanting to get closer to home," he told her.

"I'm sure you'll find another teacher. There are plenty of home economics majors out there looking for a job," she reassured him. "I just want to thank you for all the help and support you gave me while I was here at CCR. You made my job a lot easier."

"Well, so much for Carter C. Raymond," said Rick as they drove back to Pineville.

"Yes, I put in two and one-half years at that school. I gave it my best shot, but I'm not sure how much good I did. It always seems weird to leave a school and know that you're never going back. I feel a little sad about it. Most of the students seemed to like me. I hope they get a good teacher to replace me, but many teachers don't want to go to an all-black school. I think the students accepted me because I didn't treat them any differently than I would have treated students of any race. That's one of the keys to the whole thing about education. The teacher has to like their students and treat them fairly. A teacher has to see every student for who they are, not what they are or what their racial background might be."

Dianne sent up a silent prayer as they reached their apartment. *Thank you, God, for answering my prayers. It took me twenty-eight years to find my dream man but that finally came true. Rick isn't perfect but he's a really good man, and I know that he will always look after me. Now I'm about to start working at Pineville High school, in what I always believed would be my ideal job. Please be with me and help me to make it through any difficult times that might lie ahead in this new adventure in my life.*

The End

www.ingramcontent.com/pod-product-compliance
Lightning Source LLC
Chambersburg PA
CBHW021615120626
46545CB00001B/240